4 — 29   95

An ACTOR

An ACTOR Behaves

TOM MARKUS

SAMUEL FRENCH ✦ HOLLYWOOD
NEW YORK LONDON TORONTO

Library of Congress Cataloging-in-Publication Data

Markus, Tom.
An actor behaves : from audition to performance / by Tom Markus
p.   cm.
1. Acting—Professional guidance. I. Title.
PN2055.M267   1992   792'.023—dc20   92-27228

ISBN: 0-573-69901-1

Cover design by Heidi Frieder
Cover Photograph by J. A. Borowczyk

Printed and bound in the United States of America

Samuel French Trade
7623 Sunset Blvd.
Hollywood, CA 90046

for Linda

Contents

PREFACE

To write a book is to hope someone will read it. Or at least buy it and put it on a shelf in preparation for that dreary day when nothing will serve but to pull it down, crack its spine, and test its mettle. And so, dear actor, permit me to guide your hand (until your eye is ready to read my words) and to direct you to take this book home from the store and place it on your shelf snugly between Robert Cohen's *Acting Professionally* and Michael Green's *The Art of Coarse Acting*. Between the earth and water of a sensible handbook and the hot air bubbles of Mr. Green's wit. Beyond those trusty flanks, in casual disarray, I would be flattered to learn you'd placed William Goldman's *The Season*, William Gibson's *The Seesaw Log*, J. D. Salinger's *Franny and Zooey*, William Redfield's *Letters From An Actor*, Simon Callow's *Being An Actor*, and close by—but not so near as to invite corruption from my misappropriation of his title—Stanislavsky's *An Actor Prepares*.

To write a new edition of an established book is to strive to make it better. It is easy for me to list my goals and you, dear reader, will judge if I have succeeded. I have updated the information and references and tried to employ current examples: gone are such examples as Marlon Brando's work in *Last Tango in Paris*, now replaced by examples like Dustin Hoffman's work in *Rain Man*. Second, I have expanded the text to discuss topics that were not current when the earlier book came out: non-traditional casting and the impact of AIDS find their proper place in these pages. Next, I've included some new theatre anecdotes and jokes, though the funniest is not here (it tells about an experiment with three dogs, and, as a courtesy to my colleague John Harrop who shared it with me, I have left it to him to include in his new book: *Acting*). And lastly, I have given the book the title I always intended for it but which an earlier publisher shied from using: instead of *The Professional Actor* (how bland!), I hope you will enjoy *An Actor Behaves*.

To write a book is to reveal an indebtedness to more people than a preface can in reason honor. To those of you whose names should be here but are not, my apologies. I know that you know that I know who you are and that I have space here to thank only a few of the many teachers I've learned from and students I've taught and the many directors I've acted for and actors I've directed. Yet certain names will out, and I wish to extend particular appreciation to the memory of Monroe Lippman, who started me in this business; Paul Hostetler, who sustained me in moments of doubt; my son Lindsay for word-processing wisdom; Maury Erickson for nagging me to write this new version; Chuck Sachs for always taking time from his imminent career to listen to my dreams; Gordon Heath for teaching me to love the theatre; Baylor Landrum and Ira Schlosser for sharing the good years in Virginia; Malcolm Morrison and Earle Gister for their ongoing support of my errant career; Joe Varga for his brilliant designs, which make my directing seem better than it is; Bob Potter for feigning to believe I'm as good as I tell him I am; and Mike Addison who—nearly forty years on—continues with unerring accuracy and desired frequency to hit me right in the *hubris* with a pig's bladder.

PROLOGUE

"I'm going to have to let her go."

"What did she do?"

"I won't keep her. She's got to go."

"But what does she do?"

"She disrupts rehearsals. She talks all the damn time. She thinks she's too good to play anything but leads. She wants to run before she can crawl."

"Well, it's your own fault. You shouldn't have given her a lead in the *Shrew*. I never found her difficult in classes."

"No, no. She wastes time and she's impossible. No, I'm going to let her go."

This conversation took place between the general manager of a major professional theatre and the head of an important acting conservatory. I happened to be visiting, sitting quietly in the office. I've left out the names, to protect all concerned. The subject was a recent graduate of the conservatory, and it was evident, by the end of the conversation (which went on longer than the brief exchange recorded here), that a young actor was about to be fired. Not because she couldn't act, but because she couldn't behave as an actor.

One day the phone rang in my office, while I was artistic

director for TheatreVirginia in Richmond, and the artistic director of a theatre far across the country was asking me about an actor who he was considering engaging and who had worked with me earlier that season. "Well," I replied, "he was sensational in the role he did for us here, but apparently he was unbearably rude to everyone. I guess I should tell you that a delegation of my permanent staff told me that if I ever hired him again they would all quit. And I know they weren't kidding." "Thanks," said my colleague, "I'd heard that from others. Just wanted corroboration. I'll go with another actor."

Similar conversations go on around the world all the time. Young (and not so young) actors lose jobs or fail to get jobs because they don't know the rules for the profession they follow. They may be wonderfully talented and they may have received formidable training in the craft of their profession. But somehow they have not acquired the knowledge they need to work in the profession. Annually, in the United States and elsewhere, acting students leave training institutions, private coaches, or amateur theatre groups and descend on the casting centers of their respective countries seeking work. And they have talent, many of them. And skills. But without correct work habits and without a sound knowledge of professional behavior, their chances of employment are seriously reduced. There is fierce competition for jobs in the theatre, and employers don't have to waste their time on actors who can't "cut it." Like the young actor above, they're going to be "let go."

This book is a handbook, a beginner's guide to professional behavior for the actor. I hope it will provide neophyte and veteran alike with some guidelines toward professional attitudes and work habits. Now, don't expect to get work just because you've read and assimilated the notions in the pages that follow. No book can do that for you—not your how-to-act book nor your how-to-get-an-acting-job book. All this modest book can provide you with are some ways you can do your job effectively: some ways to become employable, some ways to help yourself get hired again once a job is completed.

Definitions

A first area of concern, one we'd best deal with before going any further, is a matter of definitions: actor, artist, performer, talent. What precisely is this thing that you think you are? If you're shooting a television commercial, you'll hear yourself referred to as the "talent." In the souvenir program of a resident acting company, you may find your picture and bio under a category called "artists." When you are denied a lease on an apartment, you may learn it is because you are that irresponsible and untrustworthy thing called an "actor."

Webster's Third New International Dictionary gives a good starting place: "a theatrical performer; someone that acts in a stage play, motion picture, radio or television play, or a dramatic sketch." *Webster's* defines an actress as "a woman who takes part in any affair; a female actor." I won't comment on the politically incorrect first part of that definition, except to observe that it may be just such notions that led English humorist George Moore to remark "acting is therefore the lowest of the arts, if it is an art at all."

Is an actor an artist? Only if a work of art has been created, something that exists outside the artist, that exists independent of the artist. Only if the deliberate and intentioned application of craft or skill has brought into existence something that communicates both delight and instruction. An audience must be pleased and edified before an actor can be said to have created a work of art, can be called an artist. Most would agree that Dustin Hoffman's performances as Willy Loman in *Death of a Salesman*, Shylock in *The Merchant of Venice*, and Michael Dorsey and Raymond Babbitt in the films of *Tootsie* and *Rain Man* were works of art and would therefore call him an "artist." The same is true for Laurence Olivier, for his creations of roles as diverse as Othello, Archie Rice, Andrew Wyke in the film *Sleuth*, and James Tyrone in O'Neill's *Long Day's Journey into Night*. Jessica Tandy is celebrated as an "artist" for her four decades of creating roles such as Blanche in *A Streetcar Named Desire*, Miss Daisy in the film of *Driving Miss Daisy*, and the speaking mouth in Samuel Beckett's

Not I. And James Earl Jones has earned the title "artist" for his creations on stage of Troy in *Fences* and the title role in *King Lear* and his work on the large and small screens, including the voice of Darth Vader.

The list of artists is very long. Hoffman, Olivier, Tandy, Jones, and hundreds of others may be called "artists" because they have created works of art. But "artist" is not a label actors should place upon themselves; it is not something to put on a passport in the blank space for profession. Let others give you that label—if and when you merit it, if and when you use your skills to communicate some instructive revelation that delights an audience, if and when you create a work of art. Let us, now and henceforth, relinquish discussions of actors as artists and return to considering what it is that an actor is and does.

"Acting," wrote Alexander Bakshy early in this century, "is the effort to appear different to what one really is; it is the practice of make-believe. In life we exercise this faculty of complete or partial disguise in order to achieve a variety of practical ends; some innocent, some sinister, some serious, some jocular." In life, then, we act. And on stage, an actor is one who uses this particular human faculty in a pre-planned pattern to contribute to a fiction that intends to delight and instruct an audience. The degree of each actor's effectiveness is arguable, and there are many opinions as to what is good and bad acting. Comedian George Burns, shortly before receiving an Academy Award for his performance in the film of Neil Simon's *The Sunshine Boys*, put it this way: "Good acting is when Walter Matthau says to me, 'How are you?' and I answer, 'Fine.' That's good acting. If Walter Matthau asks me, 'How are you?' and I answer, 'I think it fell on the floor,' then that's bad acting." But, wit apart, we must deal with acting in its simplest terms and return to *Webster's Third New International* to discover that acting is "the art or practice of representing a character on the stage or in a motion picture or radio or television play." If you do that, for the purposes of the pages that follow, you are an actor. You may or may not have talent; you may or may not be an artist. But you surely are an actor, and, as an actor, you need to know how to behave.

You're an actor only once you've been engaged to act. You're a professional actor only once you're being remunerated for your time—whether that is as a card-carrying member of a theatrical union or as a member of an acting commune that receives its recompense in eggs and grain from its appreciative audiences. Most of the remarks in this book will be aimed at the conventional, commercial theatre as it is practiced in the English-speaking world. As an American, most familiar with the theatre in America, my observations will have an unavoidable national bias. But as I've traveled and worked in England, Canada, and Australia, I have found no essential differences, and I am hopeful that the body of this work will be widely applicable. So: What does it take to become a professional actor? I believe there are five requisites, and each is worthy of some discussion. They are *talent, training, luck, contacts,* and *employability.* Let's look at each in turn.

Five Requisites for a Professional Actor

TALENT The world is crawling with it. The number of actors in London, New York, Sydney, and Toronto who have talent is astonishing. Exhilarating if you're trying to hire one. Depressing if you're trying to get hired. The number of talented young actors and would-be actors going through training institutions annually is astounding. Exhilarating when you're in classes with them; depressing when you leave the classroom for the marketplace. The number of people in non-theatrical professions who have theatrical talent is overwhelming: athletes, politicians, clergy, teachers. Talent, simply, is that inexplicable quality many people have that makes other people want to know about them, watch them, listen to them. It's easy to identify, but tough to define. Nor need we define it. People will tell you if you have it by casting you in roles, or seeking your company, or heeding your opinions. In the theatre, talent is easy to identify. Go see a large-cast play or a musical with a chorus of singers and dancers. See them all dressed essentially alike, involved in the same piece of choreography, or carrying the same spears. Which one do you look at?

That's the one with talent. Think about the character of Cassie in
A Chorus Line; her problem is that she wants to blend in and be
a member of the chorus, but, as Zach tells her, she stands out.
She has talent. As an actor, you won't get beyond the chorus or
the crowd of extras without talent, no matter how you develop
your skills, so it will be evident to you early in your career
whether or not you have talent. You'll be plucked from the army
and given that unenviable line, "The Queen, my lord, is dead."
Or you'll find yourself singing a short solo, even though the girl
beside you has a purer voice. But be careful. When you discover
that you have talent, that there is something about you that
others find interesting, you are likely to get a fat head, likely to
assume falsely that henceforth the world should note you well
and reward you richly for being yourself. Well, get rid of that
notion fast, or your career will end right where it began. "The
Queen, my lord, is dead" will be the zenith of your life in the
theatre, and it will be hard to convince your grandchildren, as
you sit before the fireplace forty years later, that you had a great
potential career in the theatre but that the world somehow missed
out on the chance of knowing you. The roads to Broadway are
paved with the broken psyches of talented yet unemployed actors. You need talent to be an actor, but talent is nothing you can
acquire. If you've got it, you'll learn so early on. If you're without
it, you'll learn it earlier than you wish—so try some other profession. But if you've got it, don't delude yourself that talent will get
you a career. All your competitors have talent, too. You'd better
have more in your theatrical trunk than talent if you hope to have
a life in the theatre.

   TRAINING As I write this in early 1992, the unions' current
listings of "paid up" members are 35,252 in Actors' Equity Association, 68,376 in AFTRA, and approximately 76,000 in the Screen
Actors Guild. Even if you allow that most actors belong to more
than one union and that the total number of actors is probably
closer to 90,000 than the nearly 180,000 these memberships add
up to, you realize there are a lot of actors in America today—and
all of those actors have some form of training. It may be merely
experience gained working in summer theatre, or it may be
formal training at some university or acting conservatory that

offers an intensive, three-year course in acting skills. And each year those conservatories and universities send hundreds more wannabes to Hollywood, New York, Sydney, and Toronto with some degree of training, all hoping to land a job. Some will not even know why upstage is where it is and others will hold advanced academic degrees, like the MFA so popular in American universities. But they'll all believe they're trained. How trained are you?

Aren't your chances likely to be improved in direct proportion to the extent of your training?

The conventional wisdom in the American resident theatre world today is that there are altogether too many training programs, spewing altogether too many young actors into the marketplace. As one artistic director put it at a recent meeting of the Theatre Communications Group, "Why don't they just focus on two schools? Get the very best kids in the country and put them in one school on the East Coast and one on the West?"

"Good idea," said another director, "but where would you find enough talented kids for that second school?" Their cynicism was born out of the experience of auditioning too many young actors who lacked either talent or training or both.

While it is true that your appropriateness for a particular role is likely to be more influential than your training in securing any single job, it is equally true that the more things you can do, the better your chances for being appropriate. Some years back, I auditioned a young actress in Hollywood for a role in a new play based on Chekhov's novella *Late Blooming Flowers*. The interview went approximately like this:

> Me:　Have you played any of the Chekhovian ladies?
> Her:　How do you mean?
> Me:　Well, have you seen any of the Chekhovian canon?
> Her:　Well . . . I'm not sure . . .
> Me:　What is your favorite play of Chekhov's?
> Her:　I'm sorry, I don't follow your vocabulary.
> Me:　I see . . . well, please leave your photo and
> 　　　résumé and I'll see if there's anything for you.
> 　　　　(under my breath to the stage manager)
> 　　　Hoo boy! How'd *she* get in here?

I have no idea if that young lady could act. Or if she could act any of the roles I was casting. But I knew I wouldn't have time in rehearsals to teach her all she needed to know about Chekhov. Her lack of education lost her the chance to demonstrate her abilities. Her education for the theatre was inadequate.

Your skills are never more clearly on display than during a musical audition. You can either hit Cunegonde's highest note or you can't. What is true for the singing actor is true for the black actor auditioning for a play by Athol Fugard and who needs to know South African dialect, and for the young leading man who needs to know stage combat, and for the comic who needs to know how to be hit with a cream pie. The more skills you have, the greater your chance to work.

This is not the place to engage in a lengthy discussion of variant forms of acting training or the values of education to an actor. Suffice it to say that no actor has ever had sufficient training or education and that both are lifelong pursuits for the serious actor. As a younger man, I was astounded and delighted to spend an evening with Alan Howard and Janet Suzman when they were the leading lights of the Royal Shakespeare Company and to learn that they took it as a matter of course that they should read scholarly criticism about a role they were preparing. I was equally delighted to learn that Laurence Olivier, whose voice was regarded by many as exceptional and whose athletic performances in such roles as Coriolanus were the stuff of legend, engaged a voice teacher for several months prior to beginning rehearsals for the role of Othello and a personal trainer to help help him pump iron. Training for the theatre is an unending activity, and its rewards are twofold: an ever-widening appropriateness for roles and the ability to perform roles richly.

What should *you* do about training? Get more. If you're getting roles in Hollywood and New York, consider classes that will expand your skills: singing, mime, fencing, dancing. If you're having trouble getting cast, consider going to some institution that will provide you with a basic approach to your work. If you're just starting out, select the finest and most exhaustive program your funds and time will permit you to follow. It is just common sense. The marketplace is jammed with talented actors.

Increase your odds of employment by becoming trained as well as talented.

Unhappily, talent and skills alone may not get you work. There is the tale of the young actor who arrived in Hollywood and struggled unsuccessfully for four months to get an appointment with an agent. Finally, through some friends, she got one and arrived fifteen minutes before her four o'clock appointment. She had her new photos and résumés in her briefcase and had just spent her last $45 on a trendy haircut. She was optimistic. This was the big break. She was ready to show her stuff. Four o'clock came and went. The actor reminded the battle-weary secretary that the agent wanted to see her at four. "In a minute," she replied, a hand over the phone's mouthpiece. Four fifteen. Four thirty. "My god, he'll be leaving shortly," thought the young actor, "and I'll have blown my chance." To the secretary again. "Would you please tell him I'm here?" Back to the waiting chair. The secretary buzzed the inner office. Four forty-five. Finally the agent opened the door. "Come on in, I've only got a minute." The young actor scrambled into the office, trying gamely to retain her cool, and took a seat opposite the agent. "OK," said the agent behind a frown. But the phone rang. And then the other phone. And the agent was on both. "No, Charlie, not without an outclause after the first thirteen episodes . . ." "Hello, Grace, listen, tell me the scenario. Well, read it to me now . . ." A phone on each ear, he looked up. "Go ahead, kid, show me what you can do." The young actor stood, slipped off her suit jacket, walked to the window of the 17th-floor office, opened it, and dove out. She swooped into the air, pirouetted in the air, did turns and flips out there in space high above Sunset Boulevard, and then, in a final dazzling display, somersaulted back into the office and into her seat. The agent looked at her, eyes wide. He grabbed up his pencil and the actor's résumé and scribbled on it. "Right," he said, "I'll call you when we need someone for bird imitations."

No, in show business, skills are not enough. You also can use a bit of luck.

LUCK If you're sitting in your apartment in Salt Lake City and waiting for someone you don't know in Los Angeles to discover you, just because of all those terrific notices in the hometown newspaper for your performance as the psychopathic young murderer in *Night Must Fall,* you are not likely to be chosen to star opposite Markie Post on the next episode of *Night Court.* Even though you are exactly right for the role, even though you are truly talented, and even though you have the very skills that the role demands. To be lucky in the theatre, you've got to be where the luck is and where you can help to make it happen.

Let me not deny that there *is* luck in the maddening world of the theatre. A nineteen-year-old recently acted in a college play that was invited to the American College Theatre Festival in Washington, D.C., was seen there by a casting director for day-time TV, and within a few weeks was a sustaining character on *Days of Our Lives.* A star was born! Few actors are that lucky. Most have to go where the luck is, advance themselves, promote themselves, and then hope. Too many go to their graves still hoping. Most actors get accommodated to the reality that they can call themselves successes if they can support themselves by acting. Few have any real belief they'll become stars.

But then I remember the add I found in a newspaper in Kuala Lumpur, Malaysia:

SINGAPORE FILM DEVELOPMENT (Pte) LTD.
recruiting actors and actresses.
Applicants must be above 18 years old and under 30
with at least Secondary School education.
Successful candidates will undergo training for a
short period before becoming film stars.
Please apply personally with 2 passport-size photos,
your Identity Card and personal particulars at
ORCHARD THEATRE, Grange Road
on 26th, July, 1976 (Thursday) between 8 a.m. to 11 a.m.

You might well wonder at the quality of films made with actors who have had "training for a short period before becoming film stars." I had to leave town on the 25th. Maybe that's why I never became a star.

In several places in this book, I'll be remarking on ways to help shape your luck and places to be so that luck can find you.

Here, merely accept that for those tens of thousands of talented people and those thousands of trained and talented actors, there will be hundreds of lucky ones. Be one of those. Don't wait for your luck to come to you; put yourself in its path. Become one of those hundreds that the unemployed call "lucky."

CONTACTS "It's not what you know, it's who you know" is probably truer in the acting profession than in any other. Most actors will tell you that 80% of their jobs come through friends. Not from agents, not from "open calls," and not from casting directors who see you in a college production. From friends. Who do *you* know? Don't despair—you know lots of people. Every actor you know, knew, or will meet is a contact. Everyone connected with any side of the entertainment industries is a contact. There's no telling when you'll meet that person who will give you that piece of information that will bring you to the audition that will bring you work. So, far from despairing, try to approach this subject systematically. Every class you take, every job you get, every party you go to is a beginning place for contacts. Your teacher is a contact, because someone somewhere went to school with him and is now a director looking for an actor just like you. Every student you study with and every actor you work with is someday likely to be able to do you some good. Everyone you meet at a party, who works in the business, may sometime or other know someone who's looking for an actor just like you. The number of your contacts grows exponentially the longer you are in the business and the more you do. When you're eighteen in Tacoma, you'll have very few contacts. A few years later, you'll have more than you imagine.

Of course, some folks are wise enough to be in the inheritance business, and some actors are clever enough to get born into the right families. Some years back I took a long stroll up the California beach with a student who wanted to be an actor. He had the same insecurity that all actors have. "Am I good enough?" he asked aloud. "I don't want to get work on my father's reputation. I want to make it on my own" "Grab the chance," I advised. "Not many have the opportunity to get the first job. Take it. If you're no good, the world will tell you—and in a hurry. If you're good, nobody'll think twice about your dad. You've got contacts, so use 'em." At that point, neither of us knew he'd win an Oscar for his performance in *Wall Street*. He was just another hopeful young actor with talent—and contacts.

Remember, however, that there are good contacts and bad ones. One guy who will badmouth you can do you more damage than you'd ever dream of. Think of the conversations at the beginning of this prologue. I was a visitor in an office and wouldn't want to work with that young woman in the *Shrew*. In Virginia, all I did was answer a phone and an actor lost a job. There are so many actors to choose from that no producer or director will knowingly engage a troublemaker or a nuisance. An actor who earns a troublesome reputation has two choices: be so brilliant that everyone will tolerate you in spite of yourself (and I'll bet there aren't twenty actors in America in this category) or get out of the business. Remember that, while a director is hoping you are exactly what he's looking for when you walk into the audition room, another part of him is also asking that hard-nosed question, "Do I want to spend four weeks in a stuffy room with you?" If he learns that your contacts are negative, then you're in trouble. What is the moral of this? Well, nobody expects you to be Goody Twoshoes, but the more people who like you, the more useful contacts you have. Remember, getting a job in the theatre is a bit like looking for the proverbial needle in a field of hay stacks. Any contact who can help you find the right stack has done you a lot of good.

Some actors are comprehensive and aggressive in their use of contacts. They keep a notebook of everyone they might consider a contact. Some divide the names in the notebook by function (director, actor, manager) and some by medium (stage, TV, film, regional theatre, summer festival). Some don't subdivide but function on the "blanket" theory—the more people you're in contact with, the more your contacts can help you. Surely the most admirably dogged actor I know is Bill Preston, an elderly character man in New York who sends a simple xeroxed sheet with his photo, snippets of reviews, and a reminder of his availability to a list that must exceed 500 names—every single time he works! If I don't receive two or three a year, I begin to worry about his welfare. Currently, as a resident director for the Pioneer

Theatre Company, I direct a professional production only about once a year, and I am rarely in a position to cast all the roles in that show. Even so, I receive scores of postcards seasonally from actors who've worked with me in the years when I was an artistic director and when I hired upwards of seventy actors a year. For them, I am a contact. (Which just shows you what a desperate profession you have chosen!)

Each actor must deal with contacts in his own way. And each must wrestle with his own integrity. All actors will say, at some moment or another, "I want to make it on my own." No one does! Get that naive thought out of your head as quickly as you can. Everyone takes assistance when it comes along, even if it takes the form of the agent's secretary telling his boss that you're a polite young lady and he ought to consider you. The degree to which you exploit your contacts is the only issue at hand, and you will have to work out that degree for yourself. Try putting the question in reverse. How much would you help a friend? Can you expect your friends to help you as much? Less? More? Your friends are you first contacts. And you are theirs.

EMPLOYABILITY I probably should have put this term in quotation marks to signify the large number of traits that actors must have if they are to find work. Each of these traits, in turn, is a partial answer to the pervading question in the mind of an employer, "*Why should I hire you?*" (If you can imagine that question asked by Joe Mantagna in the role of a Hollywood casting agent, you'll probably find the correct inflection for it.) The logistical truth is, nobody needs you.

"Why should I hire you?" I asked a student at a university that also sponsors a professional company. "Well, I'm cute," she replied nervously and self-consciously. "That might be a fair answer while you're still here in a school where your teachers care about you," I answered, "but you're not. And I won't." And I didn't. I was casting a production and didn't give that young woman a moment's serious consideration. There were many reasons for that, but the first reason, the first aspect of "Employability," is that she had a poor self-image.

As an actor, you've got to know who you are. A young actor once auditioned for me with one of Coriolanus's speeches. I asked him why he chose it. Was it something he had played? Had a teacher suggested it? Was he working on it in a class? "No, I just like it." I disregarded him immediately. He was 6 foot 1 and weighed about 150 pounds; he was a sunken-chested, nasal-voiced, midwestern boy and could no more play Coriolanus than could Bill Cosby. He had an entirely inaccurate self-image. That's a common problem for young actors just out of schools or training programs where they have been cast in roles they are wrong for, either because they were the best available in an impoverished talent pool or for therapeutic, "educational" reasons. This kid might have played Bernard in *Death of a Salesman*, but never Coriolanus. The realities of the marketplace are hard ones for many young actors to accept. Even older actors have trouble grasping who they are. The late Jerome Collamore was hired by Nikos Psacharopoulos to play Firs in a Williamstown Theatre Festival production of Chekhov's *The Cherry Orchard* in 1980. Collamore stood ramrod straight and had great dignity, though he was 89 years old. Really. At the first read-through, everything went fine. Then Nikos started blocking the play. At Firs's first entrance, Collamore stooped his back, smacked his lips, slurred his speech and gave a nineteen-year-old's version of an "old man." "What are you doing?" shrieked Psacharopoulos, "why are you *playing* age; you *are* age." Smacking his forehead, he raged on, "Good god, man, you were alive when Chekhov wrote the play!"

How do you know who you are as an actor? And how do you know what parts you are right for? "Is there anything in it for me?" is one of the most commonly asked questions in the acting world. It means, simply, are there any roles in the show about to be cast for which I am the right type? If there aren't, let me not waste my time and psychic energy on the audition and let me not waste the director's time as well. An accurate self-image is essential to the actor. I will be forever thankful to that wise actor who came to me during an open Equity audition and said, "Let's not waste each other's time. Either you want someone 6 foot 7 or you don't."

Your self-image has more to do with than just your physical type, of course. If you are a clown, please don't audition for

Hamlet. If you are a gorgeous ingenue, accept the reality that every straight director will want to fantasize about you and don't try to convince him you can play the wicked stepsister. If you are a highly intelligent actor and have trouble playing stupid roles, know it. If you are a particular ethnic type, audition for the plays of Neil Simon and not those of A.R. Gurney. In mid-rehearsals once, I lost the actor playing Pastor Manders in Ibsen's *Ghosts* and was having an extremely difficult time finding a replacement. And the production was to open in two weeks. In desperation, I asked a friend, "Do you think—if worst comes to absolute worst—that I could do it myself?" "Sure," she laughed, "if you want to change it to Rabbi Manders." The next day the wonderful George Ede accepted the role and saved us all from a comic disaster.

Your self-image has something to do with how good you know you are. Now don't confuse the image of how good you believe you will become with how good you have proven you are. But if you've been terrific in school plays or in summer theatres, there's evidence, in a certain small arena, of how good you are. That evidence does not necessarily mean you are ready to play a lead on Broadway or to be plucked out of school and given a sustaining role on a daytime TV serial, but it does mean that you can be confident of your work in a less competitive arena. When asked (even implicitly), "Why should I hire you?" you ought to be able to reply, "Because I have demonstrated that I am an effective actor, because for the money you're prepared to pay you'll not get anyone better, and because I am *right* for the role." If you can say these things honestly, then you've probably got an accurate self-image. If you say, "Because I'm cute," you probably have neither a good self-image nor a job.

How do you know if you're *right*? It's hard for actors to know how others perceive them. This is just as true for mature actors as it is for beginners. Here's a device that might help you learn how a director might see you when you come into an audition. Agree with three friends to watch a sequence of television shows over the course of a few days. Select a variety of shows: a soap, a sitcom like *Cheers*, a movie-of-the-week, a detective-car chase like *MacGyver* or *The Equalizer*. Agree to watch the same programs—but each of you sees the shows separately. For best results, one of you ought to videotape the shows. For each of the shows (and for each of the commercials), write down the roles any of your three friends might play. They'll do the same. Then, after you have completed these lists, get together to compare notes—play back the video recordings to see how each of you was seen by the other three. If there is a consensus among the three about particular roles you are *right* for, then you will have a starting point for recognizing the kinds of roles a director might imagine you playing. You can repeat the exercise, using plays with some literary density instead of TV programs. Select any dozen major twentieth-century plays from your own country that you and your three friends will read (the likes of Miller, Williams, Wasserstein, Howe, Guare, Wilson, Simon, and Hansberry if you're American; Brenton, Hare, Gray, Osborne, Churchill if you're English; Williamson, Buzo, and Hibberd if you're Australian). Make the same lists about your colleagues; get together to learn about yourselves. Find out the roles for which you are *right*.

Not all casting is typecasting, of course. There are exceptions to all rules, and the rule of typecasting is broken whenever a performer shows a director that the unique quality he can bring to the role is more important than his conformity to the director's preconceived notions of type. Meryl Streep's performances on stage and screen demonstrate this regularly. Is she a religious fundamentalist from Australia? a Jewish refugee from a concentration camp? a vamp? or is she a brilliant character actor who defies being typed? If *you* are a flexible character actor, your chances of influencing a director's casting by an exceptional and particular audition are very real. At the same time, you are well advised to know how others see you, to know what type of role you will most typically be cast in.

As America's theatre strives to reflect its changing population, there is an increasing effort on the part of actors to urge producers and directors to do "non-traditional casting." This phrase describes the casting of actors of surprising gender or race in roles that appear to be written for a particular gender or for an actor of a distinguishable race. Recent productions of *Death of a Salesman* have cast neighbors Charlie and Bernard as Black Americans. On TV, the proportion of female judges in courtroom dramas probably is greater than the proportion of female judges in real courtrooms. Some theatres practice "color-blind casting" and will present a play in which the parents are Caucasian and the children of another race. This strains an audience's credibility, but it may be a valuable stride towards a saner world. It is unquestionably a boon for actors from racial minorities. The sociological thrust of the theatre is sometimes in conflict with its artistic thrust, but the evolving sensibility of our times makes it possible for women and for actors from racial minorities to hope for roles that they would not have been considered for even fifteen years ago when the earlier edition of this book was written. The notion of typecasting is less narrow today.

Given a choice, I'll always work with someone I like. That's a second trait an actor needs to be "Employable"—a pleasing personality. Rehearsing a play is a difficult enough task without the added problems that abrasive personalities might add. Nobody is asking you to be a continual Pollyanna. Just be yourself—unless yourself is an abrasive, feisty, unpleasant self (in which case *be quiet!*). If you have learned through the years that the world does not find you to be an engaging and delightful social lion, then protect your "Employability" by being unobstrusive. Don't be a complainer ("The rehearsal room is too hot," "He held us two minutes overtime," "I was called today and he never even got to me"). Don't be a whiner ("Will we get a lunch break soon?" "I'm too tired to do that scene again today"). Don't be overly helpful ("Gee, I'd be happy to run lines with anybody who's having trouble"). Just be an efficient, cooperative professional. If you do that, you might find you're developing a pleasant personality, and when the director thinks, "Why should I hire you?" he may well answer himself, "Because you'll be pleasant to have around my life for the next four weeks." You will be developing that second trait the actor needs to be "Employable."

"Show me what you can do," says the casting director as she leans back with her forty-seventh cigarette of the day. Well, what *can* you do? Can you sing? Hoof? Play the zither? Can you stand on your head and drink water while your ventriloquist's dummy juggles and sings Verdi's *Otello* with a Russian accent? The more things you can do, the more skills you have, the greater is your chance of being right for the role you're auditioning for, and the greater will be your "Employability." The continual expansion of your skills is a portion of your career, of your life. A few years ago, I was doing a play by George Kelly and I engaged an actress who was an active member of the Actor's Studio, an experienced and mature performer with a substantial career on Broadway and in films and television. One day, over dinner, she confessed she had never been in a verse play, had never done any Shakespeare but hoped one day she could "get into Shakespeare." I was appalled. What did she do in her classes? Her continuing work at the Studio? Didn't she realize how she limited herself by her lack of skill with verse drama? Too many actors are like her. Too many actors wait until they have a role that will require them to learn a dialect or a skill. But when you've got the role, you don't have time to learn cockney or to fence with sword and dagger —you must use all your available time to learn the role and the fight choreography. And if you can do the dialect at your audition, and if your résumé shows that you've mastered stage combat, think how greatly you've improved your chances of getting the job.

The final aspect of "Employability" is what we can call *good work habits*. The prominent stage director Richard Ramos referred glowingly to an actor we both knew and who was a product of Catholic University's actor training program, "He is the most disciplined actor I've ever worked with." That's what the rest of this book is all about: how an actor manages time, relates to co-workers, comports himself with employers and audiences alike. How an actor goes about doing the work.

The Importance of Behavior

It is not enough to be talented, not enough to be trained as a craftsman. It is not enough to be lucky and not enough to have wonderful contacts. A professional actor needs also to know how to behave as a professional actor ought to behave—but as too few do! This book is an attempt to provide actors with guidelines to professional behavior.

The two greatest enemies to good acting are time and a lack of self-respect. There is simply never sufficient time for the actor to do his work correctly. Time is money in the commercial world of theatre and the actor needs to invest his time constructively, efficiently, and intensely. Proper work habits will assist you to use your time well. When you behave properly, you will work effectively. You will discover that you are able to maintain your focus on the real problems of acting during the hours you will be given to rehearse a role. Too many actors are destructively insecure and have so little respect for themselves and their craft that they waste their time and belittle their work by deluding themselves that divine inspiration and opening-night energy will miraculously produce results that have never been seen in rehearsals and that "it'll be right on the night." They have little craft and, therefore, few ways to assist themselves, and so they waste their time and energies on leaping irrelevant, self-imposed hurdles. Such as: "I can't work on this scene until I have have the right props." Or: "I need an audience to make me come alive." But the actor who has sound working habits knows what he can do in each rehearsal and between rehearsals. He knows how to help himself and the entire production. He knows how to respect his work, and that helps him to respect himself. That in turn helps him to use his time wisely, to behave as a professional.

A young, blonde, and attractive acting student at Temple University listened one day as her teacher discussed the importance of the actor's offstage behavior. He was describing how the Actors Theatre of Louisville tended to engage actors with compatible personalities. "My God," she exclaimed, "you mean if I want to act I've got to go to charm school?" The teacher didn't reply. He just nodded. But I could hear him think quite loudly, "Yes, you need to learn how *an actor behaves.*"

AUDITIONS

The Second Most Important Performance

Your audition is the second most important performance you will give in any role. The opening-night performance—or the one that gets reviewed—is the most important. If you act well then, you will help your career in many ways. You will contribute to the possibility of the show's having a long and successful run, and that means you'll be employed for a long time and the regular paycheck will be a welcome rarity in your life as an actor. Even if the show does not succeed, or has a fixed run, you'll have come to the critics' attention and, whenever you receive good reviews, you may be optimistic about other managements hiring you for future shows. But short of that opening-night performance, the audition's the thing with which to catch the conscience of the director. If you give a poor performance at the audition, you'll never have an opportunity to give another.

Despite this obvious truth, most actors audition poorly. I've heard actors described as behaving like alcoholics who drink to ensure they don't get the job they fear they won't get. A bad audition provides an actor with an explanation for the rejection that is the norm in the theatre. When they are not selected, they can always tell themselves they would have gotten the job if they had known the play better, or had more time to prepare, or worn different clothes, or done a more low-key audition, or a more flamboyant audition, etc. Whether or not this is an accurate interpretation of the typical actor's defense-mechanism in action, it is an observable fact that some actors come to auditions ill-prepared and that they then present themselves foolishly. As a very young actor, I arrived for auditions at the Oregon Shakespearean Festival with expurgated editions of the season's plays. I was naive enough to have taken them from my mother's library, never imagining that some texts of the plays were incomplete, or had been "Bowdlerized." When it was my turn to audition, I was unable to follow the scene being read, was unable to say my lines (many of which were not in my version), and created a dreadful impression on the directors, I am certain. I would like to believe that was a major reason for the poor casting I received that summer, though it is equally likely that my skills were deficient and that the rest of the company was just plain better than I was. (As I recall, my major role that five-play season was the small role of the aged Host of the Inn in *Two Gentlemen of Verona*.) There may be an occasional excuse for a lack of preparedness in the commercial marketplace, where frequently it is impossible for the auditioning actor to read the "sides" for a new play (or film or commercial). Or cost may be prohibitive. The reality today is that a well-prepared audition in New York for a musical role will cost the actor nearly $100: $50 for your own accompanist, $25 for two sessions with your coach, and $25 for miscellany like sheet music, transportation, lunch, etc. There may be excuses in such circumstances, but it is depressing to see this same failing among the actors in resident companies, where the season has been announced for months, and among students at schools where the script has been available for weeks prior to the audition. I cannot pretend to assess the psychology behind such self-defeating work habits. I can only urge all actors to "get over it."

Nobody likes auditions. Not actors, not directors, not producers. But it's the only system in practice. Auditions can be described in rather the same way that Winston Churchill described democracy: "Many forms of government have been tried and will be tried in this world of sin and woe. No one pretends that democracy is perfect or all-wise. Indeed, it has been said that democracy is the worst form of government, except all those other forms that have been tried from time to time." Auditions are the worst, but they're the best we've got.

Do yourself a favor. Approach the audition as a businessman would an interview. Do you think someone hoping to be engaged as an executive challenges his interviewers to discover his secret abilities behind the mask of seeming indifference and ignorance he presents? Not likely. He does everything he assumes to be correct protocol and good taste to advance himself, proclaim his abilities, and persuade the employers that he is the only person for the job. An actor ought to do the same. The protocol may differ, but the activity is essentially the same. Your task is to convince the director to select you, and there are many things you can do to help yourself.

Types of Auditions

Auditions vary greatly in type and format and they occur in a variety of places. You will be well off if you've prepared yourself for these differing experiences. If you have not had a *real* experience of the varying types and places, you can help yourself and your friends by auditioning each other in hypothetical circumstances. Indeed, by playing the game of "Auditioning," you will have a chance to sit on the listener's side of the table, where you will gain valuable insights into what the auditioner sees, hears, and thinks. Many colleges and conservatories give their students instruction in the skills of auditioning. Some of these are wonderful, but too often the instructors are not sufficiently experienced in the real world of the theatre and focus on the "acting" the students do in their audition pieces instead of the "auditioning," which ought to be the point of the instruction.

I have been auditioned in large, dark theatres, in offices, hotel rooms, automobiles, in a rented hall with a videotape camera rolling and no humans in sight, and once at the beach. Offices and rented audition halls (sometimes used as rehearsal rooms) are the most common places for auditions, but an actor needs to be prepared for any emergency. What you can do in a theatre will not necessarily work for you at the beach. The low-key reading you do in an office will differ from the open-voiced presentation you might attempt in a rehearsal room. When you are preparing material that you might use many times, in varying circumstances, you'll be well advised to rehearse it in as great a variety of locations as you can arrange. Bore your friends! Do your selections in their living rooms, their offices, in classrooms, hotel rooms, corridors, parks—wherever you can and as often as you can. Don't make the mistake of assuming your inspiration will carry you through the audition. Would you venture an opening night unrehearsed? Why audition unrehearsed?

The most common form of audition is the interview. It was virtually the *only* kind of audition until the 1920s, when the great American director George Abbott introduced the novel idea that an actor might be judged best if she actually read the lines of the role she was being considered for. The interview is a portion of all auditions and is frequently the entirety of an audition, your only chance to present yourself. That is particularly true in Hollywood, where virtually all small roles, particularly those beginners might hope for, are cast on the basis of appearance and personality—either the camera likes your face or it doesn't. Interviews are equally common in New York as an initial screening phase of the audition process. Managements are required by Actors' Equity Association to hold an open call for all shows, and typically several hundred actors a day will be shuttled through a small room before a not-very-interested casting director. What does the auditioner look for in an interview? Physical type, vocal type, appropriate skills, and personality. Ninety percent of auditioning actors will be ruled out at this stage of audition. If the role requires a soprano to hit a high C and you can't, you're out. At this stage of the process, the management is trying to select a small number of plausible actors: skilled, appropriate, pleasant.

A typical interview is conducted in the following manner: you arrive in a waiting room, corridor, or lobby and are given a number and usually an approximate time that number will be called, say 2:10 p.m. (If the number/time is for much later in the day than the present time, you're free to leave and return. Be careful to be back very early, however, as on rare occasions the casting line moves faster than anticipated and, if you miss your turn, you're out.) You will probably be asked to sign a list that is kept by the assistant stage manager (ASM) or a secretary who is coordinating the day's call. You may also be asked to fill out an audition form that typically asks your name, phone number(s), union affiliations, agent's name and number. You may be required to show your union card to some representative of the appropriate union who is there to deny entrance to non-union actors. You may be asked for your photo/résumé at this point, or you may present it only at the time you are shown into the audition. Now . . . you wait your turn! When it comes, you will be ushered into the auditioning room, and you may very well be introduced by name to the director or to whomever is present. There may be several people in the room: production stage manager, casting director, director, playwright, art director, producer, sponsor, musical director, choreographer, etc. Most will be seated behind a long table and, typically, you will be invited to sit in a chair across the table. By this time, some thirty seconds into the interview, your fate is probably already decided. The impression you have made up to this point may have determined your fate. Now the interview begins. Typical questions posed to you will relate to your training, your recent work, your agent, your experience, and any particular skills you might have that are required for the job. Do you ride horseback? can you speak German? whom did you work with last? Next you will be thanked, told that you will be contacted should there be any interest in auditioning you further, and you will leave as you came in. The entire interview will not have lasted three minutes.

The second type of audition is one in which you are asked to present prepared materials. Usually these are held by directors of permanent companies or summer companies such as the many Shakespeare festivals that have sprung up across the country. These directors are looking for actors who will be engaged for all or part of a season and cast in a sequence of roles—what is commonly called a "line" of roles: Cassio, Hortensio, and Sir Eglamour, for example. This type of audition is conducted in precisely the same way as the interview, except that you will be asked to present your prepared pieces. That may occur immediately upon your admission to the auditioning room, or it may follow a brief interview. Some directors interview actors first so as to learn a bit about them and to give them a chance to relax and get a sense of the room they're about to work in. Others feel it is faster to see the prepared selection(s) first. Then, if they're not interested in the actor, they can save the time and labor of an interview. It is quite possible that you will be interrupted in the middle of your prepared pieces. There is no way you can know what that interruption means. It might mean the director never wants to see you again in her entire life, or it might mean that you have shown what she needs to know for now and she will call you back later. Or it might mean she's rushed and must move you along, even though her mind's not made up at all. You will be tempted to interpret such an interruption as rejection. Don't. It may be, but you won't know that for certain. If you give up at this point, you'll forfeit your chances in the remaining brief moments of the audition, moments in which something about you may excite the director sufficiently to call you back for a subsequent audition. As frequently as you may be interrupted, you may be asked to present another prepared selection. A young actor ought to have a half-dozen speeches at the ready so that when the director asks for "something in verse, something comic," you can do your Viola from *Twelfth Night*, and when she asks for something serious and modern, you can do your Gabby from *Serenading Louie*. "Be prepared" is a creed for more than just the Boy Scouts.

The third type of audition is the "cold reading" in which the actor is invited to read selections from the play(s) to be produced (or from some similar play that the director feels will give him a reasonable sense of the actor's abilities). Frequently this "cold reading" follows an audition in which you present prepared materials. In most instances, you will be given the script to look over for a few minutes, while the actors ahead of you in the casting line give their readings, and then you'll be expected to provide ample space between yourself and the director's table as you read. Film and television directors are less concerned with that distance than stage directors, since the close-up is the important concern of the film director and he can see you better if you remain seated near him.

In almost all instances, there will be someone to read the other lines and to cue you. Typically, this person is an actor who has been hired by the casting director to provide this service, and a *superior* way for a young actor to learn about the audition process is to find a casting director who will hire you as a reader. When you get that job, you will be able to listen to the comments that follow each actor's audition; you will be able to observe for yourself how vital is the actor's entrance, clothing, manner, sense of confidence, and departure. And you can never know what will come of your being a reader. A director I know well once cast the young man who served patiently as a reader for five days of auditions in the leading role of a Broadway-bound new musical. (The show never got to Broadway, but the young actor had an extraordinary break.)

Some directors will coach you during auditions. Usually this happens only if the director has called you back, or if he is extremely interested in you. The late Nikos Psacharopoulos was renowned for stopping young actors in the middle of their prepared materials and saying, quite harshly, "No, no. Stop 'acting.' Just say the words to me simply. Don't give me that bullshit. Start at the top." Many actors were too unnerved to continue. But I've known actors who Nikos badgered, then hired in their first Equity jobs. Other directors will ask you to repeat all or portions of your selections, but with different actions or given circumstances pertaining. Allen Fletcher, when he was artistic director of the Seattle Repertory Theatre, caused me to repeat Didi's speech from *Waiting for Godot* ("Was I sleeping while the others suffered?") and instructed me to play this action: to share my happiness with Gogo. Of course that made no sense in terms of the play. But it was his way of learning my flexibility, my willingness to take direction, my control. (He didn't hire me.) On other occasions, directors may give you improvisations to do. This time-consuming activity is usually a sign that you are under very serious consideration for the role. Many film directors videotape all improvisations—indeed, all auditions—as a way of learning what the actor's presence on film is truly like. Stage directors will frequently resort to improvisation as a way of learning the actor's emotional range. As Robert Lewis remarks in *Method—or Madness?* (New York: Samuel French, Inc., 1958), casting must be done to ensure that the actor can reach the role's most intense emotional moments. If you are asked to do an improv, "cut loose."

Auditions are normally private affairs. Rare are the directors who will permit outsiders to sit in the room while an audition is in progress. So don't bring along your girlfriend. The audition is a meeting between you and the director—one on one (although the room may have other folks in it). And whether the audition is a limited one for a few actors the casting director has selected or that actor's nightmare, the "cattle call," the rules remain pretty much the same. You will be given a number, a chance, and an exit. It is not a cheery experience, but remember, it is your second most important performance, so you had better learn to cope with its possible rudeness, haste, and depersonalization. You must come to terms with the truth that you are one number in a "cattle call" and find ways to make the judges give you the blue ribbon.

Preparing for an Audition

At 3:30 tomorrow afternoon you have an audition. Maybe you've followed up a lead given you by a fellow actor, maybe you've learned of the audition from a notice at the Equity office, maybe your agent has made the appointment for you. No matter. You are the one who is going, whose employment rests in the balance. What do you do?

The first thing is to ensure that all the things you need to take with you are in order. These are likely to include: photo/résumé, musical instrument, accompanist, your portfolio of pictures and reviews, special equipment or props, an appointment calendar, a notebook, medicines (notably breath mints), and good luck tokens. The working actor needs to have these items ready at all times.

Your audition kit should contain several copies of your photo/résumé, your equivalent of the businessman's calling card. Just as there are many styles and formats for those little white calling cards, so there is an immense number of ways that photos and résumés are prepared. Most young actors worry themselves sick seeking the "right" way to present themselves. They are wise to concern themselves about these items, but there is a truth to be told that may ease your anxieties. There is no "right" way; there are only "wrong" ways. That is, no photo and no résumé is going to get you work—but many will lose you work. The truth here is a simple one. Each person who looks at the photo/résumé is human and subject to the inconsistencies that make us human. Each has his own prejudices and idiosyncrasies and each will pass an entirely subjective judgment on the photo and résumé. What pleases one director will bore the next. You cannot win, if by winning you mean finding a 100% foolproof model. The important thing to do is to ensure that your photo and résumé meet the common standards presently in vogue.

Vogues in photo/résumés change with the season and the city. What is true for New York this year may not be true for Hollywood. But the current fashion will be evident if you check several other actors' résumés or speak with an agent. You had best conform to the fashion, which means you must be prepared to spend a lot of money on photography and duplication at regular intervals in your career. If you have an agent, your problems are usually reduced. The agent will determine what is wanted from you. Expect, when you first get an agent, that all the photos you presently have will be discarded. The agent will require new ones that conform to what he understands the fashion to be and to the way he wishes to market you. (Beware of the agent who accepts photos only by a photographer of his choosing. He may be getting a kickback and you may be getting ripped off.)

For many years, the fashion for New York and regional theatres was for the 8x10, black and white, glossy print of a "head shot" with your face filling the entire frame, and the photo was printed without a white border or edge. The face seemed to be too large and important for the photo to hold. A couple of years ago the fashion changed, and now most head shots have a two-inch white frame around the much smaller picture of your full face, which is framed with a decorative black border. Like the

height of the hemline, these photographic fashions change—
maybe only so the photographers who support themselves by
serving actors can increase their earnings. Whatever the currently
fashionable format, the photos are usually taken in natural light
and are not "arty"—no extreme shadows, no profile lighting. The
goal is to give a clear image of what you actually look like so that
the casting director can remember you by looking at your photo.
Good = it looks like you. Bad = it could be someone else. There
is a prejudice against funny hats, eccentric wardrobe, or cutesy
pictures. The trend in Hollywood the last time I worked there
was for a 10x12 sheet printed matte with an 8x10 photo inside a
border on the front and a composite of smaller shots on the back,
each in a different pose and costume, and with the agent's name
and number printed prominently at the bottom of the sheet.
These sheets were frequently three-hole punched to fit into a
casting director's spring-binder notebook. Before you get photos
made up, decide what market they're to be distributed to and
then investigate the current fashions.

Résumés are not particularly common in Hollywood, since
what you look like is much more important than what you have
done. Frequently an agent will not circulate your résumé unless it
is a simple list of major TV shows that you have been seen in
recently and a video cassette that is available for casting directors
to look at should they be interested in you.

In New York, the regional theatres, and in summer stock,
résumés are expected. Typically, these are typed on a piece of
8x10 paper and photoduplicated so that one can be stapled (at
all four corners, *please*) to the back of each photo—making a
self-contained and easily filed credential. Many actors go the
added expense of having their photos and résumés printed, so
that they are "classier" looking, but I don't know of an actor who
ever got a job because of the "class" of her photo/résumé.

A résumé is like a piece of journalism: it must tell who, what,
where, why, and when. At the top there should be salient information: your name, address, phone and answering machine
number, your union affiliations, your age (or age range), height,
weight, color of hair and eyes. Selected evidence of your work
should be further down the page: plays you've been in, the roles

you've played, where they were produced, when and by whom, and any notable information such as the name of a prominent director or star who worked the production. Young actors frequently list items in this section that nobody cares about. Of course, you don't have a lot to list at the beginning of your career. But don't assume that quantity makes up for quality. Don't list *every* play you've been in since childhood. For example, I once played one of the Cards in a school production of *Alice in Wonderland* in which Richard Chamberlain played the Caterpillar, but that dubious credit has never appeared on my résumé. (I doubt if Chamberlain ever listed it either.) Résumés need to be revised each time you do a role that you believe will make the résumé look more impressive. Don't scribble the addition in smearable ball-point. Re-type and re-duplicate and re-staple. You may find room to list any significant training you have had (or are presently taking) and any particular skills you have at the bottom of the 8x10 sheet: dialects, athletic prowess, foreign languages. Since you are limited to one small sheet of paper and since you want it to appear neat, you will have to be selective. As with photos, the fashion in the layout of résumés changes from time to time. As long as your résumé is clear and attractive, you needn't worry unduly if it looks a bit different from others you see—and you don't have to buy the rip-off book I recently saw for sale that offers instruction for the young actor on how to prepare a photo/résumé. Look at some. Use your common sense. Take the money you would have spent on that book and go to the theatre.

Some actors lie on their résumés. Directors expect about 15% of the material on a young actor's résumé to be at least a distortion of the truth, at worst a bold-faced lie. You may disadvantage yourself if you don't include some kind of inflated material since anyone looking at the résumé will assume there's an element of fiction about it anyway. What kinds of inflation can you use safely? And what will betray you? Well, it is safe to name-drop. If any director or producer or "name" player was in any way attached to the production, make certain that's noted in your résumé. If you were an extra in King Hamlet's court when Val Kilmer played Hamlet at the Colorado Shakespeare Festival, you can say that you played "with" him. If questioned rigorously, you can explain that you were in the production, that you filled in for the actor doing Ophelia or Horatio for some of the rehearsals, and that you were asked if you could take over that role if the show extended. In other words, bluff—and don't we call that "acting?" Indicate the places you've worked by the name of the theatre, not the name of the college. Playing Judge Brack at the Lobero Theatre in Santa Barbara is more prestigious than playing him for the Department of Drama at the University of California. Particularly, in this example, because the Lobero is occasionally used as a touring house for professional companies and a director might assume the best. Overt lying cannot be recommended, but inflation is as much a part of our theatre's economy as it is of the world's. Happily, the more you work, the less you'll need to inflate your deeds. Time is on your side. You'll either develop a legitimate résumé or you'll be out of the business.

Let me underscore the problems you can get into by overt lying by relating two true stories. These are intended as morality tales—to dissuade you from falsifying your résumé and to show you how much trouble you can cause yourself. Each year in New York, Equity holds an audition called the "LORT Lottery." Each LORT (League of Resident Theatres) company is contractually obliged to hold open auditions in New York each year, and Equity facilitates this by inviting as many theatres as wish to send their casting agents to the Equity office for three days to audition the several hundred actors who have sent postcards to Equity and have had their names chosen by lot to give five minute prepared auditions. On one occasion, the directors and casting agents were each given the photo/résumé of an actor who came in, did his pieces, and went on his way. At the next ten-minute coffee break, the director of a prominent Shakespeare festival stood, got all of our attentions, held up that actor's photo/résumé and said, "On this actor's résumé it says he played the role of Roderigo in my production of *Othello*. He did not." Another added, "Well, I wasn't going to say it, but he was also not in the Philadelphia production of *Hamlet* he claims. I know, because I was." The actor's credibility and reputation were sorely damaged, and, since the actor knew in advance which directors were inside watching the auditions, more than a few of us wondered why he had been so foolish as to send in that résumé.

One day in Virginia, I received a young woman's photo/résumé in the mail. I was surprised to discover that it claimed she had played Sybil in *Private Lives* and Violet in *Man and Superman* at my theatre. I telephoned her and asked about those credits. She was vague. I responded that, to the best of my knowledge, the theatre had produced the plays only twice: twenty years earlier when, if her photo was accurate, she would have been an infant, and then two years before, when I had directed both productions and knew that she was not in the casts. Indeed, the actress who *had* played both of those roles was a particular friend of mine. The young woman faltered and confessed that she had "padded her résumé." I grew angry and told her that not only was she stupid for having sent such a résumé to the very theatre she falsely claimed she had worked at, but that she did a terrible and unethical disservice to both the actress who had played those roles and to my theatre. "Somebody might read your résumé and think I would hire you for these roles, which I would not, and that would hurt the image of this theatre," I scolded. By this time the young actress was in tears—but they were tears of her own earning.

Theatre is a surprisingly small world, and bold-faced lies will be found out quickly—and the liar will suffer.

A large number of jobs you'll audition for require you to have some musical skills. Legit plays like *And a Nightingale Sang* and *The Hostage* have songs in them, musicals are dependent on their scores, industrials are the same as musicals, and even commercials frequently hire "singers." You must insure that your needs for such an audition are in order. If you will be asked to play an instrument, you will be notified in advance. If you're going to play something (or accompany yourself as you sing), rehearse it exhaustively. The total effect of your presentation can be marred by inept musicianship. If your instrument is the tape recorder, bring along one that requires no time to set up—a transistor cassette machine is best. Make certain the batteries are new.

If you are doing a singing audition, bring your own accompanist if at all possible. At many auditions, an accompanist is provided, and he is usually a surprisingly good and flexible pianist. But he hasn't rehearsed with you: he doesn't know the tempo, or the phrasing, the shifts in volume and rhythm you will make. Singing with a pianist you haven't rehearsed with is a bit like auditioning in a language you don't really know. Don't do yourself such a disservice. Even though it may cost you money (accompanists have to eat), bring your own. If scheduling is a problem, ask to have your audition time changed. Managements are usually happy to make an adjustment if it means you can have your own accompanist. They know the difference, and they want to hear you at your best.

If it is impossible to bring your accompanist, at the very least bring your own sheet music—well marked with the dynamics that will help the pianist. Indeed, you should always carry the sheet music for at least four songs with you: two ballads, two belts. Then, in the audition that wasn't going to be a singing one but during which the director suddenly thinks, "My god, maybe I can cast her in the revue we're doing at the end of the season," you're ready. You reach in your audition kit and "voila!" Don't think this is hyperbole. During a New York audition for our forthcoming production of the musical revue *Tintypes*, director Darwin Knight and I saw a young woman who was all wrong for the show but who impressed us strongly. For the role of Anna Held, she sang a selection from Bernstein's *Candide*. Three months later, she was astounded when we called to offer her the leading role of Cunegonde in *Candide*. "When do you want me to audition?" she asked, disbelieving. "You did that when you sang at our *Tintypes* audition. We just want you to do the role." She did. She was wonderful!

There are three kinds of singers: those who can sing, those who can fake, and those who can't sing. Don't claim you can sing unless you really can—unless you have studied for a long time, can hit all the notes, and are in truth a singer of songs. It insults a director if an actor claims to be a singer and then demonstrates in the first six bars that he isn't. Directors don't like actors who fail to fool them. A brilliant musical director with the improbable name of Sand Lawn has done many shows that I've produced. At auditions, he sits erect in his tight collar, a thin pencil in his right hand, listening to auditions. When the singer can't do what the role requires, Sand shakes his head in an almost imperceptible way—the actor can't see it, but his directors can. No discussion. The singer can't sing. The singer is out.

A faker of songs is someone who knows how to sell a song, can phrase exquisitely, hit enough notes to give the impression of melody, and charm the pants off you. Rex Harrison's classic performance as Henry Higgins is the standard example of a faker. Fakers won't get cast in roles that require "real singing," but they may get cast in roles for which their skills are sufficient. A caution: a bathroom singer is not a faker. A bathroom singer is someone who is untrained—usually loud, uncontrolled, energetic, and unable to hear his own errors—though usually in love with his voice. If you are a bathroom singer, you have two choices: study to become a singer or keep your mouth shut. An actor who does not sing is just that: one who tells the director he has not studied and is not a singer. Now, if the director says "sing anyway," go ahead. And be prepared to go ahead with a well-rehearsed song that is simple, within your range, and presented without bravado. Let the director sell herself on the idea that she can make a singer out of you. If you have flatly denied being able to sing, your integrity is fine. If the director then causes you to demonstrate that you can hit all the notes of the ditty to be sung and that your voice is a simple, unaffected, untrained one, she may be very happy. And when she's happy, you have a chance to work. Directors can fool themselves into thinking they can make you into a singer, even if you have flatly denied all ability to sing, and then the problem becomes theirs. The late Robert Gerringer, a wonderful and much-loved actor, played Volpone for me. The role has a song in the sequence in which the libertine woos the innocent Celia. Bob rehearsed for hours, every day. Never was there a more tone-deaf actor, an actor less able to sustain a simple melody line. It was excruciating. Finally, we agreed he would "speak to the rhythm" and let the accompaniment take care of the musical part of the number. Bob was a marvelous faker, and he danced, pranced, and spoke his way through the song to the delight of the audiences (and to the agony of music lovers).

Some directors will want to look at your portfolio, so it is imperative you keep yours up to date and at the ready. A portfolio is merely a collection of additional photos and occasional reviews that might give the director a richer sense of you during an interview. Typically, the portfolio will contain a half-dozen 8x10s that show you in varying angles and poses: some full-body shots, some mug shots. This is the chance for you to include your cutesy pictures and your beefcake and cheesecake: take off your shirt, show your legs. You might also include shots from productions if you're in unusual makeup or extravagant costume, or if there's a "name" actor in the shot with you, or if the production was at a highly regarded theatre. Any reviews you choose to include should be from the most prestigious productions you can offer. The rave you got from the college paper for your Actor #3 in *The Dining Room* is of no use here. But the one line saying your performance was "strong" in a summer Shakespeare festival's production of *Titus Andronicus* that starred Ken Ruta is worth including; that festival is someplace where critics are supposed to apply professional standards and where other fine actors may have worked before you. Since such stars as Stacy Keach, Powers Booth, and George Peppard acted at the Oregon Shakespearean Festival, it is safe to assume that good actors work there—and that means you must be one.

Portfolios are not commonly looked at by directors of commercial shows in New York, but Hollywood casting directors like to see them because they can see how your face photographs from many angles and how differing clothes look on you. Portfolios are always expected if the call is essentially for modeling, whether you are in New York, Hollywood, or Baton Rouge. The three-hole binder is an acceptable style of portfolio, but in recent years portfolios have become increasingly elaborate. Many New York actors who seek a lot of commercial and/or modeling work carry a leather, zippered portfolio that is 11x14 or larger and that frequently has handles like a briefcase. As with photo/résumés, the fashions are subject to change. Take a look at what others are using: let conformity be your guide.

Audio and video cassettes recently have become a part of the auditioners world. Audio cassettes are for "voice-over" jobs. The standard cassette is about five minutes long. It contains an introduction in your friendliest voice in which you say "hello," introduce your name, and give either your phone number or your agent's. Next, you can read the copy of one or more actual radio commercials—tape them off the air, learn the copy, do them in your own voice—and then anything special you wish to include, like accent or dialect demonstrations. Finally, conclude with a warm and cheery salutation, thanking the auditor for listening, and re-stating your name and phone number. It is wisest to record these in a professional studio, many of which can give you broadcast quality and can support you with canned music, where appropriate. This costs a bit, but the world of voice-overs is a lucrative one, and you will have to invest time, money, and effort if you are serious about cracking it. It should be obvious that you will need many copies of this demo, since you'll be leaving it with ad agencies, casting directors, sponsors, and all sorts of potential employers. Inexpensive dubs of your original tape may be made at many stationery and photo-duplicating stores. Be certain to write your name and phone number on each cassette because it is easy for a casting agent to jumble up a dozen of them. If you are uneasy about having your phone number written and recorded on all those cassettes that will fall into who-knows-whose hands, you are wise to put an agent's name and number on them instead of your own.

Video cassettes are a slightly different item in your audition kit. Ideally, these will begin with a professional-looking title card, printed with your name and your (or your agent's) number. This should be followed with a talking head of you, announcing your name, your (or your agent's) number, and describing the items that will follow. People who view your demo tape will be interested in two things: how you come across on camera and who has hired you before. It is a sad truth to tell that faces and personalities are very different on camera from what they are on stage. Handsome lads and lovely lasses sometimes have fat faces and boring "white bread" personalities on camera. Other times, the camera turns the legendary ugly duckling into a charismatic swan. There is no predicting how you'll come across. Your demo tape will be most effective if excerpts from known TV shows follow your talking head introduction: your brief scene as an "under five" day player on *One Life to Live* and your appearance as a contestant on *Jeopardy*. As your career develops, your demo tape can expand. Actors such as the celebrated teacher Robert Benedetti have accumulated half-hour tapes of their multiple performances on major shows like *Cheers*, tapes they will play for you at the drop of a "PLAY" button. If you don't have any real TV appearances yet, then consider shooting something from a TV script or play. But these must not look like home movies. They must be as professionally made as you can arrange. Many universities have professional-caliber studios and, if you or a friend are enrolled, it is frequently possible to use these facilities to make your demo. Just as you wouldn't show an inappropriate or poorly rehearsed audition, don't show a poorly made video demo. It can hurt more than help.

For many auditions, you will need to bring along some special equipment: costumes or props. Make certain these are ready in your kit. If you're going up for a musical and you dance, make certain you bring along your dancing shoes. If one of your prepared selections requires a springblade knife, with which you can safely stab yourself, bring it along—and check it first to ensure that it is functioning correctly. I nearly cut off a finger once doing Jerry's final speeches from *Zoo Story*. The blood lent realism to the audition, but the director was more than a bit distracted by the accident. An actor once did those same speeches in an audition for me, and I was unable to take the character's menace seriously when I saw him holding not a sharp knife but a paper bookmark.

Something needs to be said here about the medicines you should keep in your audition kit. Obviously aspirin, breath mints, antacids, tissues, Band-Aids, and throat lozenges are essential. Each of you will find the ones that you prefer, but more and more health-conscious actors use those made from natural substances: *Fisherman's Friend* is a particularly fashionable brandname among many stage actors. Additionally, some actors have been known to use tranquilizers for auditions; the most popular kind are muscle relaxants that do not affect your mental capabilities but do permit you hold the script steady. But I am *strongly* opposed to actors using chemicals in their systems and, at the risk of agreeing with Nancy Reagan (one of my least-respected American celebrities), I believe we must all "SAY NO TO DRUGS." If you are well trained, you should have a technique that will permit you to relax just prior to an audition, a rehearsal, or a performance.

A well-prepared actor will keep a small diary or calendar book, a small notebook, and a pen in his audition kit. The calendar book is used to keep your schedule of classes, rehearsals, appointments, auditions, and other professional dates so that you can avoid scheduling an audition at a time you're not free. If you're asked to a callback, be certain it does not conflict with something else. The small notebook is for you to inscribe the names and phone numbers of anyone you meet (the director, casting agent, sponsor's representative) or the details of any information about casting you may learn in the waiting room.

Finally, there are your totems, your good-luck pieces. Some are religious, some personal, some clichéd—it doesn't matter. If you get comfort from saying your rosary while holding your rabbit's food, take those things with you. There's a vast amount of luck and whimsy in the casting process, and if these items will help you relax and send out good "vibes," follow Karl Malden's advice and "don't leave home without 'em."

Well, that's quite a list! Have them ready; auditions frequently come on short notice. My first New York job came like that. At 11:30 one morning a friend called and told me to hurry to the Playhouse Theatre on 48th Street. By 12:30 Jose Quintero had cast me in my first New York show. At 12:31 I was in rehearsal. And that's not a rare instance. Twenty years later, in Salt Lake City, my agent called at 10:15 a.m.—could I get to an audition before noon? I could, I did, I got the job on an episode of a CBS prime-time series. I try to be as ever-ready as a battery. You know, there's a delightful saying that's posted in a lot of business offices: "Lack of planning on your part does not constitute an emergency on my part." But in the business of show business, it does. Maybe we should post our own sign: "Deadlines don't scare me—I exist for emergencies!"

The audition kit should be a bit like a doctor's little black bag. It should have a small amount of everything you might need, and it should be ready to go with you on any call. Some actors use a briefcase to carry their things. Others prefer to appear more informal and use airline bags or the ubiquitous backpack. All that really matters is that you have what you need when you need it.

* * * * *

How much do you know about the audition you're going to? Your second task is to learn as much as you can in order to present yourself as well as you can. I am depressed when I audition actors who could know something about the job they're seeking but don't. I suppose I'm least patient with students who saunter into an audition ill prepared, mistaking their teacher for their friend, and don't realize that the teacher has metamorphosed into the director and that friendship has nothing to do with the casting of a play. These students (the most talented are frequently the greatest offenders) are teaching themselves very bad work habits. Their teachers are doing them a grievous injury by indulging such poor professional behavior. Too many teachers are shamefully insecure and need the validation of their students' adoration. They coddle their students and, under the guise of "nurturing" them, they keep them in infantile behavior patterns that will betray them when they leave the groves of academe for the thickets of the marketplace.

Sadly, many of these same poor habits are frequently found in supposedly mature professionals. I auditioned a company for roles in *Romeo and Juliet* a few years ago and discovered that about 15% of them had not read the play. When I was seeing actors for *Late Blooming Flowers*, a show adapted from Chekhov's novella, I knew that the script was not available and so I knew that no one could be fully prepared. But I thought they would have read the novella and that they would have some knowledge of Chekhov's other plays. Hoo boy, was I wrong! One actor came in, described his background as "several films with Steve Reeves in Italy," and confided that he'd never heard of Chekhov. I was dazzled by his arrogance, but I never gave him a thought when it came time to cast the production.

Where can you learn about the audition? Well, where did you first find out there was a call? If it was from one of the trade papers such as *Variety, Backstage, Show Business,* or *The Holly-wood Reporter,* you certainly have some information to use as a starter: the name of the play or film, the ages and types of the actors being sought. If it's a published property, buy it or get it from the library and read it. Next, inquire of anyone who might help you. If you have an agent, bug him until he gets you some hard intelligence. If there's a phone number with the announcement of the call, ring the people and seek whatever added information they will give you.

Get to the audition early! If the script has not been available, immediately ask for the "sides" you will be reading. Ask the other actors if they know any details about the audition. Particularly, ask those who are leaving: did they do a cold reading? did they get any coaching? what's the room like? who is inside? Ignorance is one of the actor's greatest enemies at auditions, one of the greatest contributors to anxiety. The more you know, the better off you are. Frequently the ASM can give you information—a look at the storyboard if it's a commercial; a look at the the cast breakdown; and, most importantly, the scene you'll be reading.

When you have learned all you can, consider how to costume yourself. Remember, this is a performance you're about to give, and your costuming is an important part of the effect you will make. If you know something about the play, try to wear clothes that will suggest the period or type of character you're hoping to be cast as. If you're reading for The Girl in *I'm Not Rappaport,* don't wear pants and don't wear anything with a plunging neckline. Wear an attractive and modest dress—as the script describes. Don't expect the director to be a superman whose x-ray vision can see through the denim coveralls you're wearing to the fragile soul you believe you have underneath. When an actor walks in the door, I want to see something like the character I'm looking for. Immediately.

As you'll learn from such books as John T. Molloy's *Dress for Success,* shoes are a very telling part of your appearance. Polished shoes with heels that are not run down bespeak a person of self-confidence, dignity, and importance. You may think that directors are looking at your face, but they are frequently looking at the floor—to avoid eye-contact. And what do they see there? What joins you to the earth? Your basis. Your shoes. Trendy athletic shoes may be very comfortable, ideal to wear on the way to the audition . . . but are they what the character would wear?

As with all aspects of this profession, fashions change with the seasons and the geography. Actors in Hollywood need to present themselves differently from actors in New York. In Hollywood, what you show is what you are. If you (and your agent) believe you can get work as an unshaven Don Johnson clone, fine. Go to the call looking like that. And if there's such a character in the film (and if that *Miami Vice* fashion is still current), good luck. But when you choose a particular way to present yourself, don't assume you'll be considered for any other type of role. You may read over the script in the waiting room, discover you could play the juvenile's best friend, and ask to read that as well. You're wasting your time. You are seen as what you present. So be very careful how you choose to present yourself. In New York things are a bit more conservative. The East Coast businessman wears a necktie, and as an East Coast actor you must realize that the people putting up the money are expecting you to behave as a mature professional. They want you on time, sober, and working hard. If your clothing suggests you are irresponsible, or too much of a "free spirit," you're not likely to impress them. In New York—and that's where most of the LORT companies hire their actors as well—you are seen as a talent that can be dressed to fit the role. The management wants evidence of two things: your skill as an actor and your maturity as a professional. They want to see you clean, well-groomed, conservatively dressed. In Hollywood you may get hired because you seem uniquely eccentric. In New York that will rarely happen.

Your kit's in order, you've studied the play you're reading for, you've selected your costume. Now it's time to get *yourself* ready for the audition. Get a good night's sleep. Attend to your grooming carefully. Go over your prepared selections and songs several times. Pamper yourself at breakfast to help build your ego. Arrange your day so you're not rushed or frazzled. Walk into that audition at the peak of your powers. "Go out there and kill 'em."

How to Audition

Each audition is a five-part performance; it's a very short, five-act play. Each part is a unique experience, but each retains the same structure, and you will increase your chances of success if you know what to do in each part. Let us look at an audition as though it were the performance of a play.

First, you must arrive at the audition hall. Just as Equity requires you to be in the theatre thirty minutes before curtain time ("half-hour call"), so you ought to be waiting in the "wings" for your turn to audition, well in advance of your appointed hour. You need time to learn what is to be learned from your fellow actors, to study the script of any scene you'll be asked to read, to warm up (if there's a place), to relax.

The second part of your audition performance is your entrance. As with any performance, you must have a precise sense of character, an action to play that causes you to enter, and activities you do (and lines you say) as a part of your first, entering beat. In an audition, as I mentioned earlier, the first thirty seconds can make or break you. So, decide who you are upon your entrance; get that characterization down pat. Are you the Don Johnson clone? the briefcase-bearing executive? the next Whoopi Goldberg? Don't tell me you're yourself because that's nonsense. Acting is selecting those traits of the self to be presented in a given role. Well, what do you choose to present when you are ushered before the director? The role is yours to choose, but choose it with as complete a knowledge as you can acquire of the nature of the role you're up for, the type of theatre management that might engage you, the director's preferences. Keep your characterization close to your everyday manner, as you may have to repeat it many times, and, if it is wildly improvised, you may give a bad performance at a time you can ill afford to. One of the most spectacular entrances I've ever witnessed was a little old man who came to my auditions for an off-Broadway show, shuffled across the room schlepping his wrinkled topcoat, plopped his photo/résumé on my desk, and mumbled in a thick Eastern European accent that suggested he was a refuge from 2nd Avenue, "Gut mournink." He then stepped back and gave a knockout rendering of Hamlet's "O, that this too too solid flesh." In clear diction, without accent. In excellent, youthful carriage. With fine intensity, wit, and clarity. At the end he schlumped, picked up his coat, muttered "Dank you vary much," and walked slowly out. I was in love with him. Sadly, I had nothing for him in the show I was casting at that time, but he made a lasting impression. I was delighted with his way of getting two varied and entirely credible characterizations before me. I don't know what he is like himself, but I know he can act. I can't recommend such hijinks to the readers of this book, but at that moment nothing seemed more audacious, more theatrical, or more welcome.

Here's another one, told by Paul Barry (who used to run the New Jersey Shakespeare Festival). A man came into an open call carrying a thin box, of the sort professional pool players use to carry their cues sticks. He set it down, took out three pieces, fitted them together into a fine looking Elizabethan pike, handed Barry his photo-résumé, announced "You'll recognize my audition piece," and stood with his feet apart and his left arm behind his back, the pike resting on the floor and held in a forty-five degree angle in his right hand. The very model of a spear carrying extra! Stock still for sixty seconds. He folded up his pike, said his thanks, and left. Was he really auditioning to carry spears? Was it a send-up of Paul Barry? Who's to know? It was *funny*. But it didn't get the guy a job.

Your entrance needs a clear action: to present yourself. That will lead you to focus on yourself rather than the coat or kit you're carrying, to keep your energy centered in yourself rather than bouncing about the room trying to discern which of the people behind the desk merits your attention. It will guide your improvised dialogue towards the first person singular: "*I'm* glad to be here. *I'm* Joe Doakes. *I* have my photo and résumé right here." The auditioners already know who they are; they want to learn about you. Present yourself. The beats of your first action in the interview may be labeled thusly: to enter the room, to set down what you are carrying, to introduce yourself, to take a seat. If you do this, and if you have a clear sense of your characterization when you enter, you will make a concise, energized impression. There's no way of ensuring you will be the person the auditioner is looking for, but you can be certain he has a sense of you and won't discard you as being blurred, scattered, or vacuous.

The third part of your audition is the interview proper. At this point, the auditioner wants to learn several things. Have you the appropriate physical and vocal qualities? Have you the requisite training and skills? Have you sufficient experience? Have you good professional working habits? Have you a personality she will enjoy working with? The first of these is beyond your control. You either are the body and sound she's looking for or you're not. Don't fret about this. If the interview is protracted, there's a strong chance you're appropriate. But if she cuts the meeting short, it could just as easily mean that you're appropriate, that she'll call you back, and that she simply doesn't wish to take time now to superficially do what she intends to do in great depth later. Don't expend energy trying to second-think your auditioner. Instead, accomplish *your* ends in the interview, play *your* action. She will question you about your skills and training, using your résumé as a point of reference. Here is a chance for you to elaborate. If you've studied stage combat with B.H. Barry, the brilliant and witty Englishman, slip that into your discussion. If you're a dialectician, demonstrate your skills in miniature. The auditioner will certainly question you about your recent work to assess your level of experience. Draw her attention to the most prestigious work you have done: theatres or directors or stars you've worked with. Don't assume that the director has read your résumé; she's only just now scanned it. Point out those things you're proudest of. If you've been effective thus far, the director may be concluding that you have good, professional work habits. Support that notion by asking good questions. Find out when the production goes into rehearsal and what kind of run is scheduled. If you can appear as if you're doing a mental check on your availability at that time, so much the better. This is a good time to take out your calendar. That prop is a fine way of indicating that you are an efficient and reliable worker. Ask if any of the key artists are already engaged: designer, costume designer, production stage manager. You might not have heard of any of them, but this will tell the director that you go about your affairs thoroughly. Lastly, inquire about the casting process: when decisions will be made, whom you might expect to hear from, what telephone number you might call if you have questions that come up later. Again, if you can suggest that you're awaiting word on another acting job, you will do yourself some good.

Never discuss money! If someone raises the subject, and it is extremely unlikely anyone will, be charming and vague. "Well, let's not worry about that now," is usually enough to change the subject. You want them to want you and to negotiate a salary only *then*—when you have the upper hand.

Throughout all the beats of this brief interview, the director has been wondering if she would like to work with you—if she likes your personality. All you can do to guide her to the desired decision is to avoid seeming negative. Don't downgrade any work you've seen or any actors or directors who come into the discussion. Don't pass judgments on any plays or theatres. Don't badmouth anyone. The director does not care what your private opinions are and she definitely does not want to hire an actor who stirs up trouble or creates a negative working ambiance. Don't laud everyone either. Not only might you inadvertently praise the director's greatest personal enemy, but the director doesn't want some dippy-tongued enthusiast around her. No, what she wants is a mature professional who may have firm opinions but who understands that they are private and not for the public ear.

Throughout this third part of your audition performance, your action has been to demonstrate your appropriateness for the job. The beats of that action: to elaborate on your skills, to reveal your sound professionalism, to make the director want to work with you. The more relaxed and unthreatened you seem in this segment of your audition, the better you will present yourself.

The fourth part of your audition performance will comprise the presentation of your prepared selections and/or a "cold reading." The auditioner's goal here is to learn how good an actor you are. You are working toward a common end, and you both want you to be excellent. Too frequently, actors choke in this part of an audition because they mistakenly assume the director is out to get them. Your paranoia can be partially reduced if you can remember that she desperately needs you to be right and that you are performing for a sympathetic audience. When you get the chance to be a reader for some director's auditions, you will learn the truth of this. After each actor leaves, your director will evaluate where that actor fell short of the ideal and then do everything but fall on her knees to pray that the next person coming through the door will be the *right* one. "Where's my Desdemona?" the director will whine, throwing half-hostile looks at the casting director who has selected the actors for the day's auditions. The director is desperate to cast the role and is rooting for you when you come in, as you interview, and as you read your "sides."

A "cold reading" means either that you've never seen the script before or that you've had minimal time to look at it. There is always the exception. Apochryphal or not, a newspaper reported that Charlie Sheen's famous father, Martin, secured the manuscript of the new play *The Subject Was Roses* twenty-four hours before his audition and memorized the entire role before he went in. He won the role, his Broadway performance established him as a star, and he began the theatrical dynasty that is thriving today. It is not necessary for you to be that fast a study. But there are many things you can do to aid yourself in a "cold reading." First, ask the director some questions: What are the given circumstances of the scene? What is your character's major action? What are the relationships between your character and the others in the scene? Is there a particular quality the director wants to see? In addition to getting some of the information you need to play the scene sensibly, these questions will show the director that you have an efficient and precise way of working. Your image as a professional will be enhanced.

Sometimes the director won't answer your questions. Maybe he truly doesn't know what he's looking for. Maybe he's in a hurry. Maybe he wants to see what *you* bring to the role and not what he already imagines. If you don't get responses to your questions, enjoy the opportunity to do it your way.

When you actually begin to read, there are additional ways you can help yourself. Move far enough away from the director's table so that he can see you fully. Use a chair, if the scene permits one and if there's one available in the room (there almost always is). This will tell the director that you know how to use space and objects in your work. Play your scene to the person you're reading with and *not* to the director. The interview is the time to talk to him. Now is the time to act. Unless the scene requires direct address to the audience, play to your partner. He will either be a hired reader or a stage manager, and he will read your cues intelligently and clearly, but probably won't "act" them. When I auditioned to replace as Tesman in Claire Bloom's *Hedda Gabler*, the stage manager read Hedda—in red beard and glasses. No matter. My goal was, and yours should be, to play the action of the scene. If you can be sufficiently precise in your work to make the stage manager "act," you will have acquitted yourself splendidly.

Always read more slowly than you would act. This is particularly true if you're auditioning for film work in which the actor's tempo is slower than the stage actor's; but it is also true for stage auditions. The director is not trying to learn if you can read intelligently. He wants to know if you can act—if you can play the actions of a scene, if you can fill out the subtext. If you read slowly, you will permit yourself time to play the actions, or at the very least you will indicate that you understand the task at hand. Jimmy Smits is a star now, but he auditioned for me several times in New York when he was starting out, most notably for the role of Macduff. I liked him professionally and personally, but never found any role to offer him because he wasn't very good at auditioning. His readings were intelligent, but too fast and not "filled."

Either he grew better at auditioning, or better directors than I were able to see through his inexperience and recognize his major talent. Either way, he's done wonderfully . . . but I'll always wonder how he'd have been as Macduff.

Lastly, when doing a "cold reading," commit yourself to an interpretation. Don't waffle, don't change in mid-scene, and don't generalize. Choose an action and play it. If it is the correct one, fine. If it is the wrong one, the director still will understand that you have the ability to play an action. He'll know it is his job to instruct you which action to play—and already he will imagine himself directing you. You'll be one giant step closer to employment.

The presentation of prepared materials is done in rather the same fashion as a "cold reading." Make certain there's ample room between you and the director's table. Announce your selections clearly. Too often the director misses the first part of your act because he's whispering to a colleague, trying to find out what selection you are doing. If you are doing more than one monologue, announce both in advance so that you needn't talk and the director can have a moment to think, make notes, or confer between pieces. If you haven't had an interview or a "cold reading" yet, pronounce your name distinctly, spelling it if it is unusual. Never narrate the plot of the play you are working from. Directors (at least in New York) are very well read and probably know the play better than you. And they've probably seen the same audition material many times before. I know one young actor who told the entire plot of *Our Town* to Morris Carnovsky. Can you imagine what went through that dignified gentleman's mind? If you are working from an unpublished or unproduced "original" play, then you might tell the basic situation and characters—in twenty-five words or less. If there is essential exposition, you may state it succinctly. "Gogo is asleep on the ground over here," I used to explain before launching into my audition speech from *Godot.* This prologue to your prepared selections is the place most young actors damage themselves. They become embarrassed at being themselves and mumble, shuffle, and generally fail to create the illusion of a self-confident professional. *Rehearse your introduction.* It is every bit as important as your monologues. If you think the director will be patient while you "warm up," go ahead. If swinging your arms in the air and gibbering helps you to relax and focus, go ahead. But don't take more than fifteen seconds. And please avoid all those startling moves and loud noises suggested in several of the how-to-audition books that are currently on the market. Directors have seen and heard every single one of them, hundreds of times over, and are aggravated by them. "If one more kid comes in here today and yowls 'AAAaaaaarrrrgh,' I'll belt him with my tuna fish sandwich," I heard one director threaten. But a simple, brief warm-up is OK. And it will tell the director that you have sincere and efficient work habits. Now, go ahead and do your scene as well as you can. At the conclusion, say "Thank you" and return to your seat.

A great percentage of an actor's idle time is spent trying to select good audition pieces. Here are some guidelines to help you in your hunt. Have at least five selections ready to go at all times. Two should be classical, which means anything written before 1900, preferably in verse, commonly from Shakespeare. One should be comic and one serious. The next two should be modern and realistic, which means anything written after 1920 and explicable in terms of contemporary psychology. The language of these two should be contemporary and prosaic. One should be funny and one serious. Stay away from the many speeches that revel in vulgar language. Directors are not prudes nor troubled by blasphemies, but a director is exhausted and wants to take a shower at the end of a day of listening to the abuses hurled in David Mamet plays. We have all heard about "Ruthie" twelve times too often. Your fifth piece should be a wacky one—perhaps with a song in it, or it might be in gibberish. Whatever, it must be exceptional and distinctive, like the Lizard's speech from Albee's *Seascape* or one of the Professor's lectures from Ionesco's *The Lesson.* All of the audition pieces should be selected because the characters are close to you in physical and vocal type and in age. Simply, they must all be roles you might play—that the director can believe you would play. I abandoned my pet audition speech from *Godot* the day I remembered that the character is elderly—I was not. Maybe now, some twenty years later, I could return to it. Your goal is to show what you can do now, not what you aspire to one day. If you know the roles the director is trying to cast, select something that's parallel. When I was casting Hero in *Much Ado About Nothing*, I was delighted to audition a young actor who did Juliet's "Gallop apace." In her Juliet I was able to discern my

Hero. When I was casting for the twin role of Hugo/Frederic in Christopher Fry's witty adaptation of Anouilh's *Ring Round the Moon*, I learned nothing from the young man who showed me Lenny's "mangle" speech from *The Homecoming*. Avoid doing something from the role you're seeking unless the director tells you to. The reason? Whatever you present will not be what the director imagines. Whatever interpretation you offer will conflict with the director's and he'll worry, "Oh, dear, I'll have to kick all that out of him before we can begin to work," and he's already imagining the troubles he'll have directing you. You'll be one giant step further from employment. You'll frequently be asked to bring in selections that demonstrate your versatility and variety. Don't fall for that. What is wanted is a demonstration that you are a good actor. If presenting wildly varied selections is not your strong suit, don't play. Do what you do well. That's all. Inexperienced actors misunderstand that request for variety and present their weaknesses instead of their strengths. George in *Our Town* and Danceny in *Les Liaisons Dangereuses* are both boy-next-door types, but the two present as much variety as is needed in a typical audition. If your variety is between a verse role like Damis in *Tartuffe* and Nick in *Who's Afraid of Virginia Woolf?*, you'll have satisfied the requirements of such demanding auditions as the U/RTAs (University/Resident Theatre Association).

Don't do audition speeches that are done to death. I don't care how brilliant you are—you haven't got a chance if you're the twenty-second actor doing Edmund's "Now, gods, stand up for bastards" or Lady Macbeth's sleepwalking scene. All that will be heard will be some amalgam of the hundreds of times the director has heard that speech; your audition will be obfuscated. Each year, speeches develop that are fashionable among young actors; try to avoid them. For a few years, Mamet, Durang, and *A Chorus Line* were done to death. Today, it's Shanley, Wasserstein, and *Les Miserables*. Try to pick pieces that are within your range—musically and emotionally. Don't try to bowl over the director with your power. Stay away from Lear's "Howl, howl, howl, howl." It takes about three hours of performance to get yourself to that peak and the same amount of time for the audience to get ready to hear it. At 11:30 on a sunny Thursday morning, it just plain won't work.

Where should you get your selections? From things you've played, pieces you've worked on in classes, things you've seen that you knew you were right for, plays you've read. A big danger is to select a speech from the many collections of monologues that are now published. While the editors and publishers are making a couple of bucks by selling those thin volumes to the hundreds of young actors who are desperate for audition materials and who are too lazy to read plays, they are also glutting the audition world with actors who are doing the same damn speeches that the actor just before them did. It is startling how quickly those selections become overdone. The speeches are new to the ill-read young actor, but they are frequently overly familiar to the well-read old director.

I am not alone in enjoying audition speeches adapted from novels. Somehow, I suspect the performer to be guilty of education and intelligence, and that's exciting for me. A speech from Dickens or Bellow or Roth or Borges or Angelou or Mishima— well, that can be very welcome indeed. Or, if you have the gift of words, you might consider writing your own audition piece. Last summer, a young actor did a very funny speech he had written about his own life, and ended playing Cassio in *Othello* and Hortensio in the *Shrew*. Not many have that talent, but don't be afraid to use it if you do.

No one can pick audition speeches for you, though people can and will recommend things you should consider. The more pieces you develop, the surer you will be of having appropriate ones on hand for any occasion. It's an instance of that old occidental maxim that "more is more."

Your audition is nearly over. Your fifth and final part is your exit. In olden times, a ham actor, when offered a role, would inquire about his first entrance and final exit before accepting. Everyone wants exit applause. In your audition performance, clapping takes the form of the director's leaning over to the playwright and whispering, "I hope she's OK for you, 'cause that's the gal I want." The way you do your exit may have some bearing on the director's decision, so you ought to do it well—as a professional. Its beats: to collect your things, to thank your auditioners, to go out the door. Your action: to depart. Do each of the beats briskly, but without rushing. Separate the three so that your "thank you" comes clearly and has precise focus. Your departure should be firm, assured, with no looking back and no diffusion of energy. As Bob Dylan sang, "You're an artist; don't look back."

Do you believe all that happens within a few brief minutes? You've entered, talked, acted, sold, and exited again. Whew! Time to go have a beer. If you have done your performance well, you can do no more. If you have not, you might consider where you screwed up and take the time to prepare yourself for your next chance. Under no circumstances should you fret over your chances of success! Now's the time to *forget the audition entirely*. That may be hard to do, but you must teach yourself that discipline. If they want you, they know how to find you. If you spend the next few hours in intense worry, it won't be long before you find yourself in the intensive-care ward with gastric ulcers. An audition is a little like a relationship. When it's over, you've just got to walk away. Here are some statistics that may help you accept that reality. A busy actor may average as many as two auditions a week, some thirty-five weeks a year. That's about seventy auditions a year. If you're talented, and trained, and lucky, and "Employable," you may get engaged seven times. Wow! That means that one out of every ten auditions has brought success. If only that were true. The percentages are much worse for most beginning actors: one in twenty-five is probably closer to the figure. And there's no predicting which of the twenty-five will be "it." So accept the fact that the other twenty-four are important experiences. And learn to live with the truth that your lack of employment is a statistical reality and not a personal rejection.

Nudity

About twenty years ago, there was a rage in the American theatre for nudity. Authors wrote it into such plays as *Hair* and *The Changing Room*, and directors introduced it when the authors didn't. Actors were expected to take their clothes off at the drop of a contract. It was advertised as part of the "sexual revolution," but with hindsight it seems just another device for selling tickets by appealing to the voyeur spirit in all healthy audiences. Probably the silliest instance of gratuitous stage nudity at that time was the long-running London hit *Abelard and Heloise* in which Keith Michel and Diana Rigg had a widely advertised nude scene. It went like this: Heloise comes up to Abelard's garret, they exchange a few lines, they embrace, her father enters and sees them, he has a heart attack, blackout. You don't have to be Neil Simon to know that's the stuff that farce is made of—it's a broad, standard sketch from the days of burlesque. But in London's Wyndham's Theatre, nobody laughed. A hushed, nearly reverential tone prevailed as the audience—well fortified against the supposed licentiousness with convictions of "artistic innovation"—watched as the renowned stars entered in a shadowy light from opposite sides of the stage, completely nude. They crossed to center facing one another, exchanged a few lines, lay down on the floor, and then looked up as Heloise's father entered, saw them, and had his heart attack. Blackout. Nobody seemed disturbed by the implausibility of—how shall I put it—of the limp reality that nothing was happening. A basically farce situation was made doubly farcical by what Othello calls "the ocular proof." I was wrong when I said that no one laughed. I laughed. And was shushed for my lack of reverence as surely as if I had been in St. Paul's Cathedral.

Happily, our society and our theatre seem to have gotten over an infatuation with theatrical nudity. It still appears occasionally in stage plays such as *Frankie and Johnny*, when it seems organic to the action, and it is prevalent in films, but the question of auditioning for such roles is not the burning one it was when an earlier version of this book was written. Still, it is worth spending a few minutes on the subject.

How do you feel about appearing nude? You ought to come to terms with your feelings and thoughts about it because sometime or other the question is going to be put to you and a ready answer expected. If is possible you will exclude yourself from a role if you refuse to take your clothes off—think of the plays that remain in our popular repertory, such as *Equus* and *What the*

Butler Saw, and the new ones that come along, such as *Uniden-tified Human Remains and the True Nature of Love.* If you are asked if you will appear nude, you can always reply, "I would want to see the script and discuss the scene with the director first." Any reasonable management will understand you to mean that, if their intentions are not exploitative, you'll consider going along with it. If they show you the scene, you'll have to give an answer. This is something you need to have thought through in advance.

In addition to making up your mind about performing in the altogether, you have to be ready for nude auditions. If you're auditioning for a union job, you're well protected—specific rules appear in all union contracts. Equity stipulates that you can't be asked to strip until you've already been auditioned as an actor or dancer or singer. You can't be asked to strip unless an official from the union is present at the audition. When the job is not under union governances, thing are a bit uncertain. You can never be sure which director in which hotel room is a legit employer and which is the proverbial pervert. The easiest way to handle the situation is to say, "Sure, but my manager requires that he be present for any such audition." If the auditioner is legit, he'll say fine and set up the call. If not, well, you're well protected. Your manager, needless to say, is the largest, strongest guy you know. So, if there's an unwanted advance you've got the Marines behind you.

The Casting Couch

I am writing these words on World AIDS Day, 1991. A few weeks ago, basketball star Earvin "Magic" Johnson announced that he was "HIV positive." A few years ago, film star Rock Hudson died of AIDS. Every day, the obituaries tell of more deaths from AIDS. Not since the world cringed before the influenza epidemic in 1917 have we known this fear that permeates our daily lives. Not since the Black Plague decimated Europe in the fourteenth century have we been so helpless in the face of a deadly disease for which there's no known cure. No one in the theatre or the entertainment industry has escaped losing some loved ones. There is no end in sight. Around the world, ten million are already infected. Fifty thousand are infected each day. AIDS is spreading around the world with alarming speed, striking down young and old of all races, heterosexual and homosexual of all nations. Yet the sex drive toward procreation that is natural to our species is stronger than the will to abstain. And as the round dance of sex continues, we invite our own destruction. And in spite of this, people in the theatre—people who are educated and who ought to know better—behave stupidly. Instead of practicing "safer sex," they risk their lives and they risk the lives of their partners.

The following paragraphs are dedicated to the stupid!

Casting couches are the stuff of theatrical legend, but they are more common in movies about show business than in show business itself. Still, there's always the chance that some producer or director has seen too many movies and begun to believe the myth is reality. Also, it must be confessed that the theatre is full of gorgeous people and that some employers will try to take advantage of their positions of power to lure you to their couches. What do you do? You can say yes, you can say no, or you can tease.

At the height of the sexual revolution in the 1960s, most folks said YES. Today, if you say yes—and I pray that you practice "safer sex" if you do—then you are likely to get propositioned a great deal more often than you are cast. Most theatre people take pride in their work and, while some may dangle the carrot of a good role in front of you and try to get you to follow it right into the bedroom, they're not likely to give you an acting job by way of payment. You're much better off finding your jobs on the basis of your talent and skills. And you've a much greater chance of living to a healthy old age.

The only benefit of the AIDS epidemic is that it provides you with an acceptable reason for saying NO. If you've rejected one of those directors who will only cast people he's slept with, you've probably lost the job. And saved your life.

Some actors will try to tease casting from any director who propositions them. They'll accept the dinner engagement, hint of their willingness to go to bed by using phrases like, "It's only condom sense," but finally avoid actually going there. They'll tell the director, "Oh, I really want to, but I don't want you to be influenced when you cast this role, so let's wait—and afterwards, no matter how you cast it, we can get together." This form of blackmail is about as subtle as a thunderstorm. The director who falls for it is as stupid as the actor who believes it works. Teases of this type seem to me a dubious waste of time and energy.

Who you go to bed with and why is entirely your business. The only things this book can recommend are that you ask yourself two questions: (1) is the sexual offer truly related to the professional offer, and (2) what's the danger?

Nobody hires dead actors. Don't be stupid.

Negotiating a Salary

It is difficult to work with someone if you've been fighting about money. The trust needed for theatre people to work together is extreme, and it is sometimes impossible to work together fruitfully if there have been anxieties during the negotiating phase. So the first notion about salary negotiation is—avoid it.

That's the primary function agents perform and it is a very valuable one—worth every penny of the 10% of your salary you pay them in commission. If there is to be haggling over salary, out-clauses, residuals, extra round-trip airfares, housing accommodations, car rentals, or any of the innumerable business details that are a part of the legal contract you must sign before you go to work, let the agent do it. That way, there are never bad feelings between those of you who must roll up your sleeves and go to work together.

If you don't have an agent, what can you do? One course of action is to accept whatever is offered you. You either take the job or you don't. You don't haggle. The truth of the marketplace for most beginners is that you'll be so happy to be offered any job that you'll take whatever's offered. But if you want to haggle, a ploy that's been known to work is to use the "manager" ruse again, and that can give you time to decide if you like the offer or not. (In this instance, you can select your "manager" on the basis of diplomacy instead of muscle.) Your friend the manager can negotiate whatever you instruct her to ask for. And later, once you report to work, you can feign ignorance of the entire negotiation. But sometimes you need to act on the spot. The job is offered, a salary is quoted, and you're uncertain. You want more, but don't want to damage your working relationship—also, you don't want to lose the job. The easiest way is to negotiate by introducing your salary on your previous job, which (by extraordinary coincidence) was more than you've just been offered. Here's a typical negotiation:

Them:	We want you for the show and we pay the LORT minimum of $505.
You:	Hmmmmnnn!
Them:	It's a "favored nations" contract and everybody gets the same.
You:	I don't know. Last job, I got $600.
Them:	Well, we couldn't meet that.
You:	Well, what could you do? I mean, I don't want to go backwards.
Them:	How about if we pay your manager's commission, the $50 a week?
You:	That seems fair. Sure. Thanks.

You'd better take their compromise and not haggle further.

In today's down-spiraling recession, most theatres don't have very much room to negotiate. True, a commercial production—Broadway or a tour—can still negotiate a wide range of salaries. But most LORT and stock companies have very little distance between the Equity minimum and their "top." That's what led to the "favored nations" clause. It's a guarantee to the actor that no other actor is earning more. Sometimes the clause is for the particular production, and sometimes it is for all the productions by that theatre in an entire season. It's the theatre's way of keeping down their payroll and still attracting actors who might command higher salaries at other theatres. When you are no longer a beginner and when you have sufficient credentials to command more than minimum, you can ask (or have your agent ask) for the "favored nations" salary.

A caution about kickbacks. Let's hope you never run into this, but it exists, so be prepared. It's more common in non-union theatres, but it exists in all kinds of theatres. You are offered a job and the salary agreed on is $475 a week. But the producer looks at you, with a carefully rehearsed hang-dog look, and says he can't ask you to sign the contract just yet because they're having trouble raising the last part of their annual giving campaign. He continues, sighing, that if only the damned union wasn't so unyielding and if only the actors' salaries were $100 less, he could keep his theatre open and you could all do this exciting show. Would you consider letting them hold back 100 bucks from your checks? Watch out! I fell for something like this on the first professional directing job I got. The producer promised to give me the full salary as soon as the box office receipts started coming in. He still owes me $750. I'll never see it. Some producers are more crass and more direct: "Look, we tell everybody the same thing. The salary's $525, but if you want the job, you give me a C-note under the table." Sounds like a 1930s Warner Bros. movie? Well, it happens! What can you do? If it's a union contract, report it to the union—*pronto!* If it's not, then ask yourself how much you want to do the show. What will you get from it? If you're not infringing upon any union regulation or breaking any law, make whatever decision you feel is in the best interest of your career. But measure the *real* amount you'll receive as your salary, not the fictionalized amount written on your contract. If the experience and exposure are valuable to you, if you can afford to work for what is offered and still eat, and if you're not bothered by the ethics of it, make your own decision.

"I Got It!"

The whole point of auditioning is to get a job. Everything we've been talking about in this chapter has been aimed at one moment. You've come home, punched your answering machine, listened to the messages, and yelled ecstatically for all to hear, "I got it!"

Now you're a professional. You've got a job. Unlike those

other professionals, those doctors and lawyers who only "practice" medicine and law, you're going to "do" it. You're going to work!

REHEARSALS

Repetition

Watch a runner prepare for a track meet. The event may take less than ten seconds to run, but the athlete will spend months training for it—rehearsing. Watch the kinds of things the athlete does. Here's a partial list:

- Conditions the body through a rigorous set of exercises that do not appear to have any immediate relationship to running: push-ups, sit-ups, working with weights, etc.

- Runs great distances, developing stamina: frequently alternating between sprinting, jogging, and steady pacing.

- Practices each part of the event: the start from the blocks, the early acceleration, the final spurt, the reaching for the tape, the cooling down.

- Runs practice heats—over and over and over again.

- Analyzes the work with the coach, using video-tapes as a way of viewing the action objectively.

- Studies the way others run: attending every available track meet and viewing tapes and films of the great runners of the past.

• Studies physiology to learn how to develop and control the muscles which help him run fastest.

Acting is like running. The sprint of performance requires years of training and weeks of rehearsal. The best actor, like the best runner, is well prepared for the event. His skills are honed sharply because he has known how to prepare himself. He has used his rehearsal time wisely, has known what to do in each phase of his preparation, and has focused his energies initially on the analysis of the role and only finally on the performing process.

Most actors do not know how to rehearse. Their rehearsal hours are spent in repeating rough imitations of imagined performances. They have an imperfect idea of what the final effect intends to be and they hope to arrive at it through an unstructured process of continual refinement. They're like an amateur athlete who just "starts running." They're like a sculptor who starts whacking away at a piece of marble without first having sketched the idea or without having shaped a model from soft clay. All too often, the actor's method of work is just to "try harder." Very few actors have a structured method of working that permits them to focus on specific tasks in a given rehearsal. As the runner needs to work on his starts, the actor needs to work on beginning each beat precisely. As the runner needs to study videotapes of his practice heats to analyze his work, the actor needs to analyze the script and to build a performance in a sequential manner.

Some actors don't like to rehearse; they wish only to perform, because what they seek from their work are the rewards their egos receive from public approval. Accordingly, they use rehearsal time as a mock performance, secretly casting the other actors and the director in the role of audience. Such actors don't understand the nature and purpose of the rehearsal process, and their finished work is the weaker for it. A true craftsman enjoys the process through which results are achieved. The potter enjoys the feel of the clay as it turns in her hands. The runner enjoys the feeling in her legs when the start from the blocks is smooth. The actor enjoys the rush of adrenalin when the emotion recalled is a genuine one. A true actor is one who enjoys performing, yes, but who also enjoys the creative period of rehearsals. If you are truly an actor, your love of rehearsals will guide you to help your fellow actors to build a production that will speak to your audience.

Rehearsal is an imprecise word: to "hear" over again. In *The Empty Space* (New York: Atheneum, 1968), Peter Brook reminds us of the French term and gives a fine description of the activity— to "do" over again:

> *Repetition* say the French, and their word conjures up the mechanical side of the process. Week after week, day after day, hour after hour, practice makes perfect. It is a drudge, a grind, a discipline; it is a dull action that leads to a good result. As every athlete knows, repetition eventually brings about change: harnessed to an aim, driven by a will, repetition is creative. There are cabaret singers who practice a new song again and again for a year or more before venturing to perform it in public: then they may repeat this song to audiences for a further fifty years. Laurence Olivier repeats lines of dialogue to himself again and again until he conditions his tongue muscles to a point of absolute obedience— and so gains total freedom. No clown, no acrobat, no dancer would question that repetition is the only way certain actions become possible, and anyone who refutes the challenge of repetition knows that certain regions of expression are automatically barred to him.

An amateur trusts inspiration to make the performance "right on the night." A professional trusts craft. Your acting will improve as your rehearsing improves. It is common sense. Actors who know how to rehearse will accomplish more than actors who don't. A production that has six weeks of rehearsal will be richer, deeper, and more polished than another that has only one week to rehearse. The greater the *repetition*, the greater the chances for quality. But time is money in the economic reality of the English-speaking theatre today. Rarely will you have sufficient time to rehearse your work satisfactorily. Acting is too frequently a race against time, an attempt to accomplish work in one-half or one-third the appropriate time. The actor who uses rehearsal time efficiently will help his own work and his fellows'. The actor who understands the importance of professional work habits is one who knows how an actor behaves.

Basic Etiquette

"Good morning." "Excuse me." "Thank you." "You're welcome." "Have a nice evening." "Good night now." Another civil day done. Those catchphrases by which we tell others that we respect them, their time, and their space are essential courtesies for the intense world of rehearsals. Many actors think they are witty and "with it" and intentionally omit these civilities from their conversations as a way of telling the world that they are a special, neurotic, pampered, privileged class. They use rudeness to support their puerile self-images as society's outcasts: the too-sensitive "artists" who can't be bothered with mundane courtesies. What garbage! All they are is rude and disruptive; the result is that they create an abrasive and divisive ambiance at rehearsals. Such behavior is selfish and counter-productive. If you greet someone with a pleasant and modest "Good morning" and he fails to respond or grunts condescendingly, you are unlikely to open yourself to him in the intimate scene you must rehearse fifteen minutes later. The theatre is a cooperative art form in which everyone must find ways to coexist and contribute. Civilities are the lubrication that helps the workplace run smoothly, and they create a working environment in which openness, mutual respect, and cooperation are the norms. "Excuse me," "please," "thank you," and "you're welcome" must be as basic to the actor's daily vocabulary as "line," "cue," "prop," and "make me a star."

Along with common civility, *promptness* is of paramount importance—to your own work, to the collective work, and to the management that is paying you. Actors get confused about what they have been hired to do. They think it is to act well. But the quality of their acting is a given. When the choice was made to hire you instead of the others who auditioned for the role, a decision was made that was based on qualitative grounds. You were believed to be the best available actor for the role. Once that decision was made, qualitative considerations were put aside, and time considerations became of paramount concern. Actors are hired to work as hard as they can for a specified number of six-day weeks. Your time is what has been purchased, and you have a contractual obligation to deliver it. The management has every right to expect you to be in the rehearsal hall and ready to begin work precisely on the minute you're called.

You owe it to your fellow actors to be prompt. If a play has a cast of twelve and you're five minutes late, the loss is sixty minutes of collective rehearsal time. And rehearsal time is a very precious commodity. Time is a terrible thing to waste. In addition to the real, measurable waste of collective time, your tardiness will set everyone on edge, and the subsequent rehearsal will be much less productive than it might otherwise have been.

You owe it to yourself to be on time. If you have been working wisely, if you have done your homework between rehearsals, you'll be eager to get to the rehearsal early, to explore with your fellows what you have been working on privately. Time is the enemy of theatre; to defeat that enemy, you must use your time productively and fully.

The tardy actor is unprofessional and unwanted. I have fired a professional actor who could not get to rehearsals on time. I have replaced student actors for the same reason. When a professional actor is late, I commonly begin rehearsal with someone else doing the tardy actor's role: an understudy or an assistant stage manager. It is startling for an actor to arrive at a rehearsal to find how replaceable he truly is, how easily the work goes forward without him. From fear of losing the job, that actor is prompt from that moment on. Usually, when a student actor is late, I have the stage manager inquire if she had phoned in to notify us in advance of the difficulty or if, upon arrival, she had given an acceptable reason for her delay. (Few reasons are ac-

ceptable!) If there has been no explanation, I usually say loudly
enough for all to hear something like: "You are five minutes late.
That's cost us sixty minutes of collective work and untold aggravation. Out of respect for everyone here, I have to tell you that if
you find you are going to be late again, simply do not bother to
come to rehearsal at all. I shall have replaced you before you get
here. That applies to everyone in the cast. Sorry to play the
'heavy,' but we haven't any time to waste. Now, shall we take
places for today's work, please? Thank you."

* * * * *

An actor who has "Big B.O." is either a star whose name on
the advertisements ensures sales in the box office or an actor
who smells badly. How do you smell? Would you like to embrace
you? Actors' hygiene is an important component of their professional behavior.

When you come to rehearsals, you are coming to work. Your
work necessitates that you mix with others, and your hygiene
can have an important impact on the effectiveness of that work.
To begin: bathe. The English-speaking world is fanatical about
cleanliness, placing it next to godliness in its homilies and before
everything else in its advertisements. We are conditioned to support a multi-million dollar industry that is dedicated to removing
every odor that is natural to us naked apes. We are taught to
obliterate body odor, foot odor, underarm odor, breath odor, and
denture odor. Now, you may disapprove of this aspect of our
society, but as a professional actor you must accept that you are
the "abstract and brief chronicle" of your times. In future ages,
when our theatre practices are studied by anthropologists for
revelations about our social customs, scholars will look at all
those commercials and say with confidence, "Late twentieth-
century man had an intense olfactory angst." As our society goes,
so goes our theatre. And so must you. It doesn't matter what you
believe in—if you smell bad, I don't want to rehearse with you. If
you've come to rehearsal directly from playing basketball, I don't
want to embrace you. If you've just enjoyed an exotic Indian
dinner made in forty cloves of garlic, I don't want to kiss you. At

best, bathe before—even if you're pressed for time, even if you've been at school or a job all day prior to rehearsal. At least, spray yourself with something inoffense and gobble down some breath mints. That's why you keep them in your rehearsal kit.

If you are offended, day after day, by the odor of garlic that surrounds a fellow actor, hestitate before you complain to the stage manager. Try discreetly to learn more. It is possible that the offender is "HIV positive," and is following the advice of a doctor. Currently, medical science is unable to do much to help the stricken, and some doctors believe that the rate of deterioration can be slowed if the patient eats a lot of garlic. To some, this may sound as fantastical as the notion that garlic wards off vampires. But to a person fighting to save his life, everything has to be tried. If that is the instance you've encountered, then let your human compassion take precedence over your artistic needs. For once, no matter how much you are bothered by the scent, live with it. AIDS will not soon go away. We must all live with it.

After you have ensured that your body is purged of its anti-social odors, attend to your grooming. The clothes you wear to rehearsal will have an effect on both you and the actors you work with. You should always come to rehearsal in relatively clean and tidy clothes, and you ought to select clothing that provides you with some semblance of the "feeling" of the character and period you're working in. This will assist you in your own work and it will make it easier for your fellow actors to relate to you. If you are playing Lady Sneerwell and you arrive in Levi's, boots, and a halter-top, you are not likely to "feel" particularly Sneerwellish, and the gentlemen in *The School for Scandal* are going to find it difficult to imagine your character. If you are playing Biff Loman and you arrive in Danskins, you're going to seem silly trying to pull that length of rubber hose out of your pocket. And the incongruity of your gesture will impede the desired flow of the rehearsal.

In addition to your clothing, you must pay attention to your hair: that on your head and that on your face. Too many actors disadvantage themselves and their fellows by arriving at rehearsals with their hair unkempt: unwashed and covered in dandruff, or recently washed and still in curlers. How can Romeo say, "It is the East and Juliet is the sun" when he's looking at a head covered with hardware? How can Juliet reply when she's looking at a two-day beard stubble? Since the mid-1960s, when men's fashions in hair grooming embraced all variants of facial and head hair, male actors have become self-indulgent and counter-productive in their work by placing their private preferences above their professional needs. I was directing George Kelly's *The Show-off*, the American comedy set in the 1920s (when the fashion in men's hair was quite short and close to the head), and I had an actor who resisted haircuts and rehearsed in a ponytail. He was not cast as a pony, I frequently remarked, and, after a week of rehearsal, I was obliged to offer him the choice of a haircut or dismissal. I don't know or care why he delayed—he knew his hair had to be cut and that it would one day grow out again; it was clear that this actor was painfully unprofessional in his approach to his work.

* * * * *

There are four R's to remember as basic etiquette: *Respect the Space, Respect the Time, Respect the People, Respect Yourself.*

RESPECT THE SPACE   You will work best if you treat your working space as just that—a place to work in. That means the only things in it ought to be items related to your work. Here's a list of items commonly found in rehearsal halls and theatre auditoriums that are destructive to good working conditions: partially eaten sandwiches, paper cups, cigarette butts, tea bags, old books, abandoned clothing, crumpled cigarette packs, dogs, babies, friends, newspapers, umbrellas, correspondence, notebooks, used chewing gum, unused chewing gum, stage mothers, photo albums, telephone books, and diaper bags.

Think of your doctor's examination room. Do you remember seeing any of the things on this list in his examination room? How about the conference room of a legal firm? A chemist's laboratory? Those professionals seem to keep the spaces they reserve for group work in sensible order. A place of work is not a clutterbox nor a dumping ground for personal refuse. Historically, actors have had (and undeniably earned) the reputation for being slobs. Perhaps their slovenly behavior has resulted from that same attitude that has made some of them rude.

Acting students are among the worst offenders. Perhaps they are at an age of social rebellion. They may have only recently left home environments in which they misinterpreted their parents' requests for commonly accepted social behavior as parental constriction, and are now living in dormitories or apartments where no one forces them to pick up after themselves. Perhaps they import that adolescent behavior into their working environment. Or perhaps they are spoiled by the availability in most schools of a labor force of underpaid custodial staff who will pick up after them. Whatever the reason, the work habit is a deplorable one and debilitating to the group's goals. (In schools, where the teacher-director has some authority, it is desirable to build a "policing the area" call into the end of each rehearsal. That will relieve the student stage managers from unpleasant duties that are not properly their responsibility but which too frequently fall to them by default. It will also help the actors to learn mature, professional behavior, and, if they are serious about acting, they won't wish to use valuable rehearsal time in custodial work, and they will begin quickly to monitor their own behavior so that such "police" calls become unnecessary. It will also prepare them for the union workplace where the stage manager has some very real authority—and is not shy about using it!)

An actor's working space extends beyond the rehearsal hall or stage itself. It includes the auditorium of the theatre, the toilets, showers, makeup rooms, and indeed any part of the rehearsal or performance complex. Actors spend an immense portion of their waking hours in the rehearsal space and frequently mistake it for their living quarters. They forget that the space is owned by someone else and that they are guests and ought to behave accordingly. An actress at Temple University's Stage Three grew very angry when she discovered her makeup had been removed from in front of the mirror she used nightly. She had forgotten that the theatre was also used by a company performing children's theatre, by musicians preparing a concert, by the management of a cinematheque, and, on occasion, by the University's celebrity guest lecturers. She had forgotten that she was not in her own home.

RESPECT THE TIME Promptness is a postulate of mature, professional behavior that applies throughout the rehearsal period. It means that a one-hour lunch break finds the actor returned, warmed up, and ready to rehearse fifty-nine minutes after dismissal. It means that a ten-minute coffee break is no longer than ten minutes. It means that the actor who just exited a scene in rehearsal does not wander off immediately and, should the director choose to repeat the scene, waste the company's time looking for her. It means that the actor who is not in the scene being rehearsed at that moment is precisely where she has told the stage manager she is and can be summoned without undue delay.

Actors must respect the time of everyone working on a production. That means that the actor must be prompt for the costume fitting and for the interview that has been arranged with the newspaper reporter. In rehearsal, when it is the actor's time to work, you have the right to expect the full concentration of the director, stage manager, and other actors. When it is someone else's time to work, you must not intrude on their time. Sometimes it is a bit difficult to know when it is your time, but a bit of sensitivity melded to a bit of experience will help the beginner to reach an awareness of the rehearsal's progress. A common error is for an actor to complete a scene and to want—right then—to get the director's response. But the director may wish to proceed into the next scene, saving her responses for a later moment in the rehearsal. The actors who are on stage and working do not want their time interrupted. The exiting actor should assess the situation before blurting out, "Hey, was that what you wanted?"

RESPECT THE PEOPLE A camel is a horse that has been designed by committee, the old saw has it, and a performance is an event that has been shaped by a cooperating group of theatricians. If the shape is elegant, proportionate, and efficient, an audience will know the group has worked well and respected the mutual contributions of all members. If a performance is as lumpy as a camel, the audience will know it is in for a bumpy ride. A one-hump camel may occasionally succeed in the race for large weekly box-office receipts, but a two-hump camel is usually scratched before the race begins. The actor can help the group avoid creating a deformed dromedary by respecting the efforts, intentions, and accomplishments of all fellow workers.

Two general practices the actor ought to observe in dealing with all fellow workers are abstention from offering advice and aloofness from the rumor mill. For inexplicable psychological reasons, many actors like to express their opinions on all sorts of subjects about which they are ignorant. The nature of theatrical advertising, the structuring of the rehearsal period, the construction of sets, costumes, and props, the skills of the photographer, the layout of the program, the length of intermissions, the prices of tickets, the literary style of press releases, the ushers' uniforms, the skills of the choreographer, musical director, and dialect coach: these are a representative sampling. Haven't you heard an actor sound off on most of these? Sadly, most actors' comments on other people's work is negative and it seems as though they are seeking to lay the blame for a show's possible failure on someone else's shoulders. Well, don't do it! If someone asks your opinion of his work, you have three ways to reply. You may be complimentary; you may confess you don't know anything about the work and decline to comment; or you may offer concrete advice. Offer advice *only* if you have done that type of work yourself professionally and are *certain* the advice you're giving is accurate and applicable and constructive. If the costume cutter asks what you think of the skirt she has just fitted on you, you might be complimentary and say "terrific!" If the PR director asks your opinion of the design for the poster, you may be non-committal and say, "I don't know anything about how to sell a show—I sure hope this will." If the stage manager asks you the best way to give an actor a visual cue in a blackout, and if you have stage managed and dealt with the same problem, you might say, "When I did it, I turned my flashlight on for the warning and then off for the 'go,' and it seemed to work OK." If no one asks your opinion, don't offer it! You don't want a lot of unqualified non-actors telling you how to express credible terror in your big scene, and others don't want you telling them how to do their jobs. They are professionals, hired because they know their work. So are you. Respect each other.

In every show, in every company, in every theatre school, on every tour there is a rumor mill. Nobody ever knows how the rumors start, but everyone has seen how they fly, multiply, develop, and disrupt. The actor is usually one of the least-informed people working on a production. Administrative decisions are made without your awareness and artistic decisions are made without your consultation. Accordingly, you are the last person to learn truths and facts. At the same time, you live in an intense world that is all but hermetically sealed from the rest of the production's workers and, within this tight little world, you actors begin to believe that the show is all about you. Aren't you actors the life of the play once it opens? Aren't you the ones who must go out there and face the audience? Aren't you the ones who risk everything? Well, not exactly. For example, you actors rarely risk any of the $350,000 it takes to get the show open in a regional theatre (or the $7,000,000 if it's a Broadway musical). And, despite the possible embarrassment you may feel should your performance be poorly reviewed, you don't risk the career damage the playwright does. And there is more than a modicum of truth to the cliché that good plays are well acted while bad ones are poorly directed. Directors are at risk, as well, and so are designers. The actors' belief that the world revolves about them is probably what makes them actors, but it does not necessarily make them sensible members of a company—persons who resist believing in, propagating, and encouraging rumors.

Rumors tend to deal with either events or people. Either they suggest that the opening is postponed and the costume fitting canceled, or they suggest that the director is being replaced and the spear-carrier recruited from the football team is sleeping with the ingenue. To believe rumors is naive, to start them is corruptive, and to support them is divisive. When you hear a rumor that troubles you, ask the most informed person you can of its accuracy. That will be the stage manager if it deals with events and the director if it deals with artistic decisions. If they are responsible professionals, they will tell you the truth if they know it and are permitted to share it. They will tell you they don't know if they don't know or if they are constrained by their employers from discussing the matter. In either event, you must then function as though what you've been told is what you need to know—and go about your work. I was in a show in California and heard a rumor that an actor was to be replaced—yet I saw him at the rehearsal. I approached the director at a break and discreetly asked about the situation, since I had to rehearse a scene with that actor when we started up again. "I'm not free to discuss it," said the director. I understood him to mean that it was probably true, but that he and I should continue as though it were not. The reason? There were several scenes remaining that day in which the actor's character appeared. Everyone needed to function as though no change were imminent, so that efficient use could be made of the valuable rehearsal time. If the actor who was to be dismissed knew he was about to be canned, the rehearsal would have been awkward and minimally productive. A cruel business? Yes. But remember, it is a business. I helped all of us get on with our business by keeping my mouth shut.

RESPECT YOURSELF Actors are a little bit in love with death. Think how many catchphrases suggest it. "I'm going to kill 'em tonight." "I'm dying out there tonight." "The show died last night." "Breathe some life into it, will ya?" "If I go out there like this, they'll murder me." "It'd be suicide to play it that way." There is something about the actor that is self-destructive, that flirts with death. There is something about the actor that welcomes failure, and it takes a strong-willed actor with a lot of self-respect to overcome the temptation to fail. Self-respect is gained by improving one's skills, by experience, by longevity, by meeting challenges. The challenges the actor meets during rehearsals are many, and your work will be good in relation to the way you meet them—in relation to your degree of self-respect. Many of the challenges have to do with the art of acting and are not my concern here; others have to do with the habits of rehearsing, and are.

The sprinter can't run until he's warmed up and the actor can't rehearse until he's warmed up. The warm-up exercises you use are different, but the relationship between preparation and execution is identical. Actors are a kind of athlete. The great French actor Jean-Louis Barrault describes actors as "affective athletes" ("The Theatrical Phenomenon," *Educational Theatre*

Journal, May 1965, pp. 89-100). The actor needs to warm up his body to make it flexible, responsive to his needs, and quick to respond to stimulation. Most actors learn a set of warm-ups during their training and then, sadly, abandon them ever after. When they do so, they are telling death they can be seduced. Of course, there are difficulties with doing the kinds of physical exercises that most actors know: there's rarely an ideal place to exercise, and other actors may ridicule you. If that bothers you, do your exercises at home, before you come to rehearsal. Then you will need only a few brief, selected exercises to be ready to work. On the other hand, if you respect your work enough to bear their ridicule a couple of times, you might shortly find others joining you. Your self-respect might be contagious.

The actor needs to warm up the voice, to loosen the muscles, to clear the resonating chambers, and to re-tune the ear. Your exercises may take five or thirty minutes, depending on the type of role you're rehearsing. If you sing, you should warm up that carefully trained instrument for a long time. If you're doing a prosaic modern play that requires few stretches of your vocal instrument—something like A.R. Gurney's *The Dining Room*— you can get by with running a few scales and doing a couple of tongue twisters. Again, if you're embarrassed to do this in a corner of the rehearsal hall, do it at home, in the car, or in the bathroom. But do it. Respect your work enough to prepare yourself for it.

The actor needs to warm up his sense of observation, concentration, and emotional recall. These exercises can be done privately and in almost any location, even while riding a subway or waiting for a bus. If the emotion to be recalled is one required for the role being rehearsed, think how ready you'll be when "places" is called. Think how you will have met the challenge of rehearsal and how you will have built your self-confidence and increased your self-respect.

You must come to rehearsals in optimal physical condition. That means you need to have had sufficient sleep and a sound breakfast (or supper if it's an evening rehearsal as is common in most training institutions). It is common to see an actor's energy flag during a rehearsal because of insufficient sleep or nourishment. When that happens to you, you have only yourself to blame. But your poor work will affect those you work with and the collective work suffers as well. So get to bed on time and eat sensibly. As an actor, your body is your instrument—respect it. Treat it properly and it will do what you need it to do. Punish it, and it will fail you—help you to fail, help you to die.

The most common forms of self-punishment actors enjoy are liquor and drugs. Separately or in combination, these can reduce your effectiveness and help you to achieve the failure you seek when you use them. All actors indulge their adolescent fantasies and pretend that they are superhuman, immortal, and that "drugs, sex, and rock 'n roll" are the artist's way of life. Carried to the logical extreme, this adolescent behavior will become the artist's way to death. Jim Morrison of *The Doors* is a bad role model.

It may be comforting to blame liquor and drugs for your bad performance, but that delusion only lasts a short while. Finally, you know you are doing it to yourself so that you'll never need to discover if you are as good as you boast you are and as you must be to succeed. The blame can always be laid on the bottle and the joint. "Man, if I'd a been straight, I'd a been terrific" is the empty rationalization of the actor who has so little respect for his work, for the theatre, for his fellow actors, for his audience, and for his very self that he will do almost anything to delude himself. The lore of liquor goes all the way back to Dionysian revels, and the liberation it can provide is strangely like the exaltation that great acting can provide. We all seek that "high." But more often, we use liquor to dull our senses and to protect ourselves from our fears. There's an old story that has been attributed to many celebrated actors—Edmund Kean and Richard Burbage probably had it told about them. I heard it ascribed to Victor Jory, but it's probably apocryphal. It's also a pretty good story. A young actor has his first job and is wildly nervous on opening night, pacing backstage. The five-minute call comes over the dressing-room speaker and he decides to head for the wings, to get ready for his first entrance. He passes the star's dressing room and stops in his tracks, jaw slack open at the sight of a half-empty bottle of booze on the star's table. The star looks up and sees the kid. "Hey, come on in," he waves cheerily. The young actor enters past the glittering gold star on the Number One dressing room door. "Your first show?" asks the star. "Yes, sir, and I'm really nervous." "Well, have a drink," says the star, pushing the bottle and a glass towards the youngster, "it'll calm you down." "Oh, no, sir. Thank you. I'm afraid it might affect my performance." The star squints up at him, knocks back a tumbler of whiskey, and says in awe, "You don't mean to tell me you're going out there *alone?*"

Liquor is essentially a depressant. It is a stimulant for the first shot or so, but swiftly the muscles lose their edge of coordination, the mind loses its ability to concentrate, the sense of time and the judgment of distance become impaired. In short, the very controls you need to act are debilitated. All the lies about "It's just to relax my throat," "It gets me warmed up," "This much doesn't even affect me" are just that—lies. *If you drink—don't act!*

A drink *after* a rehearsal is wonderful. I'll race you to the bar. But I know I have a full night's sleep ahead and my body will have a chance to recuperate. And I'll be able to respect the work I do the next day. But to arrive at work with a glow on—well, that's just plain stupid.

The most common kind of drug is marijuana, and it is also the only one I can speak of from personal experience. It's purpose, and indeed the primary purpose of most popular forms of drugs, is to adjust the sensory and temporal controls of the mind. Well, it must be obvious that to do so is to render your work useless. Have you ever been on stage with someone who was loaded? I have. It was awful. Suddenly there were long pauses that he believed were either significant or not so long as I and the audience knew them to be. Suddenly there were changed line readings—the result of some associative mental image that was unrelated to the action being played.

A major trouble with using drugs during the rehearsal period is that the effects of the chemical may not be short-lived. The temporal and sensory adjustments might not go away with a short nap. Watch out for that.

It's not my intention here to moralize, to tell you how to live your life, or to explicate the complicated laws of our society in relation to drugs and alcohol. It *is* my intention to urge self-re-

spect upon you. To remind you that it is achieved through meeting professional challenges, not through avoiding them. You may
be very successful and totally dissolute. Others have been before
you. But they were never the actors they might have been. Read
about Richard Burton and you will read about an actor who
permitted alcohol to keep him from achieving his potential. Read
about Jason Robards and you will read about an actor who
overcame his dependency and gave some of the great performances of our generation. A wonderful, though fictional, description of the alcoholic failed actor is the character Charles
Paris in the series of entertaining murder-mystery novels by Simon
Brett. (And they're terrific fun to read when you're trying to relax
after a strenuous day at rehearsal.)

One final caution. Don't believe you'll fool anyone. If you're
drunk or spaced, the director will know. Maybe not the first time,
but she'll learn fast. And when she does, you'll be out on your
ear. And not just from your present engagement, but from any
subsequent show she—or the stage manager, playwright, designer, producer, or "gofer"—might be working. You'd be startled
how fast your reputation can precede you. A reputation as a
drunk or a "user" will find you out of the profession and back in
your father's grocery business fast.

The theatre is a social art, one that requires people to work
together under extreme pressure. The norms of society are mir-
rored in the working situation and the rules that apply for success in most walks of life apply for rehearsals. You can help
yourself if you remember how an actor behaves.

The Political Structure

You're in rehearsal—in the intense quiet of a darkened, sequestered room. There's only the director, the stage manager, the
playwright, and the other six actors. Here's where it all happens.
Where the creativity flows. Where the play is made. Nothing else
matters.

If you believe that, it is no wonder you have a strange view
of the theatre. As an actor, you seldom see the others who are

working every bit as hard as you are. You're wrapped up in the harmonious and fertile crucible of rehearsals and need have no other concerns. You believe that you are the advance guard, the infantry that will combat the enemy of the audience, and you may forget that outside, beyond and (notably) above the rehearsals, are many professionals working at fever pitch to ensure the production's success. You are not alone.

Outside the rehearsal room there is an entirely different world. A world of business. And whenever you cross into it, you ought to know about it. You ought to know the people who work in it, the jobs they perform, their relationship to you, your obligations to them, and your place in the huge machinery that is a production company.

The production company is a business with offices and officers and follows the basic principles that guide all businesses. Its intention is to turn a profit or, if it is a not-for-profit company (an institutional theatre), to balance its books. It is an organization that deals in money, although the production it is marketing is a service instead of a commodity. You are a very small part of the company, not much more important to the business's success than the exhaust system on a new Buick is to General Motors. The Buick needs an exhaust system, but if one doesn't function well, another will replace it. General Motors goes on. The theatrical production company needs you, but it will continue to do business if it has to replace you. Inside that rehearsal room you may seem essential to the company, but inside the producer's office you are not.

Do you know about the late Arnold Soboloff? He was a fine actor, playing the pirate Smee in Sandy Duncan's triumphant Broadway production of *Peter Pan*. At one performance, he made his exit at the end of Act One and dropped dead in the wings. Heart attack. His understudy did the second act and the rest of the run. Arnie was *essential* to the production while he was in it, and he was replaced before the audience could finish their intermission cup of coffee. The production company goes on. Just like General Motors.

Your relationship to the company is best illustrated by the sample organizational charts for a theatrical production company that are on the next pages. Some variant of this chart exists for every production. If you're a member of a resident professional theatre company, the configuration may vary slightly, and there may be other minor differences in a university or training school. I've included organizational charts for Temple University's Department of Theatre and TheatreVirginia from the times when I was artistic director for each. I think these will illustrate some of the possible differences. But certain truths apply in all instances, and they are what's important for you to keep in mind.

First, recognize that more people are engaged in mounting the production than in performing it; members of the administrative staff, marketing staff, design, construction, and backstage staff outnumber the performers heavily. Second, note the place of the actor on the organizational chart—at the bottom. This does not mean the actor is the least important member of the company, necessarily. It means that the actor is the least important in regard to administrative and financial and artistic decision making. Simply, nobody consults the actor about anything. The actor is engaged to act. Your opinions and preferences about operating policy are unwelcome and irrelevant. When you have absorbed these truths, you will find you are happier in your work. All the energy you might direct to worrying about the poster campaign, the number of preview performances to give, the colors for the gels, and the number of overtime hours to rehearse can be directed toward your own work. You will be freed to concentrate on your acting. *Your* job.

As an actor, you have five members of the company you must go through when you have needs. The director will attend to your artistic needs; the production stage manager will attend to your working needs in both rehearsals and performances; the company manager will attend to your business and personal needs (housing, banking, transportation, medical); the publicity director will attend to your photographic, press, and program needs; the Equity deputy will be your liaison to the producer about extraordinary problems related to your working circumstances. Don't go to anyone else with your problems unless you are directed to do so by one of these five. If you need house seats for your agent, go to the company manager, not the box-

Temple University
Department of Theatre

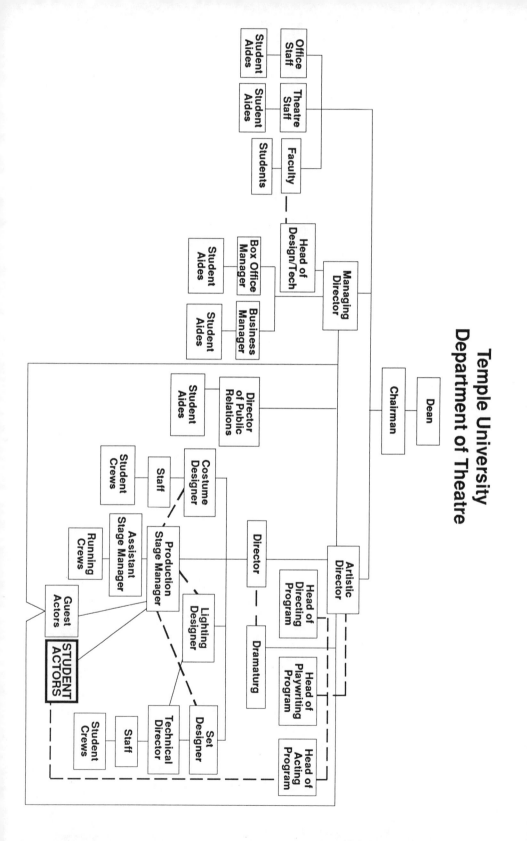

TheatreVirginia

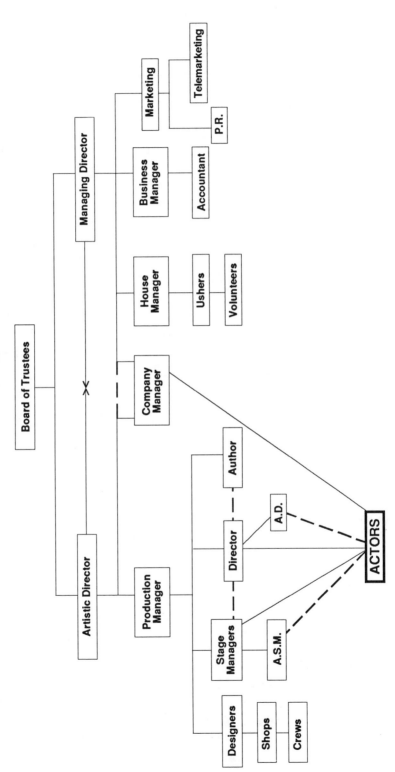

office treasurer. If you need a pocket in your costume, go to the production stage manager, not the costume designer.

Each of these five has a direct channel to you—and you have the same direct line to them. Everything you need to know will be told you by one of the five, and every question you might have should be directed to one of them. And of the five, the production stage manager should be the first person to whom you pose your questions on all subjects except how to act your role. She will probably steer you to whichever of the other persons can best treat your needs, but you should begin with her. The production stage manager is your primary contact with the huge number of people who make up the production company.

Once you have learned the political structure of the company that has employed you, once you know both the people and their jobs, you will begin to perceive the unique nature of the company. You'll find out how *they* work: who is strong, who has taken on tasks not traditionally a part of his job, who gets things done, who is hopelessly overworked. You will begin to learn those deviations from the standard political structure that might affect you; you will begin to learn who on the production has the "muscle." (Unquestionably the finest discussion of this aspect of the actor's world in found in the chapter entitled "Muscle" in William Goldman's *The Season* (New York: Harcourt, Brace & World, Inc., 1969). The details and names in that extraordinary book may now be a bit out of date, but the essential work remains invaluable.)

* * * * *

Sexual politics exist in the theatre just as in other walks of life. The sensational media coverage of the 1991 U.S. Senate hearings on the confirmation of Clarence Thomas's appointment to the Supreme Court and the powerful testimony by Professor Anita Hill may have heightened our sensitivity to the pervasiveness of sexual harassment, but that does not mean that sexual politics are any the less prevalent. You will work best if you are alert to the most common forms of sexual politics in the theatre and if you guide your para-theatrical activities with an alert eye to their influence on your acting. The myth and reality of the casting couch have been discussed earlier, but this is a good place for a few notions about sexual politics in rehearsals and performance. Freud taught us that the sex drive is frequently sublimated into other drives. The drive for wealth, military or political power, religious authority, intellectual superiority, and public acclaim may be surrogates for the sexual drive. Inversely, a position of superiority or authority is frequently expressed through sexual acts. The boss has his secretary, the senator his aide, the rock star her groupies. Indeed, most of us are sexually attracted to people in positions of authority. They have what we call "charisma."

In the intense and sequestered world of theatre, many opportunities exist for the sexual exploitation of political power. The director can seduce the actor who wants his approval of her acting and will go to any length to achieve it. The actor can seduce her leading man so that he will perform their scenes as she wishes them interpreted. The stage manager can seduce the bit player by dangling hopes of an understudy's job. The critic can seduce the playwright with promises of good reviews. The producer can seduce them all with promises of employment.

You have an obligation to yourself, your fellows, and your work to measure how your possible sexual activities might impede your work. And it can be very hard to keep your lusts and your professional aims separate. It is very difficult to discern which motives should guide your behavior, since you can be quite capable of deluding yourself that the exercise of your political muscle is in fact "true love."

The very nature of the rehearsal circumstance obscures our vision and confuses our feelings, even in non-sexual relationships. Some years ago, Jon Jory, Producing Director of the Actors Theatre of Louisville, described to me his years as a guest director around the LORT circuit and explained why it was destructive to his social sanity. His comments have been echoed by many other directors in the years since I first heard them. Jon said that he would arrive in a city knowing that he would be there for only three and a half weeks. The first day he would meet the dozen or so people he would work with and immediately plunge into intense working relationships with them—relationships in which the emotions are high, the nerve endings exposed, the trust imperative. Within a week, the group was very friendly. A year's casual acquaintanceship had been compressed into one week. And during that intensive first week, the outside world had not intruded. They had all lived a rarefied life with the creative work as its center and bond. In the second week people became dear, old friends. They knew each other's life story and had shared ecstasy and despair. Then came the third week. Just as he needed to work most closely with the actors professionally, he and they perceived the imminency of his departure. Both sides pulled back from the relationship, from the friendship. Both sides were striving to protect themselves from the pain of separation that is a necessity of the transient director's life. "It can screw you up," Jon said. "I was glad to get done with it." If your social sanity can be abused by the rehearsal rhythm, imagine what can happen to your love life. If you're playing Ophelia and you have a huge fight with Hamlet and he moves back into his own apartment three days before you face the critics, you're going to have a terrible time rehearsing and performing the show. (Although you may find a richer feeling behind your line, "Oh what a noble mind is here o'erthrown.")

Similarly, avoid getting involved with your directors. They are charismatic, energetic, mature, forceful, all-knowing, patient, all-caring, and, as a result, they are damned attractive. What's more, in the heat of work, they can be attracted to you. Both of you are of the theatre and supremely gifted at self-delusion; you can play the roles of "lovers" with great conviction. But directors spend their public hours being supportive, caring, forceful, witty, and energetic. Privately, they may need someone who will be those things for them, when they collapse at home after a tough day's rehearsal. Do you really have the strength to rehearse all day and then nurture an adult who can need your domestic but *not* your creative instincts? Can you leave the rehearsal together and suddenly reverse roles? The strain can be incredible. And beware of "opening nightitis." It is a birthing, a delivery. As an actor, you are a child about to be born, bursting with the energy of new life and crying out for a hearing and for attention. The director is the parent who experiences post-partum depressions.

The wisest behavior would be restraint. Particularly in this age of AIDS when the dangers of short-term affairs are so great. But if you are going to pursue your private life, if you're going to try to live a normal and healthy life, then at least wait until the show has opened. Then your world will slow down a little, and you can explore your feelings sensibly. If you still think the director is terrific (and if he's still in town), get together. In short, try to separate your work from your pleasure. Try to behave so as to ensure your best working circumstances and your happiest private life. Avoid the blurring of theatre and life implicit in John Barrymore's oft-quoted response to the interviewer who wanted to know if his interpretation was developing as the production toured from city to city and asked if Barrymore believed Hamlet was sleeping with Ophelia. "Not since we left Chicago," he quipped.

The People You Work With

Come out of the rehearsal room and meet the people you work with. There are clerks and craftsmen, administrators and advocates. Each actor will encounter a long list of people during the rehearsals for a production, and your work will go well and your life will go pleasantly if you know how to relate to your co-workers. Each is a professional, conscientiously doing a job, and each is working under pressure and adverse conditions that equal yours. None is there as your servant or underling. The overriding principle guiding your working relationships should be *mutual respect*. If you can learn to put aside your insecurity and ac-knowledge others' importance to the show's ultimate success, you will do well.

ACTORS The greatest percentage of your time will be spent with your fellow actors. If you think for a moment what you need from them to help you do your job well, then you will realize what you must do to help them—you will learn how an actor behaves toward other actors.

Respect their work habits. They are frequently strangers to

you and it is safe to assume a great many will go about their work in ways quite different from yours. You need only watch a play in performance to witness the truth of this. All actors develop their own variants upon the myriad of methods of acting that are presently taught in the English-speaking theatre, and one of the distressing truths about our work is that we rarely create a cohesive production because the actors have no common approach to their work. Have you ever seen the film of Shakespeare's *Julius Caesar* that features Marlon Brando, John Gielgud, James Mason, Edmund O'Brien, and Louis Calhern? All the name players give brilliant performances, but each appears to be in a different play. The same applies to Sidney Lumet's celebrated film of O'Neill's *Long Day's Journey into Night*, with Katherine Hepburn, Ralph Richardson, Jason Robards, and Dean Stockwell. Each has a different accent, rhythm, appearance, and acting style— so much so that it almost seems that the tortured members of the Tyrone family have never met one another, let alone endured the long years that lead to their long day's journey.

You have no control over the selection of the actors you must work with and no way of anticipating how each works. If you are flexible, however, you will not only aid your fellows but you may learn ways of working (techniques of the craft) that you may wish to incorporate into your own future work. Let's say that an actor comes to you before rehearsal one day and says, "I hope you'll go along with this. Today, during the first run of our scene, I want to concentrate hard on the physical realities of the environment: climate, time of day, that sort of thing. Oh, I'll be right with all the lines and blocking, but don't be disturbed if my concentration isn't on you and if I don't seem to be listening to you the way I have been." Can you handle that? She's giving you the skeleton of what you need to get through the scene, and she's obviously bringing to the rehearsal the results of her homework, and she's giving you the chance to work on whatever you need to work on, and she's giving you a demonstration of a technique that you may one day wish to explore. Can you handle it?

At the same time, don't abandon your own work habits. Don't be so cooperative that you never get your own work done. Don't spend your rehearsal time poorly. The major conflict of interests in regard to the use of rehearsal time will probably not come between you and another actor, but between you and the director. And his preferences will normally prevail, so you must learn to be flexible if you are to accomplish your own ends. For example, if you are an actor who likes to learn the words and the basic moves within the first few days so that you can forget those external concerns and get to what you feel is the heart of your work—if you're like Olivier (as Peter Brook described him), an actor who achieves his freedom only after the tongue muscles have been externally conditioned to say the correct words and the director decides to spend the first seven rehearsals improvising the offstage scenes referred to in the action—what will you do? Well, what you cannot do in rehearsals you can do at home or during rehearsal hours in some other space. Spend your offstage rehearsal time and your at-home rehearsal time doing what *you* need to do. And learn as much as you can from the exercises the director is pursuing. Actors waste a sad amount of their available rehearsal time just sitting around. Not "waiting to go on," just sitting around bored. Or reading magazines. Or playing cards. You ought to use that time to advantage. If you can find an actor you play a scene with, go to it in the hallway, basement, or out in the lobby. Even if you have to work alone, work. If you have a particular order to your own rehearsal process, stick to it. You will profit from the company's joint effort as often as it corresponds to your needs. But when that luxury is denied you, you can still work in your own manner and at your own tempo.

Never give another actor unsolicited advice! Don't suggest how he might say his line, pick up his cigarette, or bring forth real tears. Don't explain to him what the director has just said. Respect the actors you work with by letting them do their work while you do yours. This is a common fault of young actors who have not yet learned how an actor behaves; it is particularly true of those trained in universities where some sort of "let's all get together and do a play, guys" mentality has prevailed. They step beyond their actor's job and naively assume they are directors. Or at the least, they think they are in some summer-camp conclave where everyone's opinion is equally important. But the theatre is not a democracy. Egalitarianism does not obtain. The director talks with each actor individually. What is true for the star is not true for you. And you don't want others telling you how to do your work, so you must respect them by restraining your impulse to advise them. You may believe you are speaking for the common good, but it is widely thought to be very bad manners for one actor to coach another. Frequently a seasoned veteran will snap at a beginner who breaches this code of conduct, and I've seen tears, wasted energies, and wasted rehearsal time result from just such a professional blunder.

Occasionally you will find an actor who asks for your help. Be careful; she is probably only asking to be told she's wonderful. Most actors don't want advice, only praise. Actors are single-minded and self-centered and only truly interested in themselves. There's the old joke about the actor who's at an opening night party and talking with the bankers, lawyers, doctors, and other philanthropists who make up the theatre's board of directors and their friends. After boring a group of listeners with the story of his life, the actor realizes he's dominating the conversation and that he'd better change the subject. "But enough of talking about me," he says. "Here I am in your city, and I'd like to learn about *you*. What did *you* think of my performance?" So, if an actor seeks your advice, tread carefully. If you can determine that he truly wants help, then offer it delicately. You might try describing some occasion where you wrestled with a similar problem. "Yeah, crying is hard for me too," you might hear yourself say. "I've tried everything from putting soap under my fingernails and then squeezing it into my eyes to trying to recall how I felt when I learned I was going to be divorced. I'm not much good at it. How are you working?" By revealing your own limitations first and then returning the ball into his court, you've initiated reasonable, craft-level discussion. If you can be of help to the actor, great. But don't ever be condescending. Don't ever boast, "Oh, I've learned how to do that one. You see, what you do is . . ."

Another gaffe of this type can happen when you are rehearsing a role you've done in an earlier production of the same play. The temptation is to say, "What we did here, was . . ." or "If you give me that line fast and then I do a slow take, the audience howls with laughter." It is offensive to the other actors to impose what you did somewhere else on what they are working to create new. After all, they are different actors. The theatre, the director, and the audience are different. *Your* performance is going to be different as well. You don't have to forget what you learned in your earlier experience, and you may even repeat a great deal of your earlier performance, but just don't talk about it all the time.

On occasions, you will need an actor's help. Perhaps what an actor is doing is keeping you from achieving the quality you are striving for in a given scene. That can happen on a simple, technical level or on a profound, interpretive one. You may simply need him to come in with a quick cue so your transition to your next beat will fall right rhythmically, or you may need him to play a very different action in a scene if your characterization is to remain coherent. The first of these problems can be dealt with between actors. Broach the subject by seeking mutual help. "Listen, I'm having trouble with this moment. Can you figure out what I might do here?" More often than not, the actor will provide an answer that changes what he does, and thereby makes your joint scene go properly. You will have accomplished your own ends diplomatically. If a major interpretive issue is at hand, raise the subject with the director and not the actor. Use rather the same tactic. "Here I am, Lady Anne, on my way to bury my husband, and Richard interrupts me. I have to resist his advances. Well, I find I'm having trouble doing that, because I don't feel he's really advancing. What do I do?" Then the director can do what she's been trying to do for several weeks, namely to correct Richard's false interpretation of the famed wooing scene.

This isn't just an abstract example. Have you seen the very funny movie *The Goodbye Girl*? Neil Simon wrote it for his second wife, Marsha Mason. The way the story was told in New York at that time is this: Marsha Mason was rehearsing Lady Anne at the Lincoln Center and she'd come home to Neil Simon at night and unload her frustrations with the actor doing Richard. Simon took what she told him, elaborated it with his unique comic imagination, and came up with the wildly funny sequence in which Richard Dreyfus is being directed to play an extremely "camp" King Richard. Those of us who saw that Lincoln Center production saw the parallels. It made the film doubly funny.

There are times when you just have to be assertive, though you should turn to that only after you've tried every polite and diplomatic device you know. I was playing Benedick in *Much Ado About Nothing* and had trouble with a short scene late in the action. Benedick has formally challenged Claudio to a duel and is happily returning to tell Beatrice what's he's done and to woo her. He encounters Margaret, young Hero's confidante, who tries to flirt with him. I understood my action: to get to Beatrice. The obstacle was Margaret, and the way of overcoming the obstacle was through wit, through badinage. It was, I felt certain, a scene to be played swiftly. But the actor doing Margaret knew this was one of her largest scenes in the play and wanted to go slowly, to show the audience her stuff, I suspect. I tried discussing it with the actress. No change. I discussed it with the director, who agreed with me. He rehearsed the scene carefully and we made good progress. Then we did a run-through and Margaret reverted to her slower tempo. I spoke with the stage manager, who spoke to the actor. No change. I knew the scene played swiftly was charming and witty and kept the drive of the latter portion of the show going. I knew that the scene played slowly was uninteresting and irrelevant. What to do? Having exhausted all my other options, I started playing the scene at the correct tempo. That meant I'd say a line, wait the appropriate time, and say my next line. I'd begun my next line before Margaret had concluded hers. After a couple of these overlaps had happened, she was all in a muddle, unable to get a cue, or hear herself, or play the scene. She had to hurry up to get her lines in. From then on, she did. In every subsequent rehearsal and in performance.

"Let me play the lion's part," says that greatest of all ham actors, Bottom the Weaver. Bottom wants to play every role and to tell his friends how to play theirs. Don't be Bottom, for you too may suffer his fate and turn into a jackass.

Respect your fellow actor's working space. Don't lounge in front of him reading, smoking, knitting, chatting, sleeping. If a show is rehearsing in a small room where the director's table is only a few feet from the edge of the playing area, never intrude into that space. Never walk between the actors and the director!

And keep the working space free of clutter. Leave your umbrella and backpack somewhere else. If the rehearsal is in a theatre, stay out of the front part of the auditorium, where the onstage actors can see you—where their concentrations can be shaken by your presence. Don't walk from the waiting area to the playing area on a path that intrudes on the other actors' concentration. Acting is hard enough to do without some unthinking clod marching about in front of you.

I directed a show a few years back in which such an extraordinary breach of etiquette occurred that I remember it vividly today. The scene was an office with two basic areas: a desk area and a lounge area. The script called for an intense scene between two central characters around the desk while a group of characters in the lounge watched a TV monitor and made occasional remarks that provided an editorial counterpoint to the main dialogue. During one rehearsal, as I concentrated on the dialogue scene stage right, I kept hearing low conversation from the other side of the stage. I discovered that one of the actors in the lounge area was going over his lines for yet a different scene in the play. He was not playing his action (which was to study the TV playback), and he was disrupting the other actors' work. I just turned and stared at him in astonishment. So, shortly, did the other actors. After a moment, he realized the silence, looked up to see everyone staring at him in disgust, and quickly shut up. We were able to go on with the rehearsal.

Respect your fellow actors' time. When you are working, you wish and need the director's and stage manager's full attention. When your fellow actors are working, they need it. Don't intrude on the concentration of anyone who is at work; don't waste their precious time. What you have to ask the director can wait until an appropriate break in the rehearsal.

Be on hand when your turn to work comes. Don't be in the coffee shop, the tobacconist's, the costume shop, or the rest room. Be alert to the rehearsal's development and be prepared to make your entrance when your scene comes up. Your mutual enemy is time. Join to defeat it.

Respect the seriousness of your fellow actors' work. Don't give in to any childish or childlike impulses. Don't play pranks. It is true that a portion of acting is "playing" and that one of the things that makes you an actor is the exuberance you have. But don't disrupt serious work to gratify your private, non-theatrical needs. Can you rehearse Maggie's opening monologue from *Cat on a Hot Tin Roof* if someone has drawn a smiley-face on the mirror you use? Or can anyone effectively rehearse the Gwendolyn-Cecily tea scene if you have replaced the sugar cubes with bouillon cubes? Don't denigrate an actor's work by playing silly pranks. That's the stuff amateur theatricals are made of—not a part of mature, professional behavior. (For a delightful and rich discussion of amateur theatricals, read Michael Green's *Downwind of Upstage, The Art of Coarse Acting* [New York: Drama Book Specialists, 1980].) Respect another actor's warm-ups and pre-entrance preparations. A brilliant young actor I know goes through the entirety of his role, on stage, before every performance. It sometimes takes him hours. You'll rarely encounter such a zealot, but if you do, respect him. What he's doing is no more than what you do; he's just getting ready to do the show. In his own particular way. And if you meet such an actor, be aware that he might just grow up to be the next George Grizzard—who did all of Hamlet, on stage by himself, in the afternoon before he opened the famed Tyrone Guthrie Theatre in Minneapolis in 1963.

If an actor you're working with spends five minutes vocalizing before each rehearsal begins, let him. Don't intrude on that time to ask about your scene with him. What he's doing is a portion of his work process and merits your consideration. It's what he needs to do. Don't be guilty of judging its value. You have no grounds for such a judgment.

Nowadays we seldom encounter hard and fast Actors Studio-trained actors, but if you work with such a performer, be alert to and respectful of those working habits. I engaged an actor once, a member of the Studio, who made it very clear that she was not to be called by her own name once a rehearsal began—she wanted to think, feel, and respond only as the character. You may share my belief that "that way madness lies," but she's entitled to her beliefs and practices every bit as much as you're entitled to yours. There is no single correct way to achieve results as an actor, and you must be tolerant of whatever habits, warm-ups, and pre-entrance preparations your fellow actors do. After all, as Jerry says in *The Zoo Story*, "Sometimes you have to go a long distance out of your way in order to come back a short distance correctly."

When you are rehearsing scenes of violent action, you must be especially careful of your working manners. Here you may not merely offend a colleague, you may break bones: theirs or yours.

In the fifteen years since an earlier version of this book was written, there has been a welcome addition to our theatre. Fight choreographers are now a commonplace, and rare is the production that does not have one creating and supervising all stage combat—from the simple slap Willy Loman gives Biff to the complicated battle of Agincourt in *Henry V*. And many younger actors have received formal instruction in stage combat in their universities and conservatories. Still, stage violence can be dangerous, and how you behave is of vital importance. Safe practice includes three things: (1) a qualified fight choreographer who is given appropriate rehearsal time, (2) appropriate weapons that are made available to the actors from the first rehearsal on, and (3) the mutual cooperation of the actor-fighters. This last item is your job. If you feel there is insufficient rehearsal time being allotted for your fights, ask your stage manager to talk to the director. If you don't have the appropriate weapons, do the same. But the task of cooperating with your fight opponents is yours and yours alone.

In the rare instance that you will be asked to "work out the fight" yourselves, you must approach the fight as if it were a piece of dance choreography. Each fighter must learn each move of the fight as precisely as a dancer learns each step of a dance combination. Fights are commonly divided into beats and are as precisely counted out as the steps of a tap routine. If you work slowly and cooperatively with your partners, and if you take sufficient time, you will be able to "work out the fight" safely and effectively. But watch out for being overzealous. In a recent *Henry V*, two young actors were permitted by the fight choreographer to work out a sequence on their own. What they came up with was exciting and appropriate, and they went through it time after time after time to perfect it. Then they showed it to the fight choreographer and the rest of us in the cast. And, in their enthusiasm, they made a tiny miss-move—and one of the actors got a broken nose! Fights are intended to excite the audience, not the actors.

You have no control over the selection of the play or the length of rehearsal time, but you can help yourself and your other actors by observing sensible professional behavior in the preparation of fight scenes. Don't let someone's exuberance intrude on sound working practices. At the Oregon Shakespearean Festival, in the pre-fight choreographer days, I had an upstage sequence in the middle of a large battle. My partner and I were to execute a *corps-à-corps* (or what Michael Green calls "the eternal parry"), and then a very simple pattern of thrusts and counters. My partner was new to acting, much enamored of a misunderstanding of Stanislavsky's teachings, and liked to believe he *was* his character. In the midst of a rehearsal, as I was dutifully counting 1-2-3-4 and 1-2-3-4, he abandoned the rehearsed pattern and came for me! I stepped aside and swatted him with the flat of my rapier, as hard as I could on his thigh, raising (I learned later) an ugly welt. "You see," I explained, "we must follow the pattern as carefully as if it were dialogue. That way I can avoid hurting you." The fight went well from that welt onwards.

The greatest danger in fight sequences is that they are under-rehearsed. Once again, time is the enemy of theatre. That's what's behind the English superstitions surrounding *Macbeth*. English actors frequently will not mention the title, referring to it as "the Scottish play" and to the title role as "the thane" or "Mackers." They hold that quoting lines from it in the dressing room is bad luck. It is also believed that some terrible accident will occur during any production of the play. Frequently, this is explained by alleging that the invocations spoken by the witches are real, but the more sensible reason is this: the play is frequently produced without sufficient rehearsal time. It's a short script and can be learned fast. And it is usually popular at the box office. But producing *Macbeth* in three weeks is asking for trouble. All those fight scenes! Small wonder there are many accidents!

And accidents aren't just "accidents" any longer. They can be deadly—which leads to some brief comments on the reality of AIDS in the workplace. Probably no group of workers is more sympathetic to the victims of this terrifying disease than are actors. Most of us have lost many friends and loved ones. Yet the disease is spreading through our profession at a terrifying speed. And there are some realities we must be awake to.

The first reality is that medical science doesn't know very much and that, as long as a bigoted and smug morality governs our society and announces that this plague is God's wrath upon the immoral, it is unlikely that much money will be spent on research or that we will swiftly find a cure.

The second reality is that because our knowledge is little, our fears lead us to foolish forms of protection and to a continually changing set of behaviors. A few years ago, when it was believed that AIDS was transmitted through saliva, writers on daytime "soap opera" television were instructed to write out *all* kisses. Hugs were encouraged, but kisses were forbidden. The actors were afraid. The producers didn't want their star actors dying. Today, we believe AIDS is not transmitted through saliva but through blood. Do we have a fear of blood in rehearsals? You bet we do. While writing this chapter, I came upon a newspaper item about an Englishman who had contracted the fatal illness in a fist fight, trying to keep some univited guest out of a wedding reception—a guest who was later diagnosed to be HIV "positive" and whose broken lip bled onto the host's hand and got into his system. And what, I suddenly thought, of the blood on my opponent's knuckles when I accidentally hit him with a sword while rehearsing our combat? And what of the wardrobe staff who pin costumes on HIV "positive" actors during fittings? We have a fear. We do not have answers.

We can only be compassionate. And careful.

I'm going to stop writing for a while. I urge you to stop reading. Let's both start up again when the mood is cheerier.

* * * * *

Not all actors you work with will be humans. Some will be our friends from the animal kingdom. Your way of working with animals, your behavior toward them, is an important portion of your entire comportment as an actor. It can also have an immense impact on your effectiveness in performance.

If you are to play a scene with an animal that is unfamiliar to you, request some expert advice. If you're in *Oliver* and must follow the trained dog across a scaffolding to seek out the hidden Bill Sykes, learn as much as you can about the dog from its trainer. If you must carry a chicken across the stage, as I did once in *My Three Angels*, talk to a farmer about the best way to carry a chicken. I didn't. I tried to keep it upright under my arm, like a football, and got pecked repeatedly—until an actor who had grown up on a farm taught me that if I grabbed the chicken by the feet and carried it upside down, it would become a hypnotized, calm, and cooperative actor. Years later I gave the same business to the actor I was directing as Jacques in a production of *The Miser,* and he handled the bird very successfully, despite indignant cries of some city-bred young women in the cast who viewed themselves as politically correct and who cried out that we were guilty of "chicken abuse."

Just as you must get along with human actors offstage, you must spend time offstage getting to know your animal-actor. This is particularly true if you are a bit afraid of the animal. A young actor was engaged by the Disney people to play in a TV western; he lied and said that he rode horses well. He was flown to the location in Kanab, Utah. His first shot of the working day required him to mount, ride about 200 yards into the distance, and then ride past the camera, as though he were en route somewhere. He was terrified of horses but in love with paychecks, so he gamely mounted and rode off toward the distant starting place. But the horse bolted and ran amuck, knocked over two expensive cameras, and scattered people and gear until it was captured by the wrangler. The young actor received a bus ticket back to Hollywood. The moral: talk to horses. Had he taken the trouble to befriend that horse instead of revealing his fear of it, he might have gotten away with the scene. Might have been retained on the film.

Animals need a lot of rehearsal time because they are, as a rule, not as bright as human actors. You will reduce your animal partner's anxieties if you repeat the actions from rehearsal to rehearsal with great consistency. Newness confuses animals. Improvisation encourages catastrophe. You may be bored doing a scene a particular way, but the dog at your side is loving the security of knowing what to do. Don't flirt with danger.

Try, as best you can, to anticipate the audience's reaction so that you can be prepared to assist the animal in performance. If, for example, you're doing Launce in Shakespeare's *Two Gentlemen of Verona* and you know the audience is going to howl with laughter at your dog Crab, ask the director to have the company laugh a lot during Crab's scenes, so he gets accustomed to the idea and doesn't start barking at the braying audience on opening night—or worse, grow frightened and lift his leg against yours.

Not all experiences with animals can be anticipated, and there are no guidelines to help you with the unpredicted. You're on your own when they happen. Bats may swoop from the grid, moths get hypnotized in a spotlight, stray dogs may saunter through your love scene, pigeons may drop on your doublet, and crickets may underscore your soliloquy. The strangest of these, in my own experience, occurred one summer during a performance in Hollywood of an outdoor passion play. Happily, I was in the wings. (I was playing Judas for Equity minimum and thirty pieces of silver a week.) Jesus and his disciples were on stage. Suddenly, an immense and unattractive spider entered from the other side of the stage and casually worked his way toward Our Savior, whose blood had rushed from his face at the sight. Deftly, and with an act of devotion that surely rivaled his namesake's, John the Beloved strode across the stage and placed his sandaled foot on the intruder. Scrunch! The show must go on!

* * * * *

Animals require one kind of treatment. Stars another. Your behavior in a production with a star may differ from your regular behavior. And with good reason.

A star is any performer whose name assures the production will attract an audience. In Hollywood terms, a star is "bankable"—money for production can be wrestled from a studio if a star is featured in the film. For Broadway, a star is that person whose name will create a pre-sale big enough to keep the play open for a few weeks, until it can build an audience. In summer stock, a star is anyone whose name will sell tickets. That may well be some TV personality from a game show who is not necessarily correct for the role and who may even perform a mini-nightclub act following the play to reward his faithful fans. If you are a star, you know it.

In the LORT circuit, the emphasis is on the "play," and billing is done alphabetically. There is a resistance to acknowledging a star. Until a real one arrives on the scene. I was producing a new play written by Alfred Drake, the star who had created the leading roles in *Oklahoma!*, *Kismet*, and *Kiss Me, Kate*, and who had played Benedick opposite Katherine Hepburn and Claudius opposite Richard Burton. Drake was also directing the play and playing the lead. On the phone with Drake's agent, my managing director explained that in the LORT contract, actors are listed alphabetically, and we had no above-the-title names in the program. "Since 1943," replied the agent, "Mr. Drake has been above the title. This is not open to negotiation." It wasn't. We complied. And Drake (who by the way is an immensely pleasant man) and his agent were right. People bought tickets to see Drake and not our LORT company. The audience expected the star's name to be prominently displayed. *They* wanted to celebrate the star.

Your goal is employment, and to the degree that the star creates the possibility for you to work, he merits particularly courteous attention. Also, the star is working with a lot more pressure on him than you are. He is certainly playing the leading role, which means he's got more to master than you have—more scenes, more lines, more business, more time on stage to fill with credible acting. It means if the show is a new script trying out, he's got more changes to learn from night to night. It means he has more demands on his time for public-relations work. He has to go to TV interviews, do press conferences, have luncheons with entertainment editors. He must give over valuable working time for the purpose of promoting the economic venture that is paying your salary. He must lose additional working time being social with the show's backers—the angels who have capitalized the production. And he has the extraordinary pressure of delivering a performance that is good enough to merit the name he has earned over the years, good enough to carry the show, to live up to his own reputation. You see, under adverse conditions and with extreme pressure on him, the star must do more than merely act the role well: he must be the figurehead, center of morale, and touchstone for the entire venture. Anyone who does all that merits an adjustment in your work habits; after all, your employment depends on the star's success. If he succeeds, you eat, even if your performance is only mediocre.

Accommodate your work habits to the star's. I did a Molière with Tammy Grimes a few seasons back, and she began every rehearsal with a speed-line run-through of the scene to be worked. I guess she needed it as a way of warming up, focusing her work on the segment of the script to be attacked in that rehearsal, or maybe just as a way of learning the lines. Whatever. I was playing quite a small role and those line run-throughs were of no use to me. But my work habits were of no consequence. We did line run-throughs. And I did my damnedest to do them the way she liked.

Don't be surprised when the star gives you notes. If just any actor were to give you notes, you would be justified in telling him where to put them. But the star is concerned with the total success of the show and will frequently become something of a second director on the production—a first director on some occasions. Some stars reportedly give notes after almost every performance. Take the notes. Smile. If the notes contradict what the director has asked you to do, discreetly discuss this with the director or stage manager and inquire how to proceed. If the notes make sense, incorporate them into your performance. Good advice from a more experienced player ought to be welcome. Usually, such notes will relate to the way you give cues to the star. In a production of *Taming of the Shrew* I did with Tammy Grimes, she would advise how she wanted me to feed her certain lines, and she knew what she was talking about. She knew when a fast or slow cue would best set up her punchline, and I was happy to comply. But some stars can be unwise and selfish. The late Howard da Silva didn't want anyone to get laughs in his scenes. My entrance did—just the way director Dan Petrie asked me to come down the steps invariably got a laugh. Da Silva gave me notes after almost every performance. Ed Flanders shared my dressing room and he wisely advised that as a young actor, and an actor in a supporting role, I should never fight the star myself. "You'll lose," he said. And he was right, of course. Don't be so filled with "artistic integrity" that you gain the whole note but lose your career. I took da Silva's notes to the stage manager. He told me to do what the director had set. I was in the middle, and I couldn't find a way out. Happily, the run was a short three weeks.

The star will expect and receive special treatment. Stage management will have a chair for the star, ice water, candy, and a battery-operated fan. And you'll get the floor, a break during which to buy your own soda, and you can fan yourself with your script if you're warm. Don't worry about that. If those flatterings are necessary to get a good performance, don't begrudge them. Remember the star's pressures. And if you're ever successful enough to merit such attention, you'll get it. For now, be professional and do your job. And part of your job is contributing to a happy environment. If you complain about the star's special treatment, you're counter-productive—not to mention stupid.

Most stars are pleasant. They're hard-working actors who've achieved their status because they do their work well, and they know their work includes creating a good working ambiance. But occasionally you might work with a louse. Someone who is so insecure that he needs to boost his own petty ego by making everyone feel inferior. This is unpleasant when the offender is a star. When he's just another working actor who has delusions of stardom, it can be enraging. What to do? Stay clear! Don't get in the way, don't contradict, don't compete. This too shall pass. Be thankful you have the job, and do it as well as you can without causing any additional sparks to fly.

If you are any good as an actor, if you have any future, somewhere along the line you will work with a star. As you ascend toward the heights of your profession, you will find yourself playing scenes with actors whose names have always dazzled you. You'll discover that stars are good actors and bad actors, nice people and grouches, but always, always stars. Actors who merit and require your best behavior.

And if you get to be a star one day? Try to remember how an actor behaves.

*   *   *   *   *

"Who is going to be Deputy Dawg?" I heard asked on my first Equity production. The phrase was borrowed from a cartoon figure on TV that was particularly popular at the time, and the real question was who would be elected to serve as the Equity deputy. This is a job one of the senior members of Equity will perform on every production, in every company. It is an important job, but actors usually make light of it. It is sadly traditional to elect anyone who is not present. If you go to the toilet at the wrong time during the first rehearsal, you may be it.

The duties of the deputy are clearly defined in the Equity handbook and, under most circumstances, are simple to do and don't require more than a few minutes a week to fill out the weekly report and mail it in to Equity. Essentially, the deputy represents labor (you) in negotiations with management (the producer). The deputy can help you in many ways. At the Great Lakes Shakespeare Festival one summer, the producer suggested that we should all wear body makeup for our production of *Troilus and Cressida*. Most of us had deep suntans and believed we didn't need it. None of us felt we needed to come to the theatre an hour early for each performance to dob that streaky body paint all over ourselves. Out came the Equity handbook and up spoke our deputy. The rules forbade the producer's requiring it unless he provided us, on the premises, with hot showers. The theatre didn't have them, and we didn't wear it. Hooray for the deputy.

The election of deputy should be taken seriously. Vote for someone who is experienced, who is mature in manner and will command the management's respect. Then, you can go to your deputy with any problems you are having with the management. She may tell you that it is an artistic problem and you should go to the stage manager or director with it; she may tell you it is a personal problem and you should go to the company manager with it; she may tell you you don't have a problem and that you should shut up and go back to work; or she may tell you that others have mentioned the same concern and that she'll act upon it. If, for example, the director is frequently holding you five or ten minutes overtime at the end of the day, and is doing the same with others, it is the deputy's job to discuss this with the management and either see that the proper hours are observed or that the actors are compensated for the overtime. Your deputy is an actor, like you, and can help you through some of the rough times on the job. Support your local deputy.

* * * * *

Remember when you took your clothes off in that audition room and agreed you would do the nude scene? Well, now it's time to rehearse it. How will your fellow actors behave? How would you behave if one of them were about to "take it off." Nudity in public makes most of us pretty nervous and, as a result, we sometimes behave stupidly. Here are some notions on behavior for the rehearsal of nude scenes that may help you through your first experience.

We are all a conflicted mixture of socially and culturally conditioned taboos and childlike desires to be exhibitionistic. That is part of what identifies us as actors. We want to show off our bodies and we are afraid to show off our bodies. This conflict within ourselves causes us to behave uncertainly in any circumstance in which the conflict between the desire and the taboo is made public. Rehearsals of nude scenes are just such situations.

Happily, there is much truth to the homily "familiarity breeds contempt." The more we look at bodies, the less they seem extraordinary. Doctors manage to confront nudity all day long and perform as professionals. So can actors, once they have looked at nudity all day long—or often enough that the novelty has worn off and they can return to the professional tasks before them, the playing of their actions. Think of such plays as *Hair* and David Storey's *The Changing Room.* Whatever uncertainty of

behavior might have affected the casts at the beginning of rehearsals was surely absent by the time those shows were ready
for an audience.

The first few nude rehearsals create the tension. The sooner
in the rehearsal period these occur, the better the subsequent
rehearsals will be. If you have to do the nude scene in Peter
Shaffer's *Equus*, ask the director when she would like to introduce this element of the show into rehearsals. It ought to come
after you have learned the scene sufficiently to play straight
through it without stops for prompts, discussion, and coaching.
That way the initial "exposure" can be brief and you can dress
and get on with your work without undue dwelling on the
nudity. Certainly, you should work nude well before the dress
rehearsal as that normally comes too late in the rehearsal period
for you to get over your nervousness sufficiently in advance of
opening night.

If you are doing a nude scene, make certain that your costume is presentable. Bathe! Dirty feet on a nude body can be as
disruptive to a rehearsal as inappropriate clothes on a costumed
one. If the nude body seems inappropriate, the actors who play
the scene with you will be distracted and will begin to focus on
you instead of on your character.

Bring some sort of robe or covering with you so that you can
be clothed before and after the scene. That way, you'll support
the notion that the character is nude, but that you, the actor, are
not. Also, you'll help prevent yourself from catching a cold in a
poorly heated rehearsal hall.

Try to hold down your exhibitionistic impulses. As a way of
covering your nervousness, you might parade around in the
nude, luxuriating in your "freedom." (I've seen this happen.) All
you succeed in doing is making the rest of the company as
uneasy as you are. That's disruptive rather than constructive.

As you rehearse the scene, focus on the given circumstances.
Your nudity ought to be as appropriate to the scene you're
playing as an evening gown would be in a Noel Coward play. If
you are playing your actions correctly, you'll reduce initial un-
easiness.

Ask the director if you might rehearse the scene a few times with only the actors who are in the scene present—until the novelty has worn off for them and they and you can play the scene without undue self-consciousness. Then, when the actors, crew, and production staff see a later rehearsal, you'll have a degree of self-confidence in yourself, your fellow actors, and the scene that will make it easier for you to go about your work productively.

If some other actor in the production has the nude scene, you can help by going about your business knowing that the actor's skin is the appropriate costume for the scene. Relate to the nude actor as you ought to in the context of the scene's given circumstances. Are you, as your character, shocked by it, excited by it, indifferent to it? Play your action truthfully and keep your attention on the character, not the performer. As yourself, relating to your fellow actor before or after the scene, refrain from the temptation to make witty remarks.

In all your dealings with your fellow actors, simply remember to employ the Golden Rule: Do unto other actors as you would have other actors do unto you.

STAGE MANAGERS   After the actors, you will spend the largest part of your time with the show's stage managers. The production stage manager (PSM) is so-named because he joins the production in its earliest stages of development, well before the actors are engaged and the rehearsals begun, and because he is the chief authority for running the production through rehearsals and performances. The PSM has a huge responsibility, and Actors' Equity Association has appropriately established a higher minimum salary for PSMs than for actors. The PSM may have a number of stage managers and assistant stage managers assisting him. On a large musical like *Les Misérables*, there could be more than four stage managers. The ranking of the company's stage managers will become evident to you immediately. The PSM will delegate responsibilities, convene and terminate rehearsals, and conduct all "business" during rehearsals (announcements of fittings, changes of scheduling), and will take primary responsibility for the prompt book, that "bible" of the developing production that will govern the show through its performances. As the chief of his division of the production team (and it is a large

division that includes you), he merits your respect and cooperation. So do all the stage managers. They are there to make it
possible for you to do your job well. You need them.

There are four phases to the stage manager's work, and you
need to understand these. The first is the pre-rehearsal phase,
during which much of the play's formative work is completed:
concepts achieved, re-writes undertaken, designs approved, and
personnel engaged. It is only in this final area that you might
encounter the stage manager. When you come to auditions, you
might meet an ASM (assistant stage manager) taking names and
giving out scripts. In the audition room you may meet the PSM
collecting photo/résumés or even reading the other characters'
speeches for your cold reading. During this first phase, stage
management is very busy and is beset with friends and acquaintances who are seeking employment. What can you do? Be efficient in your use of the stage manager's time, courteous to her
(thank her for reading with you), and businesslike in your ex-
changes. If she asks for your phone number, don't say you'll find
it later. Say, "It's 474-1010, and it's on the top of my résumé.
There's an answering machine, and I check it regularly." Let her
know, without being overbearing, that you are a cooperative,
responsive worker. You would be astounded at the influence
that a PSM has on casting. Think of it this way: She's been hired
already. The producer and director trust her with what all theatre
people know to be a huge and difficult job. They are likely, as a
result, to trust her opinion on many matters. If she knows you or
is impressed enough by you to commit herself on your behalf,
you will be considered seriously. Also, if she is turned off by you,
you're through. One whisper of "look out for that one" and your
photo will go directly into the circular file.

The second phase of the stage manager's work is the rehearsal phase, the weeks during which the show is shaped.
During this period, the stage manager is concerned with compil-
ing a correct prompt book, ascertaining all the cues to be called
(for lights, sound, fly floor, conductor, etc.), administering the
smooth flow of work (seeing that actors get to fittings and photo
calls, that props are available for rehearsals), and establishing a
healthy spirit within the company. That last item usually means

that the stage manager is eager to keep everyone happy, to head off personality conflicts, and to establish proper discipline from the outset. To do so she may jump on someone for tardiness or for being too slow in learning lines, and she will attempt diplomatically to guide everyone to a respect for the working space and working process. But mostly she will be your obliging, cheery, and helpful co-worker.

The third phase of the stage manager's work begins the day the company moves onto the set, into the theatre. This phase continues through the rigorous and tiring technical and dress rehearsals, all the way to opening night. From the beginning of this phase, the PSM is the chief executive on the show—even the director takes instructions from her. It is the PSM's responsibility to make the show run correctly, and her concerns are larger than those of any other person. The writer's desire to cut a line must be cleared with the PSM to ensure that no cue is affected by the change; only then may the actor be instructed to drop the line. The actor may not decide to sit on the arm of the chair instead of the seat until the change has been cleared with the PSM, who may be taking a visual cue off the action. (The university-trained actor is frequently confused at this stage of a production's development. In most university situations, the stage manager is a student, inexperienced, and most often poorly trained. The director is most commonly a professor who assumes responsibilities that go beyond what a professional director does. As a result, the director frequently runs the final phase of rehearsals, and the student actor learns the unprofessional practice of ignoring the stage manager. The stage manager is shunted to an inferior position by the professor-director's need to get the show ready by opening night. When this happens, the actor learns very poor work habits and may well get confused on his first professional job by the sudden switch of authority from director to PSM. I have seen more than one young actor being read the riot act by an impatient PSM.)

The final phase of the stage manager's work is the performance. Throughout the run of the play, the PSM is responsible for the smooth running of the show *and* for the maintenance of its performance standards. The PSM is responsible to ensure that actors are in the theatre on time, that wardrobe is sent to the cleaners each week, and that the electricians do a nightly check for burned-out lamps. It also means she gives the actors notes on their performances and, if she feels it essential, she calls brush-up rehearsals. The PSM is the boss who "manages" the production and her authority is unquestionable.

In case you're mistakenly envious of the PSM's authority, remember the truth that everything that goes wrong on a production is the stage manager's fault. And on occasions, the PSM runs into hateful responsibilities. Perry Cline, PSM for the roller-skate musical *Starlight Express*, had the terrifying responsibility for cuing all the moving scenery. One tiny error and the skaters' very lives could be in danger. He said almost every single performance had a "swing" skater in it because there was almost always one of the "first cast" out with an injury. A "swing" skater's speed or rhythm might be slightly different, and that made Cline's calling of cues that much more difficult. Or consider the case of the PSM for a production of Neil Simon's *Prisoner of Second Avenue* I directed at the Walnut Street Theatre in Philadelphia. After the show opened (and after I'd left) the two leads' violent disliking for each other led to bizarre events. They would do hateful things to one another on stage nightly, and then they would each complain about the other to the long-suffering PSM. Who knows who was "right" or "wrong?" Both, probably. But the PSM had to listen to all that aggravation, from each in turn, and then go talk to each in turn requesting that he or she *not* repeat whatever it was that the other had complained about. In such hateful circumstances, to borrow from the lyrics of W.S. Gilbert, the stage manager's lot is not a happy one.

As swiftly as you can, learn the PSM's working habits. Each works differently, and you will ingratiate yourself, save valuable time, and contribute to the smooth flow of rehearsals if you can adapt. This will not ask much of you as most stage managers understand that they are employed to make your life easy, that they are to be flexible and cooperative, and that your needs are to be respected. That means the stage manager will go 80% of the way. Now if you'll go 30%, imagine how cheerfully and smoothly things will run.

Right off, learn the important telephone numbers and get them written down where you can *always* find them. You'll get a "contact sheet" in the first few days of rehearsal—a page with the names and numbers of the company on it. But before it is duplicated and distributed, learn the stage manager's number(s) and those of the production office, rehearsal hall, and wardrobe department. Inquire if the stage manager minds being called at home in the case of an emergency. He'll invariably say, "Call me at any hour of the day or night, but only if it is *really* an emergency."

Next, learn the rules he enforces at rehearsals. Does he restrict smoking to onstage actions? Does he like all coats and umbrellas left in another room? Does he like you to ask questions of him or of the ASM? In short, be sensitive to his working habits and respect them as far as you can without intruding on your own. Yours are finally more important and he knows it. But it is unlikely there would ever be a conflict over honest work habits. Usually, if he requests some change from you, it is the result of his attempt to please one of your fellow actors. So cooperate. If, for example, you wear either contacts or regular eyeglasses and he asks you to wear your contacts, it may result from the director's remark that the worklights bounce off your glasses and he can't see what you're doing in your big scene.

Most important is the way a stage manager communicates information. If he makes spoken announcements at the beginning or end of each rehearsal, be certain to be present at those times to learn what you need to know and to avoid making him repeat himself. If he posts all notices on a callboard, then check it at your arrival and departure for each rehearsal.

The stage manager does many things for you. He will be pleased if you use his services. He's a supplier of writing aides like pencils, note paper, erasers, and scotch tape. He's a supplier of medical aides like aspirin, breath mints, ice packs, bandages, and antacids. He's an aide in line-learning (he'll hold book for you or find an ASM who will). He'll transmit your needs for props or costumes to the appropriate people (if you need a rehearsal prop or if your costume ought to have boots tall enough so you can hide a knife in them, tell your stage manager). He'll assist you to learn your role by going over line changes and blocking with you—using his prompt book to show you what the correct line or business is. He'll serve as a personnel manager; if you're having a personality conflict with a particular actor, discuss the difficulty with the stage manager. He'll solve 90% of such problems and be happy to be of service. Finally, he'll prompt you during rehearsals. Prompting merits a brief discussion.

The better the stage manager, the better the prompter. A good prompt is given very loudly so that your concentration need not be broken as you strain to hear what's been said. It is given only when you ask for it or when you are obviously stumped. It is always given in a clear and correct manner. It will include a long phrase, and not just two or three words. A stage manager will try very, very hard to accommodate to your habits and needs as he gives prompts. His goal is to help you. There are some ways you can help yourself.

Be consistent in the way you ask for a prompt. "Line" and "yes" are the two most popular requests. The English and Australians tend to use "yes" most often. "Line" is most popular in America and seems the less confusing of the two. I've often speculated on the madness that might have arisen during rehearsals for David Storey's *Home* in which many of Sir John Gielgud's lines were "yes." I fantasized an exchange in which the initial line is spoken correctly and no prompt required:

JG:	I see. Yes.
PSM:	Yes?
JG:	Yes?
PSM:	(mistakenly repeating the prompt) *Yes.*
JG:	No. I know. It's "Yes," yes?
PSM:	Yes.
JG:	Oh, I see. Yes.

Well, who could work his way out of that confusion? I prefer and recommend the consistent use of "line." Inexperienced, impetuous, and self-indulgent actors sometimes snap their fingers, or moan "Oh . . . oh . . . oh . . . don't tell me . . . oh . . ." Rude actors say stronger words than "dammit." All such manners are undesirable as they confuse the prompter and offend your fellow actor.

Don't ever ask for a repeat of your *incorrect* delivery of the line. Don't say "What did I say just then?" A good prompter will *never* repeat your error, so as not to support it in your mind or ear. He'll only give you the correct line. You'll confuse everyone and stall the rehearsal by asking to hear lines spoken back to you that are not in the text and which can only confuse both you and the actor whose cue is your correct line.

There are some things you can do to help the stage manager. Never interrupt the stage manager while he's working. Wait for a break in the rehearsal. You may not think he's doing anything as he sits over his prompt book watching a run-through, but he's working. Perhaps he is counting the seconds in which a scene shift must be executed or a costume changed. Whatever, respect his work. You don't want him stopping your scene to discuss lighting cues, so don't you stop his work to inquire about your needs.

Instruct the stage manager of anything you learn about the flow of performance that relates to your work and that he will need to know. For example, if you have only twenty seconds of dialogue and a ten-second scene shift to cross the stage, change costume, beard, and grab the leash on a pack of bloodhounds, you're going to need assistance. Tell the PSM and he will build that off-stage maneuver into his production plan and you will get the help you need. Less dramatically, if you need to have a prop off-left and the actor who handles it before you leaves it off-right on her exit, tell the PSM and he will arrange to have it where you need it. Or, if the low volume of a line makes it impossible for you to hear your entrance cue, tell the PSM so he can arrange a way to ensure that you get your cue. The PSM takes pride in a well-run show and will appreciate your help. He'll regret working with the actor who begins every statement with, "This is wrong." Or with the actor who whines and snivels, "I can't hear my cue," "I can't make that change," and "Somebody lost my prop." But he'll want to work often with the actor who notifies him during rehearsals of the problems that may arise and courteously asks for assistance.

Keep the stage manager alert to your whereabouts during rehearsals. If you're working on a scene with another actor, or if you're at a PR or costume call, make certain the stage manager knows about it. You can save aggravation and wasted time if the stage manager knows where you are.

Respect the stage manager's rules. They're set with an eye to keeping everybody happy and the show running smoothly. If you like to smoke and have been asked not to, don't. Which do you place more highly? Your work or your personal habits? If it is the latter, don't be surprised if nobody want to hire you.

When the third phase of rehearsals begins, the stage manager has no time for you. For several weeks he has joked with you, catered to you, prompted you, maybe even gotten drunk with you. Now there is a sudden shift in his attentions. You are one small and very insignificant part of the show. He's concerned with cues and sound levels, the duration of scenes shifts, and the logistical management of scores of people who you've never seen but who are just as important to the show's success as you are.

For a short while your relation to the stage manager must shift from co-worker to boss-employee. He needs you to be present, on time, consistent, cooperative, and, above all, silent. Do not expect favors from him. Do not be slighted by his seeming disinterest in you. Once the show has opened, if it runs a week or a year, he'll be able to re-engage in his friendly relation with you. For now, he's too busy to deal with you. You can help him and help yourself by knowing this and by doing your job well. And by being silent. As time is the general enemy of theatre, time and noise are the enemies of those final, complicated, nerve-testing rehearsals.

THE DIRECTOR "What does your dad do?" the seven-year-old was asked. "He's a play director." "But what does he *do?*" "Well, at the theatre he tells everybody where to go and what to say and how to say it." From the mouths of babes, the proverb has it, comes wisdom.

The director is responsible for the "artistic" standards of a play. He's responsible for the designs, as he approves them; for the actors, as he selects them; for the script, as he undertakes to direct it; for the music, the lighting, the tempo, the tone. For the whole thing. One part of his responsibility, perhaps the most visible part, is the performance of the actors. The director is responsible for what you do. You'll earn the credit for what you do well. The director will earn the blame for what you do poorly.

The director selects you because he believes that you are the best of the actors available to him. Once he has selected you he has two ways to achieve the desired performance: coach you to do it or fire you and get someone who can. This simple truth ought to lead you to several eye-raising discoveries. The standard Equity contract permits management to fire you during the first five days of rehearsal without paying you a separation fee. If you're retained past five days, you can't be fired unless you're given two weeks' notice (or given two weeks' salary and told you're not needed at rehearsals any longer). That five-day clause is your union's recognition of the basic principle underlying your engagement: the assumption that you can act, can do the job you've been hired to do. When a cab company hires a driver, they assume that he knows how to drive a car and can reach the assigned destination if he's given a route. It's assumed that he knows the traffic rules, is licensed to drive, knows enough to stop for gas when it's needed, and will normally avoid accidents. The actor, it is likewise assumed, knows how to rehearse, how to do his makeup, how to learn his lines, how to behave, and how to reach his destination: a good performance. The actor is expected to know *how* to do his work. All the director will do is tell him where he's headed and attempt to assist him when he makes wrong turns along the way. If the cab driver can't drive, he's out of a job. The same thing is true for the actor who can't act. This proves a confusion for many young, university-trained actors who are accustomed to their directors being their nurturing teachers. In most school situations, the director tries to teach at the same time she directs, and the student-actor unhappily grows accustomed to the idea that the director will help him learn to act while helping him to meet the challenges of a particular role. This work habit is a tough one for many young actors to break. They come into a commercial situation and are puzzled when the director does not take time to help them—to teach them their craft.

Just as an actor might be replaced if he cannot arrive at a good performance, he might be dismissed if he does not know how to behave. Let's assume an actor is always late, or talks during rehearsals, or interrupts when the director is talking, or disappears on coffee breaks at inopportune moments, or backbites about everyone's performance, or in other ways displays bad professional behavior. Such an actor might well be let go, as the opening dialogue of this book reveals.

He might just as easily be let go because he doesn't know how to rehearse. He doesn't learn his lines, say. Or he can't do improvisations. Or he can't adjust to changes in blocking. Or he's so clumsy that he stumbles over furniture or lets his horse get away from him and run amuck through the camera equipment.

If you cannot do the job, you'd be wise to turn it down. If the role calls for a swordsman who can speak several passages in credible French and you're only at home with Turkish and a switchblade, discuss that with the director before you accept the job. He'll respect you for speaking the truth, and if he hires you he'll never blame you for what you can't do. He knows the responsibility is his. If he doesn't hire you, you can be happy in the awareness that you've earned his respect and that he'll probably hire you the next time he seeks someone of your age and appearance. And you've saved yourself the embarrassment of being fired—as you surely would have been whenever the first fight rehearsal was ended.

Not many actors are fired, and perhaps I'm guilty of scare tactics here. But my aim in this handbook is to provide guidelines that will help actors to work. I've only had to release three professional and two student actors in the more than 100 plays I've directed, and one of the students was a sixteen-year-old who always missed his entrances because he was off necking in the bushes behind the outdoor summer theatre. When I met him again, twenty-five years later, he was the head of a prominent PBS TV station and I'd entirely forgotten the incident. With great good humor, he reminded me. And then he thanked me profusely for teaching him to respect his work. Some stories end happily.

As an actor, you must understand that the moment you sign a contract you are subject to the legal cancellation of that contract.

The director's relationship to you should always be seen in this light. In the school circumstance, the director-teacher has a responsibility to help you improve during the rehearsal period. In a professional circumstance, the director has a responsibility to get a good performance from you. He will try every device his skill and time permit him to try. He won't give up on you hastily, if only because it will cost the management a lot of money to replace you. But he'll drop you the moment he's convinced that you can't make it.

* * * * *

The actor proposes, the director disposes. From your study of the script and your other homework, and your discoveries during rehearsals, you develop your performance. The director tells you when you're doing well and/or poorly—when you're on the road toward a good performance, and when you've strayed onto the backroads that lead nowhere. If he says nothing, you may assume he is delighted with your progress, or else he's willing to accept it because he doesn't know how to help you to make it any better.

Of course, the truth is that the process isn't so cut and dried, nor so one-directional from you to him. The director will regularly "direct" you what to do, where to go, and may even give you line readings from time to time. When you get specific directions, your task is to do them and to make whatever justifications you require in your internal development of the character's actions that make those movements and those line readings "correct." Sometimes the director needs you to move to a particular place for entirely pictorial reasons—your body is a part of a visual composition that communicates to the audience the essential meaning of the scene. You must find a reason for your character to move to the assigned place if the director doesn't provide one. Sometimes he needs you to speak a line slowly, so as to help build the audience's suspense; the justification for that action is yours to find. The director tells you what to do, and you need to find out how and why. If you're having a hard time, the director will try to help you. There is, of course, the old tale about the Broadway director of musicals and farces who was directing an Actors Studio-trained juvenile. The actor was told to cross to the window and look out on a particular line. For days the actor did as told, but felt no justification. Finally he approached the director. "Sir, I've been doing the cross just as you told me, but I don't understand it, and frankly I don't think it's a motivated cross, and could you please tell me my motivation?" "How about your salary?" retorted the director.

One way to get along with your director is to be prepared for the day's work. Know what is to be rehearsed. Work on that particular segment of the play as the focus of your homework. Come to the rehearsal with your lines, business, actions, images, and recalls all in order. The actor who wanders into rehearsal and asks, "What scenes are we doing today?" is ill prepared.

Each director will hold his own kinds of rehearsals and will try to get from you the individual and group performance he desires through a variety of methods. The most common kinds of rehearsal are show-and-tell, discussion, improvisation, games, speed rehearsals, reading, and psychophysical exercises. The extent to which a director will employ any of these will depend on the script being rehearsed, the time available for rehearsal, the groups he's working with, and his own strengths. Jonathan Miller, the prominent English director, confesses in his perceptive book *Subsequent Performances* (New York: Viking Penguin, 1986) that he spends a great percentage of his rehearsal time in discussion. Elia Kazan, the great American director of such plays as *Streetcar Named Desire* and *Cat on a Hot Tin Roof*, hardly ever discussed things with his actors—he held that *doing* is the way to discovery. "Don't talk about it, *do* it," might well have been his creed. Directing *The Member of the Wedding* with a cast I'd never met before, and with only two and a half weeks to rehearse that long and emotionally difficult play, I indulged in two improvisations and spent about fifteen minutes in something that might be called a game. Directing a student cast that I knew well in Strindberg's *The Father*, when I had a five-week rehearsal period, we did improvisations almost daily, played games frequently, and explored many rehearsals using recorded sound effects to help establish the desired moods. Different situations dictate different practices. The director will try to be sensitive to the company's needs and abilities, but he will finally use the techniques he judges wisest. Your task is to work within the framework he establishes. If you have gone through formal actor training, you will be experienced with many forms of rehearsal. The more directors you work with, the wider will be your experience of rehearsal procedures. What you owe your director is a willingness to try whatever he chooses—an openness to new techniques that may help you both achieve your ends. If you resist and fall back on your own devices, you will impede the production's organic development. Correct professional behavior dictates that you explore all approaches to your work and that you do so enthusiastically.

Most directors give notes. Some write them down and distribute them; others say them to the assembled cast since most notes affect the work of more than one performer. Write down all the notes that affect you, even if they have not been directed to you specifically. You should infer from this guideline that you ought to have pencil and paper at all rehearsals. One sure difference between the professional and the amateur is the seriousness with which directions are heeded—and notes are the most concrete form of direction. The actor with sound working habits writes down all the notes she gets, works on each prior to the next rehearsal, and improves with each day's work. The actor with poor habits listens inattentively, remembers what she can, and makes many of the same mistakes rehearsal after rehearsal. Nagle Jackson, then artistic director for the Milwaukee Repertory Theatre, was directing a group of students. I asked him what some of their deficiencies were. "Well," he smiled gently, "I'd forgotten that you have to give student actors the same note twice."

* * * * *

One breach of good behavior common to young actors of all ages is to start directing. This is sure to offend the director, the stage manager, and the other actors. Yet, many do it all the time—until someone puts the offender in his place. Somehow actors get the mistaken idea that theatre is a democratic art.

Perhaps this results from the actor's egotistical need to seem an authority on all subjects. Whatever its source, it is offensive behavior. Theatre is a benevolent dictatorship, not an egalitarian commune. The director does not want your suggestions about interpretation, staging, timing, or execution. Either the director knows her business and you're a nuisance, or else she doesn't know her business and you're a threat. In either case, your unsolicited advice is disruptive to the director, troublesome to the stage manager, and insulting to your fellow actor. When that innocent urge wells up in you to say, "Hey, do it this way," keep your mouth shut!

Similarly, don't direct yourself. Don't stop in the middle of a run-through to discuss the appropriateness of your interpretation or your physical business. Don't anticipate the director and stop a scene to look out front, waiting for her reaction. Act! If she wants you to stop, she'll say so. You are not the only person in a scene, and it may be that the others require continuity more than you need discussion. Regardless, the choice lies with the director, not with you.

Don't start directing others' scenes in the lobby. Restrain your enthusiasm and let the actors do their acting and the director do her directing. And you mind your own business. In all likelihood, you have more than enough work to do on your own role.

Some directors are bad directors. You will meet them, and it won't take you long to realize that they are bad directors. I have worked for three different directors with prominent Broadway credits who have fallen asleep during rehearsals. I have worked for a director in a resident theatre who, during three weeks of rehearsal for *Escurial* (de Ghelderode's extremely complex two-person play), stopped petting his dog long enough to say only four things to me, one of which was, "Could you do the final part faster?" Oy! I have worked for directors who have given me incorrect definitions of words that appeared in my speeches. Sad but true, many directors are bad directors. And you need to know how to protect yourself and how to behave toward them.

Begin by knowing when to say "No." However politely, however firmly, you must at some point say "No." There are times when you must refuse to do what a director instructs you to do.

You must never do this for reasons of ego, but only for reasons of intelligence, taste, and craft. You must never refuse to execute a move or line-reading because you "feel" it is inappropriate. You must be able to state firmly and clearly the reasons the direction is inappropriate, and you must be prepared to counter with a sensible and defensible alternative. When you are prepared, you may engage in justified debate and strive to win your point. Don't waste valuable time in endless debate, and don't be a continual talker, but do protect yourself. A couple of examples may clarify this notion.

I was playing Albany in *King Lear.* I was suspicious of the director because I felt she had miscast me badly and that I should have been playing Cornwall. After all, I'm a tall man with a dark complexion, a dark baritone voice, and (as a friend said) I look like I put out people's eyes. But I tried to put that behind me as we went into rehearsals, and I determined to play Albany as well as I could. In the early rehearsals, the director was staging the show. Late in the action, Albany confronts Gloucester's bastard son Edmund, who has presumed to set himself up as commander of the armies that Albany properly commands, since he's a Duke and Edmund is an untitled upstart. In the midst of the battlefield, Albany says, "Let's, then, determine with the ancient of war on our proceedings." Translation: let's get together with our wisest and most experienced military advisors and determine how to conduct our battle. Edmund replies, "I shall attend you presently at your tent." Four brief lines later, they all exit. The director told me to go out up right and Edmund to exit left. "Excuse me"—I'd like to think I said this politely—"but we've got to exit together. And since we're headed for my tent, shouldn't we go out the same direction I entered from?" A brief exchange, and I realized the director wasn't clear what the lines meant. I shut up. But I went home and did some work. First, I photocopied the appropriate passage from the *Oxford English Dictionary* that states what the word "presently" meant at the time Shakespeare wrote the play. As I had been taught, and as the *OED* confirmed, the word meant "immediately." The inference was that Edmund (sincerely or hypocritically) says, "I'll meet with you without delay." For him to exit in a different direction didn't make sense, and I wrote out my understanding of the lines and the scene to give to the director in an attempt to persuade her to stage the scene properly. I wrote out my arguments, so I wouldn't waste rehearsal time. As a safeguard, in case she didn't accept my argument, I offered her three ways I could play the scene if Edmund went off a different direction from me. Well, I probably shouldn't have done all of that. I suspect I threatened her unduly. Basically, she said she didn't want to discuss it and that she wanted to stage it as she wanted to stage it. It wasn't the best way for her to regain an actor's confidence, but there we were. The problem became mine again. How to cover for some bad direction? I resolved finally to look away as Edmund exited, so that I wouldn't see him go, and then turn to discover he was *not* going to do what he had just told me he would do, and then I exited in a spirited rage. I always feared an educated audience would find this funny, but it was the best solution I could come up with. Sometimes you win, and sometimes you lose.

Another example. I was playing Macduff. We were rehearsing the final scene in which Macduff confronts Macbeth. "Turn, hell-hound, turn." Macbeth got to the line "Before my body I throw my warlike shield . . ." and tossed his shield down on the ground. "Ah ha," I thought, "I'll cleave him from his nave to his chops." But the director told me to throw down my shield as well. "Hang on a second," I said. "I've come here to kill that swine, and now I've got a perfect opportunity." The actor playing Macbeth said he had thrown down his shield because the script had indicated: "Before my body I throw my warlike shield." I knew that the line meant "I put my warlike shield up in front of me for protection," but I knew better than to tell the actor playing the title role what his lines meant. So I just held the ground of my argument. "If he throws down his shield I will simply chop him into messes. Unless he runs away, which seems hardly in keeping with his warrior-like speech that follows." The director argued that the gentlemanly code of chivalry would require me to throw down my shield if he had thrown down his. Not only was that historically inaccurate, I replied, but "my action couldn't be clearer: to kill Macbeth." We debated this for several minutes (the debate was more interesting than the battle we finally staged, I assure you). I was trying to protect myself from what I knew was a directorial blunder. My argument had a lot to do with my craft and very little to do with my ego (although I did not relish being laughed at, as I suspected would be the case if we staged the scenes as the director was requesting). Ultimately, the director said the magic words, "Never mind about all that: I'm the director and do it like I said." I complied, as I was contracted to do. The director is boss, and you must comply with his directions. But you must first do your damnedest to protect yourself from his stupidities. And if your "No" is backed up with good reasoning, you'll usually win your point. In the case of that scene in *Macbeth*? Well, sometimes you win, and sometimes you lose big.

Bad directors seldom lead you to confrontation and the examples I've just used are rare. More commonly, as with the director of *Escurial*, they don't do anything, or else, like the director of *King Lear*, they don't appear to recognize that you're doing your best to protect yourself. If that's the case, don't seek confrontation. Just try to think through your role, beat by beat, and create the best performance you can. When in doubt about a choice, make the least conspicuous one. Without a good director out front disposing of what you propose, selecting from among the actions you're exploring, it is easy for you to make a choice that will stick out like the production's proverbial sore thumb and make you noticeable to the critics who will hang you by it. Anonymity is the better part of valor.

* * * * *

One last thought about your working relationship with your director. What happens when the director is your friend? That happens often. In the hours you will rehearse together, across the shows you may do together, you will come to know her very, very well. I count among my warmest friends some of the actors I have directed and some of the directors I have acted for. But those friendships should not intrude into the rehearsal. I don't suggest that you both suddenly put on somber masks and work with austere aloofness. I mean that the friendship must not influence professional judgment. Don't ask to play a role you know you're wrong for. That will only strain your friendship. Don't bring your personal squabbles into the rehearsal hall. That will only mar your work. Separate your friendly director from your friend the director. Respect both.

THE DIRECTOR'S ASSISTANTS There are specialists who direct portions of a production. Though they frequently have titles that describe their functions, and though their names may appear on the title page of the printed program, they are essentially assistants to the primary director. You must relate to them exactly as you do to the main director. Five common types of assistants are the musical director, the choreographer, the vocal coach, the fight choreographer, and the generic assistant director (someone with no speciality but who has been engaged to work with you while the director works with others). It is common for an assistant director to work with the members of a crowd, for example, or with the chorus in a Greek tragedy. On *Romeo and Juliet* I was fortunate to have a choreographer for the dances, a fight choreographer for the combat sequences, and an assistant director to whom I gave the primary task of coaching the title characters, particularly in the textual density of their two love scenes. Fred Adams of the Utah Shakespearean Festival once directed *A Midsummer Night's Dream* with one assistant directing the fairy sequences and another directing the mechanicals while he directed the young lovers and the court scenes and supervised his assistants. (This is a particularly fine way for young directors to get their apprenticeship.) In films, the first and second assistants have particular and clearly defined jobs that have very little to do with you as an actor. You are more likely to get coaching from a dialogue director, particularly if you are an inexperienced beginner, so that the director can be assured that you know your role before you step in front of the camera.

The director's assistants have specific jobs and the responsibility to help you learn a particular portion of your role. They may teach you dance steps, parries with the broadsword, the dynamics of singing your songs, or a South African accent. Whatever their task, they will treat you as though they were the director, and you must strive to cooperate with them fully.

Assistants are commonly engaged because the primary director does not have time or particular skills. One director won't be able to choreograph a dance and the next won't know her épée from her epaulet. But she will know someone who does, and that knowledge helps to make her a good director. You can learn much from the assistants, and you will develop a full performance if you apply yourself as rigorously to their rehearsals as you do to the director's. Some additional thoughts: assistants frequently grow up to be directors, and you may further your career by impressing the assistant. Most directors of musicals began as choreographers, as Tommy Tune did. Some fight choreographers, like B. H. Barry, are beginning to direct. When they reach that higher step on the theatrical ladder, they have the authority to say the magic words, "Do you want a job?" So respect them accordingly.

Assistants necessarily have different personalities and work habits from the director, and you must be flexible enough to work for both without revealing your preferences. How do you behave if you receive contradictory directions? If the musical director, for example, guides you to a harsh and angry singing of a song and the director (while staging the book scenes) keeps alluding to the gentle mood that will follow your song, then you're in trouble. You can make things worse if you engage in a squabble. You can make things better if you bring the contradiction to the stage manager's attention and let her bring the two directors together to resolve how the song should be done. When caught in the middle, pass the buck!

You'll rarely be in the middle, happily. Typically, the director will lay out his intentions to his assistants quite early. Additionally, he will check in on all the sub-rehearsals periodically and will catch any deviations early. But once in a long time you may find yourself the pawn in a power struggle between the director and an assistant who is ambitious to become the director. When that happens, duck! And never take sides. You don't know who's going to win, and you want to keep your job no matter what happens. If the director and choreographer are screaming at one another (for the producer's benefit, no doubt), just turn to the stage manager and ask, "How do you want me to do it?" She'll get you out of your pickle, and, because she's not an artistic decision-maker, there's little likelihood she'll fall in any purge that may hit your troubled show. But I'm describing a rare event. You're likely to complete a long and rewarding career without ever suffering through such a scene.

PLAYWRIGHTS Exciting rehearsals happen when the playwright is at your side. All rehearsals have an invigorating fusion of creative energies. When the playwright is among you, reshaping the script to exploit your particular gifts, the experience is wonderfully dizzying. Your sense of danger is deliciously heightened because you know that nobody has played your role before. There are no paths to follow, only trails to blaze. Your sense of responsibility is great because you know your creation of the role will influence every actor who plays it in productions yet to come. We remember Richard Burbage because he created Hamlet and Helene Weigel because she created Mother Courage and Sidney Poitier because he created Walter Lee Younger. In the most ephemeral of arts, originating a great role is your fleeting chance for immortality.

The *genus playwrightus* is an enigmatic being. In the 1960s— the heyday of group creativity and of The Living Theatre, The Open Theatre, and The Performance Group—some thought the playwright was an endangered species, the victim of an ecological shift. Throughout theatrical history, he has been the spokesman of the devil and the darling of the gods. As society changed, so did its attitudes towards its playwrights. For actors as well, the playwright has an ambivalent status. He's that nitpicking wordmaker who fusses over details. And he's that dark visionary who gives us our feelings. In the Italian comedy of the Renaissance, the *commedia dell 'arte*, he fused with the actors completely. In the literary salons of the Roman Empire, he banished the actors and read the scripts himself, proclaiming the ascendancy of closet drama. In our own time, and for a long time to come, he is our most exciting co-worker, for he brings us the stories, characters, and actions we play. He merits our respect, love, and tender care.

The practices governing your working relationship with the playwright during rehearsals will be dictated by the director and must be observed by you. Typically, the director will forbid the playwright and actor to talk to one another. You may find this strange, since you have much need of the playwright, but it is a practice which has developed out of much experience and it makes good sense. You cannot be directed by two people at once, and you'll become either schizophrenic or traumatized if you are not protected. The director know this, and hence sets up a communications link with himself at its center. He understands that you are focused upon process, while the playwright is focused on product. And the director has to be the one who ensures that your process results in the playwright's production.

Anything the writer needs to tell you must go through the director, so he can head off any notes that conflict with what he's telling you and so he can translate into "actorese" any notes that might confuse you. Any questions you have for the playwright must go through the director so he can screen out questions that he can better answer himself, and so that he can translate into "writerese" any of your requests that might confuse the playwright. If the director knows and trusts the playwright, he might relax this rule, but even so you are well-advised to tread cautiously. Don't get caught between conflicting guides.

The playwright is rarely a good director. Indeed, his creative process is quite different from yours, and if you understand this, you will see why problems arise. In psychological terms, as Philip Weisman discusses in *Creativity in the Theatre* (New York: Basic Books, 1965), ". . . actors often suffer from an undeveloped self-image and intensified conflicts around exhibitionism, whereas the dramatist has the tendency towards enactment (inclusive of acting out), from which he dissociates himself in his capacity as an artist and utilizes its contents for his dramas." Simply, the urge to express himself leads the actor to public display, but the writer sublimates it into the private act of writing. Think of your preparations for your work. You exercise your body to warm up, jumping about the room, chanting, gibbering, and generally making a spectacle of yourself. Think of the writer's. He withdraws from every external stimulation, finds a quiet space, and directs all his energy toward thinking. The impulse to enactment is translated into the impulse to think—to write down the thoughts. If he is well disciplined, he may have lost his urge to act things out, and he may be a poor judge of how you go about your work. The director knows this, understands the ways that both of you think and work, and is the necessary link between you. That's why he separates you, and you must observe his rule.

When the director permits you to speak with the playwright, ask for *information* about the character, the given circumstances, and your relationships to other characters. Where was you character before this entrance? Why did you pick up the apple, as the script dictates? How many hours have passed since your previous scene? What's the temperature in the room? Who is your closer friend between your brothers? Playwrights have what they call a "backplay," a huge amount of information about the characters, situations, and locations in their plays—information that never appears in the play, but which they have had to think about in the process of writing the script. Get that information and you will have a more solid sense of what you are doing than if you invent things about your character. Your subtext, your grasp of the given circumstances, and most importantly your motivations, need not be in doubt. The writer may not have thought out all the details that you will ask about, and some of your questions may cause him to lift his eyebrows reflectively and confess, "I've never even thought about that." But the answer ultimately provided is an absolute one, for only the playwright has the full experience of the play. After all, it came out of him.

Make suggestions about your role and dialogue. These must never be made thoughtlessly, nor in an attempt to build up the size of your role. Restrain your ego and apply your craft. Your request should never begin with "I want." Instead, say "If there were a different speech here, I could do what I have to do in the next scene with greater conviction." You may discover that the writer has left out a necessary step in your character's emotional development, and if you draw this to his attention, you may receive changes that will help you to do your job and, coincidentally, will help the audience enjoy the play. Equally, you may discover that you're doing things and saying things you don't need to say or do. Perhaps your subtextual development is hindered by a speech. Discuss this with the writer. He may have a textural reason he needs you to do what he's written, but more than likely he will be delighted to learn that some cuts can be made—that you can enact what he has only described.

If you're having real trouble with a particular line or phrase, you might ask the playwright to re-phrase it or to re-cast his ideas. Be careful here that you don't mistake your laziness for a real problem. Your reason for a desired change should never be "I can say it easier this way." Actors frequently confuse their characters with themselves and want all dialogue to sound as *they* would say it. But the writer has not written you. It is your job to act the character he has written—a character who speaks as the written lines suggest, no matter how unlike you they sound. In the press of rehearsals, actors commonly look for shortcuts, and changing dialogue to make it sound "natural" is a common and destructive shortcut. The writer's work must be respected. You're not the writer. The greatest offenders here are film and TV actors. In those media, the human emotion seen in extreme close-up is the primary means of communication, and as a result the actor must appear comfortable. Commonly actors are permitted (even encouraged) to paraphrase. (Writers have usually made some painful accommodation to this practice and are wounded but accepting. They rationalize that the huge fees they receive for writing movies and TV compensate for their loss of artistic integrity.) But in stage work, either say the line as it's written or offer the playwright a sound reason for a change. As a rule, don't offer an alternative. Don't try to do his job. Just ask for his help. Don't discuss actor-problems with the writer. Don't describe to him the imagistic pattern you're using in a scene and don't tell him the emotional recall you're using at your big moment. And never talk with him about your invented subtext. These are all tools of your craft—as balance, internal rhyme, counterpoint, and imagistic juxtaposition are tools of his. To act the role, you don't need to know that the apple you bite is a verbal metaphor for New York, and he doesn't need to know that the recollection of sour milk is what brings that exquisite expression of agony to your face. You see, the director does have to serve as a translator.

Throughout the rehearsal period, the playwright will fiddle with the script. This will always be done in consultation with the director, and you will be expected to accommodate these changes quickly. It's a part of your job. Many of the changes will be tiny—subtle adjustments of syntax or additions or deletions of phrases that give the script its desired texture. These will not alter your actions, subtext, imagistic pattern, or stage business. Take the changes, learn them, do them. Other changes will be major. In a new play headed for Broadway, you may well be required to play a scene each evening in script "A" while each afternoon you rehearse script "B." When "B" is ready, it is then inserted into the next evening's performance. On rare occasions, there may be four or five variants on a sequence and you'll suddenly find you're re-rehearsing script "A"—the one you thought had been abandoned a week earlier. When that happens, you are in a wild and desperate situation. Study hard, concentrate clearly, and do your best. Your best behavior must be displayed in such trying circumstances. Remember, nobody is trying to please you. Nobody cares which way you like to play the scene. The director, playwright, producer, composer, lyricist, and playdoctor are all trying to learn which way the *audience* likes the scene. That's the only measure of appropriateness. Your task is to remain cheerful, cooperative, and hard working.

This kind of harried experience came to some of the actors in a recent Broadway revival of *Macbeth*. It starred Christopher Plummer and Glenda Jackson. Shakespeare was long dead, so the responsibility for the text—the playwright's authority—devolved to the director. But the production went through four directors before it opened, and each had a different notion about the lines each of the three witches should speak. At night they'd have one set of lines to perform, and during the day they would rehearse a different set. They all ended knowing all the witches' lines, but sometimes in performance they got confused, and long silences accompanied their furtive glances to one another as they tried to figure out who said the next part of an incantation. May the ghost of Thespis protect us all from such nightmares.

Rehearsals for a new play breed love and great affection. And yet, the playwright is not your friend. Playwrights tend to be very much like people. There are shy ones and brash ones, pompous ones and frightened ones, battle-weary veterans and bright-eyed newcomers. Their professional admiration for your professional accomplishments will be sincere, and their feigned enthusiasm for your inept performance will be phony—and you won't always be able to tell one from the other. Both of you know that the good morale of the company is an essential part of any show's success, so you'll hug each other, compliment each other, buy each other beers, and all this seemingly personal behavior is merely professional manners gone berserk. In fact, you don't know each other and are not friends. You will be drawn to his charisma as the creative center of the project, and you are likely to mistake his public graciousness for private friendship. But opening night will reveal the truth of the situation.

If the show is a flop—he never knew you. If the show is a hit—he returns to his friends, his activities, his private life, and he may never see you again. His work on the show is completed and yours goes on. He may pass you on 45th Street and not recognize you. Don't be offended. You have been an important and wonderful part of his life, and he of yours, but a life in the theatre is made up of time capsules—one for each show you do. A few of your co-workers may become your friends, and all will become your professional acquaintances, but don't be hurt when one doesn't invite you home for dinner. The playwright is probably the first who will remove himself from your daily world. Respect his removal.

SCENE DESIGNER   You may never meet the scene designer. Her work is normally completed before you are hired and done in studios and shops far from where you rehearse. If you do meet when she drops by rehearsals to watch a run-through and to learn if there are any problems developing (the director has you climbing a trellis that is only decorative and won't support your weight), be enthusiastic about the design. If you meet during tech or dress rehearsals when she's putting finishing touches on the set, be appreciative of her contribution to the production. Designers usually like actors. They have little commerce with them and are consequently fascinated by them. You, in turn, can widen your horizons and your contacts by chatting with the scene designer. (Like the PSM, the scene designer is hired onto a production in its earliest stages and her opinion is a valued one. I have hired actors on the recommendation of a designer. For every one I've hired that way, there must be many others.)

You can help the designer by describing the way a setting or prop is used in performance to her—if she asks you. Don't run up panting to tell her what she already knows. Discretion must be employed. Let her introduce the subject. Or if you're worried about how to use a part of the set or a prop, ask the designer a question. "What are the spreads on Stanley and Eugene's beds going to be like?" can alert the designer to the real problem you are thinking about: can you get into the bed for the scene in which you're supposed to have a fever?

Don't offer your opinion about her work. I had an embarrassing car ride some years back. I had engaged the director Davey Marlin-Jones, and he was staying at my home until he found satisfactory accommodations. He rode with me to the airport as I picked up an actor just arriving to the city, and we drove to the theatre together. "Who is designing the set?" she inquired. I told her. "Oh God," she whined, "his work is so tacky." Davey's eyes turned slowly to me. He had just met the designer and didn't yet know that the man was brilliant, swift, and cooperative—didn't yet know he would be delighted with the set. The actor's naive and thoughtless remark gave him an unwarranted scare and, worse, it made him wonder what kind of an actor this might be whose behavior was so awful. He later discovered she was a talented actor, but a young and bad-mannered one. She should have kept her opinions to herself. She knew nothing about scene design. Most actors know nothing about scene design.

Don't presume to give the designer instructions. If you have a particular problem with the set, if you have to come down a stairway that has no handrail and you're afraid of heights, tell the stage manager your problem. Stage managers solve problems.

LIGHTING DESIGNER Lighting designers receive very little praise for their work, though their impact on a production can be significant. Most reviewers, if they mention the lighting at all, give it a short phrase toward the end of the review. Something like, ". . . and the graceful lighting by John Doe." Worse, lighting designers are sometimes the butt of audience abuse, since they are physically present in the auditorium during dress rehearsals and previews. When Mitch Dana was lighting Caryl Churchill's taboo-busting comedy *Cloud 9* for me, some patron who had sat through the (free) invited-audience dress was offended by the play and, at the end, looked about for someone to complain to. I was backstage giving notes to the actors. But Mitch was at the tech table, re-writing cues. The irate patron accosted him and told him what he thought of the play, using the same abusive vocabulary he had found offensive in the play. Mitch smiled up at him and replied, "I don't have to like 'em to light 'em."

Lighting designers live a rather lonely life—they travel from theatre to theatre and are with a production for a few days only, at a time when you actors are most self-absorbed with getting your performances ready for opening night. So the two of you rarely get to know each other; you may never even meet the lighting designer. If you do, it is unlikely his work will be altered because of anything you do. You do not interact with him in the way you interact with the costume designer or with your fellow actors. You job is to accommodate what the lighting designer has done. His job is to achieve what the director requests. The director worries about how the lighting affects you. That's the circular structure of the working relationship.

You may meet the lighting designer at a run-through in the rehearsal hall or just prior to one of the final or technical run-throughs. If you arrive early and are checking over the set or some of your onstage business, you may find the lighting designer at work. Introduce yourself. He'll probably already know who you are, as he'll have watched some rehearsals. Chat with him. You may make a friend, and you can certainly help your performance by learning from him.

Ask him some professional questions. Find out what colors he's gelled the lamps with—this can affect your makeup. Ask him where certain lighting areas drop off—this might guide you to tiny adjustments in your blocking that will keep you well-lit. Ask him if there's anything you can do in your performance to help him achieve the effects he's striving for. Let's say you're Banquo's ghost, and you pop up from a trap door. Let's say you've been told that there'll be a large green light directly over your head, though you've not yet seen it. Let's say that the lighting designer teaches you that by leaning back slightly as you pop up, you'll look appropriately ghostly, his lighting will look terrific, and the audience will get a thrill. By behaving professionally, by asking the right questions of the right person, you will learn how to improve your performance and the total impact of the production.

Don't offer your opinion. If you think the lighting is lousy, keep it to yourself. If you're acting, you're inside the show and can't possibly see what it looks like, so don't offer an unqualified opinion. Even if you're right, why create ill will, make enemies, spread uncertainty through the company, and undermine your collective efforts? The lighting designer is not qualified to judge your acting and you're not qualified to judge his lighting. If both of you are good, fine. You'll both contribute to the show's success. By remembering how an actor behaves, you can advance your career.

COSTUME DESIGNER You will definitely meet the costume designer, and you will meet her assistants: the cutters, tailors, and wardrobe crew who create and maintain the costumes you will wear. These people are of immediate and continued importance to your work, and you must behave in a manner that will make you friends. Remember, "Apparel oft proclaims the man." Your visual impression on the stage is mightily significant. Cyrano's nose and Claire Zachanasian's wooden leg are only extreme examples of a continuing theatrical reality—you must appear appropriate if the audience is to believe in you. Sensibly, you must cooperate with those who have a great impact on the way you appear.

The costume designer will probably have completed her designs long before you are hired and her rendering may not look like you, though once in a long while a designer's rendering will anticipate the actor's appearance uncannily. That usually means that the director was influenced by the rendering at the time he was casting the role. When you first see the renderings, try to grasp the "feel" of the whole production. Let's say you're doing Marianne in a production of *The Miser*, and you're shown wearing a blond wig though you're naturally a brunette. Look at the other renderings to learn how your blond wig helps to tell the story. You'll probably find that Cleante's wearing a blond wig as well. If the rendering shows a silhouette very different from yours, if your body varies greatly from the director's and costume designer's preconceptions, you can be confident that adjustments will be made (or an entirely new costume designed) to ensure that you look good. The costume designer wants you to look "right" for the production. You will normally meet the costume designer at an early fitting. During this and subsequent fittings, you can do much to help her—and she to help you. Give her any information about your body and coloring that might be helpful. If you have one leg that's shorter than another, or if you're a redhead and know that certain colors of red look terrible on you, share that information. But be careful not to tell the designer what you do and don't wear. Rather, phrase it indirectly. If you're broad in the beam, say, "I've been told I look better in pleated skirts than straight ones." Work *with* the designer, not against her.

If you are developing a particular interpretation for your character, make certain the designer understands what you're doing. Once, I was rehearsing Parolles in Shakespeare's *All's Well That Ends Well*. The costume designer had presented his designs at the first rehearsal, and they were glorious. I was to wear a white "ice cream" suit with colored handkerchiefs coming out of all my pockets. I wore a sports jacket to rehearsals and hung handkerchiefs from all my pockets. After a couple of days of rehearsal, I was confused. All the characters in the play kept calling me "Captain," and they were all wearing military uniforms. Why wasn't I? I asked the director. He was a good director and I liked working for him. A lightbulb went off over his head. He realized he had missed this obvious point, that Parolles is in the army! A quick huddle or two and the costume designer designed an entirely new costume for me. This is a rare instance, and you should not seek to have the costume re-designed to suit your whimsy. But it suggests the positive results that can be achieved when a good director and an inquiring actor work cooperatively with a talented and flexible costume designer.

As you rehearse, you will have a sequence of fittings. Even if you have given notes to the stage manager, which you have good cause to believe have been communicated to the costume designer, these fittings are an excellent time for you to repeat them. Are you introducing a particular physical carriage? A limp or a stooped walk? Has the director given you explicit business that the designer might not know about? Do you carry a weapon or climb a rope? Do you carry a torch and are you concerned to know that your costume will be flame-proofed? Is there a hat in the production that was not seen in the rendering? Has the fight choreographer given you moves that require the costume to move freely? Do you have any particularly fast costume changes? These are all things you should raise with the costume designer. She will know most of them, but if even one is news to her, then you will be helping her to help you. In short, share with the designer anything that has developed since the designs were approved by the director.

She can help you by explaining how certain garments ought properly to be worn (most applicable in period plays), what stances or actions will show you off to advantage, how the colors and textures of your costume relate you to other characters in the play and help to tell the story, and how you can manage such difficult actions as a deep curtsy or a wrestling match in the garments you'll be wearing. If she doesn't volunteer such advice, ask questions. Costume designers typically have a huge body of research that you are welcome to look through—art books, manuals of deportment, and historical documents that you will find extremely valuable. A designer will be happy to find an actor who's eager to learn what she has to share. You'll be making a friend of a very important colleague. Then, parade about in your costume to get the feel of it. Try out some of the things you'll have to do in it so that you won't be surprised later. I made the mistake, during a fitting for a production of *Henry V* that I was acting in, of not exploring the way my armor would fit. When I had to wear it in the complicated fights that had been choreographed, I found that it rose up over my nose whenever my arms went over my head. It had to be changed and that caused a lot of extra labor for the designer at a time when she was very, very busy. If I had followed the guidance I'm offering here, I would have helped the designer as well as myself.

The costume designer is one of the few people working on the show that you are expected to question directly, without the stage manager as an intermediary. Perhaps this practice results from her particular expertise or perhaps from the fact that your initial encounters with her occur outside rehearsals, in the wardrobe shop or in some rental company's dressing room. No one else is about, so it makes sense for you to discuss your common problems. This will hold true throughout the rehearsal period. Even in final dress rehearsals, when you may be receiving your costume notes through the director, it is correct behavior for you to ask specific questions of the costume designer or her assistants.

The cutters, tailors, and milliners are those craftspersons who actually build the costumes or rebuild old costumes to suit the present needs. These are among the unsung heroes of most productions and merit your politest behavior. For inexplicable reasons, most costume departments are placed in rooms without natural light or sufficient ventilation. Usually they are deep underground. Also, all costume departments are under-equipped, under-staffed, and given too small of a working space. Result? Bleary-eyed moles with bleeding fingers who are justified in feeling martyred, neglected, and generally malcontented. You are their pipeline to the outside, just as they are your lifeline to a good costume. You can help each other.

Visit the costume shop, even when you are not called. (This pertains only if the costume shop is a part of your company. If costumes are rented, or if the shop is far from the rehearsal hall, forget this.) Your goal is to keep them abreast of the show's development, to help build their morale. Consider this as a social call that will have pleasant repercussions—special care will be taken with your costume, or yours will be available for use earlier than others'. In these visits, always be supportive and constructive. Compliment the craftspeople on their skills. Bring them goodies: a cardinal rule in the costume shop is *chocolate's always welcome*! Despite temptation, don't engage in divisive gossip. Because they are isolated from rehearsals, costume shops frequently become Gossip Central in a theatre. As the staff grows increasingly tired, the gossip grows proportionately vicious. Don't contribute. Bring only good reports of the show's development.

Your major contact with the costume staff will come at fittings. Here, as earlier with the designer, ask questions and relay information. Since your last fitting, has the director introduced the idea of blood bags for your death scene? Has the stage manager gotten this information to the costume department? Have you introduced a handkerchief into a scene and do you need a pocket for the dressing robe you wear in Act Three?

Additionally, you should observe some common courtesies in all fittings. *Be prompt!* Actors are notoriously naughty about being on time for fittings. Since the costume department is even more pressured than you are, you must respect their problems and get to your call promptly. *Don't rush the fitters!* Never mind that you want to leave shortly. Their work takes time, is exacting, and serves you. Plan to spend relaxed time at your fittings. *Be clean!* When you come to a fitting, the staff has to work with and around your body. Make it presentable. Wash. Make certain your breath is inoffensive. Be certain to have on clean clothes, particularly clean underclothes: socks, bras, etc. Make certain you bring with you any support garments that might be necessary to the proper fitting of your costume. Women, bring your long-line bra so that your gown can be properly fitted, and if you have long hair, bring a ribbon or barrette to tie it up out of the workers' way. Men, bring your dance belt if you'll be wearing tights. *Respect your costumes!* It is essential that you handle your costumes carefully. Hang things up after you've tried them on. Keep all your costumes and accessories tidily together so that no time is lost in looking for stray belts and shawls. Finally, *thank the people* who've helped you. When you leave, they're going to work on your costume; a courteous "thank you" is never amiss. If they like you, they will go the extra mile to insure your costume serves you. If they dislike you, watch out for the pins left "accidentally" in your armpit or crotch.

At the dress parade, you first encounter the production's wardrobe crew, the dressers and menders who assist you through all costume rehearsals and performances. You will have daily commerce with this crew, and you will get service in direct ratio to your courteous behavior. If you're polite and treat them as the co-workers they truly are, you'll find your shoes shined regularly and your dresser in place for your quick change. These workers take pride in their contribution to the show and do not like being treated as second-class citizens. If you bark "that's wrong" at them, like the actor I heard of in a recent production of *The Mystery of Irma Vep*, you may expect them to lose interest in helping you, and suddenly you'll find yourself desperately trying to make that quick change all alone.

At the dress parade, follow instructions. Typically, you'll be told to put on one costume, come to the wings, take your turn on the stage, then return it to your dressing room and follow the same procedure with all your other costumes. Don't waste time in this tedious but all-important exercise. You will do a lot of waiting around, but don't you be the cause of anyone else's waiting around. You may feel excited to be in your finished costume for the first time, seeing other characters in theirs, but don't rush about showing yours off to your friends. The goal of a dress parade is to make a nearly final check of all costumes so that adjustments may be made before the first dress rehearsal. The director and costume designer are out front taking notes and nobody needs you to preen about interrupting and wasting time. You can contribute to a quick and valuable dress parade by being quiet! Your excitement will tempt you to gabble. Resist the temptation. There are people working who don't need their concentrations muddled by your small talk. And finally, don't panic. True, your pants aren't ready and you look silly in your doublet and blue jeans, but it is precisely to create a list of work to be completed that this parade is being held. Don't rain on it.

When your turn comes to go on the stage, do so quickly and simply. You'll be given instructions like "turn around," "put your hands over your head," and "wear the cape in Act Two." Typically, you'll be asked for any notes you have. Report any incompletions: no shoelaces, no cufflinks. Report problems: "I really can't sit down without splitting the breeches," and then demonstrate the problem. Ask questions: "How should the hat be worn?" "What jewelry should I wear?" "Which scenes do I use the raincoat in?" If there is a lull in the session while the director and costume designer confer out front, move about in the costume to demonstrate for them how it hangs and moves. When you are told "Thank you, next," leave the stage and make room for your successor.

Return all parts of your costume to their proper places. Hang up all costume pieces that should be on hangers. A sure sign of an amateur is a costume piled thoughtlessly on a chair. Make certain that all accessories are carefully stored: hats, swords, boots, collar pins, barrettes, etc. Your job, not to mention your performance, requires you to attend to your costume. What do you do when an expected alteration has not been done? You're still in rehearsals, and not everything can be done at once, so before you throw a hissy-fit because the sleeve that ripped out at the last rehearsal is still out, check with the wardrobe department to learn when they will get to it. If they think they've done it and you know they haven't, don't help the dresser to pin it closed so no one will notice. That'd be proper if this were a performance and you wanted to hide the problem from the paying audience. But this is still a rehearsal, so instead of hiding the problem, flaunt it. Wear the costume on stage, and contrive to make the problem very visible. The director will give a note to the costume designer, who will give a note to the costume shop . . . and the repair will get done. And no one will have behaved badly.

Observe all rules for the care of costumes. It is common for actors to be told that they may not eat or drink or smoke in costume. The younger the company, the more these policies will be stressed. The producer doesn't have the money to pay for a new costume after you squirt the ketchup from your McBurger all down your front, and the costume shop doesn't have the time to build you another. A sensible way to accommodate any such rules and your own habits is to bring along a dressing smock to wear over your costume when you want to eat or smoke.

Take good care of your costume. Report any problems to maintenance quickly. Usually, a sheet of paper and a pencil is posted in your dressing room for just such notes. Shine your shoes if your character would have well-shined shoes. The audience sees your feet and measures you, in part, by their appearance. Management is required to have your costumes laundered and dry cleaned regularly, usually on Monday, the day off. That means things are getting wilted toward the weekend, when your largest and highest-paying audience sees the show. Care enough about your work to give them their money's worth. Put on your makeup *before* your costume so that you don't get liner, rouge, and powder all over it. If you have to touch up your makeup during a performance, cover yourself with a towel or smock. In short, deal with your costume as carefully as you do all parts of your performance.

CREWS Suddenly, a lot of people working all around you. For four weeks you were an intense band of actors in a quiet rehearsal hall. Now you've moved into the theatre where there are electricians, stagehands, flymen, prop men, and an entire army of skilled, efficient workers. They don't know you and they ignore you. It was bad enough in school when the crew were all frightened seventeen-year-olds. Now they are all fifty-five years old, smoke pipes, tell rude jokes, and are openly disinterested in what you're doing. How do you adjust to this? How do you behave?

Sadly, the typical young actor assumes a nose-in-the-air attitude. "After all," he feels, "I am young, talented, beautiful, and the artist without whom this show cannot go on." If those thoughts go through your mind and influence your attitude toward the crews, you're in for a bad time. For a moment, think what they're thinking. "Who is this punk? I've worked this theatre for thirty-five years. I've worked with the greats like Dustin, Meryl, and Jimmy Jones. I know more about theatre in my broken little finger than he'll know in ten years—if he's still in the business, which I doubt." The experienced stagehand is a part of the theatre family, an old and proven member. You are the new kid on the block. The distinction between crew and cast is mostly in the egotistical mind of the performer. From the management's point of view, both are important workers. They need to get along together.

Two guidelines to your behavior with the crews: first, respect their work. The crews know their jobs. Unlike the seventeen-year-old prop-mistress who rattles easily and is doing her job under protest because she really wants to be an actress, a professional prop master knows his job, does it without flap, and enjoys doing it well. He probably belongs to a union, and that means he gets paid handsomely for doing it. (He'll work many more weeks a year and no doubt will earn substantially more than you will. In a commercial world where your value is in part measured by your ability to earn, he has much better credentials than you have, so forget the notion that you are more important because you're "an actor.") In a union house, there are a lot of things you are used to doing that you can no longer do. If you want your prop pre-set by the entrance and not on the prop table, you have to get the prop man to do it; you can't move it yourself. You can ask the stage manager to ask the prop man, or, if you have won that old hand's respect by your courteous behavior, you can ask him directly. But pick it up yourself and you'll find you've created more problems than you can believe. Second, be courteous. Unless you're playing a leading role (and, as a beginner, that's not likely), you'll spend a lot of hours backstage. If you make friends with the crews, you'll enjoy a sip of coffee, an occasional cigarette, and some pleasant small talk. Your time will pass pleasantly, if you're a member of the family. And when that emergency comes up and you really need the crew to help you, they will—because you've become family, and family knows how an actor behaves.

PRODUCERS   You might be cast in a show, rehearse it, perform it for thirty-five weeks, close it, go on a twenty-week national tour, return to New York, and never once speak to the producer. You will have seen him (or them, since it takes several producers to raise the money in today's economy for a commercial production), but you may never have been introduced. The producer is the businessman who sits on top of the economic, political, and artistic pyramids. You are near the base of that pyramid, as the earlier organizational charts revealed. You are one of the building blocks with which the producer has made the show happen.

There are many types of producers, from the tough dealers of the Shubert organization, to the grizzled veterans like Manny Azenburg, to the former whiz-kids like Rocco Landesman, to the elitist gentlemen like Roger Stevens, to the former actors like Ken Marsolais. Producers come in all shapes and sizes, and what they have in common is that they are responsible for everything. The producer raises the money, chooses the show, hires everyone, and works to improve the script, the performances, the advance sales, and the company's morale. He lives in a continual world of crises: the set won't be ready on time, the critics have a conflict with another show and the opening date has to be shifted, the star has a cold, the theatre parties aren't selling, and the director needs to work the company overtime, which costs money, and there isn't any more! By comparison, your complaints that the dressing rooms are dirty and the box office treasurer rude seem rather petty. Small wonder the producer is remote from you; your responsibilities are on very different planes.

There are three times you're likely to meet the producer: during casting, during rehearsals, and on social occasions. When he is casting a show—when you are auditioning—he is the boss and you are the job applicant. He doesn't want to hire anyone he hasn't met and personally approved, so he will probably sit in on your final audition. He is the capitalist who will exploit you if he possibly can. Also he is the lover, in love with the forthcoming production, and he wants to make you happy and welcome. So he will be all smiles as he offers you less money than you were hoping he would. But you also are a lover, hoping the next weeks will stretch into months and that the affair will be a wonderful one, so you smile, too, as you compromise yourself. After all, a happy job at five bucks over minimum is better than no job at all. If you are wise, you will have learned the producer's name before you meet him. But your encounter will normally be limited to a handshake and a three-sentence exchange of banalities.

You will next encounter the producer when he shows up at a rehearsal. And he will, whether he is producing a $7,000,000 Broadway musical or an experimental production in a university drama department. You can get a feel for what the producer's visit to a rehearsal is like by watching Bob Fosse's film *All That Jazz*; there's a wonderful sequence in which the producers come to watch and the whole show goes to pieces. In a LORT company, the producer might be the artistic director or the managing director or even the president of the board of trustees. At a university, he is typically the chairman of the department. Whoever he is, and no matter how unobtrusively he enters, he sends everyone into a panic. The higher up the pyramid you are, the more nervous you will be to have the boss looking over your shoulder. The director and the star will be the most nervous because they have the greatest responsibility for the way things are going. As a supporting player, you will feel relatively unthreatened, and yet in the back of your mind you'll know that if he hates what you're doing, he may talk with the director about replacing you. So now you're panicked. What to do? Pretend it is a performance. Everyone will say, "It's only a rehearsal, just go about your business as usual," but no one will believe that. You're not ready for a public performance, but give one anyway. Turn on your performance concentration, your public calm, and act the hell out of your scenes. By doing so, you'll achieve several ends. You'll make it possible for you to get through the day. You'll show the producer what he came to see, a preview of coming attractions. And you'll help settle down the actors who share scenes with you. You may not actually talk to the boss during this encounter but your behavior can have an important influence on your working relationship with him.

Lastly, you will meet the producer at social gatherings. These may be at the beginning of rehearsals or at the inevitable opening-night party—whether that happens on a darkened stage with communion wine from the cathedral next door, at the elegant home of a rich patron of the theatre, or at Sardi's on 44th Street. At any social gathering, the producer is both host and star. The center of attention. Around him, in concentric circles, are the backers (or Board of Trustees if it's an institutional theatre), the director and the stars, the producer's professional and personal friends, the producer's staff, and lastly you actors. If he enjoys mingling among the masses, you may exchange a greeting or two and shake his hand. During such gatherings, it is wise to remember that the producer believes that he has created you. You're his toy, and he may introduce you to his acquaintances or to members of the press as though you were his private possession. He's a seventeenth-century benevolent despot and patron of the arts who keeps you about because he believes in culture. You can resist this relation if you wish to endanger your chances of working for him again, but you'd be wisest to tug at your forelock and smile at his patronage.

PUBLIC RELATIONS   You are part of a business. You are a commodity to be marketed, both as yourself and as a component of a show that must be sold to a resisting public. When you deal with your show's PR department, you must temporarily put aside all notions of yourself as an "artist" and recognize that the same devices that lead you to buy one brand of soup instead of another are the devices that will guide some ticket buyer to come to your show instead of to the one across the street. We live in an advertiser's world, and we succeed to the extent that we realize this truth and do our PR work well. Accordingly, as an actor, you should cooperate fully with the professional PR people who've been engaged to promote you.

Volunteer for any promotional activities you can. Exposure is a valuable aid to your career, and if you can get an interview in the paper or if you appear in a TV spot, you'll do yourself and your show a world of good. Be generous with your time. At the same time, you need not totally sell out your own sense of taste and dignity, and you don't have to do anything that you find emotionally frightening. If you're asked to promote your summer stock production of *Harvey* by dressing up in a bunny suit and riding on a float in a Fourth of July parade, you can decline if you'd find that experience mortifying. They'll find someone else to do it. Or if they ask you to do a TV interview and you absolutely freeze when you're asked to be spontaneous on camera, you can decline. They'll find someone else. If you *can* do these things, of course, you'll endear yourself to your fellow workers, and you might just advance your career.

Recognize that PR people are professionals who deal in the business world regularly. They respond to promptness, courtesy, and clarity. If you've been scheduled to meet with the guy knocking out a news release about you, be on time. He has a deadline that can't wait upon your whimsy. Come prepared. Bring with you some photos (more than one pose if possible), some copies of your résumé, and anything that gives him a particular angle for the story: have you broken your leg during rehearsals? is this your first visit to Cleveland since your family moved away when you were four? did you get cast because you were the only one-legged Lithuanian to audition?

Write your own bio for the program. You'll commonly be invited to do so, but write it even if no one asks you. That way you can be certain that it says what you want it to say and in the tone you wish to use in advancing yourself to your public and to other possible future employers who might read it. And for pity's sake, make certain there're no mistakes in your bio. You will not believe how often actors get the title of the plays they've acted in, the names of the characters they've played, and the names of the theatres they've worked at wrong. It is exasperating to the PR staff to re-write the bio you've written because you've gotten your facts wrong. You didn't play Angel in *School of Wives* at the Huntington Boston Company; you played Agnes in *School for Wives* at the Huntington Theatre Company. Get it right. If you're joining a permanent company, check past programs to learn the length and tone of their bios. If you're in a commercial production, inquire of the PR head what kind of bios will be used. As a rule, I bring mine with me to the first rehearsal. At that time, I know I'll be asked to fill out a brief form for the PR department. I simply attach my bio to that form.

Photography is a major part of public relations work, and you will be photographed many times for each job. Some photos may be taken during rehearsals, to be used for press releases or in souvenir programs. Over the years you will grow accustomed to photographers moving about you, clicking away as you work. Your stage manager and/or director will normally protect you from overzealous photographers and intrusive cameramen, particularly those prone to use flashes. Modern lenses and film speeds permit photographers to work in poor light, so photographers may roam in front of the stage (and in the wings) during runthroughs and final dresses. Your task is to go about your business. Pretend you're in a performance and the clicking sound is some unidentifiable audience noise that you will not allow to disturb your concentration. But if your work is really being disrupted by a photographer, a brief word to the stage manager will set things right.

Photo calls are another matter. These are special sessions dedicated entirely to the photographer. They may occur on the stage, at the photographer's studio, on location in some park, or anywhere the photographer and producer agree on. A photo call is a part of your working day. Your union stipulates the amount of time permitted for a photo call and it is reasonable. Particularly if you remember that the primary use for all photos is to promote your show. If you suspect you're being asked to spend too much time at a photo call, inquire of your Equity deputy. If you're right, you may receive overtime pay. It's standard to have a photo call during the final week of rehearsals, perhaps following a run-through. This is for promotional and/or archival photos. You'll be tired, anxious to get your notes and a shower, but you'll have to hang around while some outsider snaps away. If your stage manager is top flight, the session will be well organized and progress smoothly. A list of the photos to be taken (the points in the action will be identified by lines of dialogue) should be posted so you'll know in advance which shots you're in and how many costume changes you need to make—and in what order. Good behavior on your part will get you through this session gracefully. Don't waste time. If you have a costume change to make, complete it by the time your next photo is called. Don't wander off and make someone come searching for you. Keep quiet. Keep your wisecracks *sotto voce* and entertain only those closest to you. Deal with the photo call as an important segment of your working day. Respect the photographer and his problems. Who knows, the picture he snaps may end up in the front of the theatre and lead you to stardom. Or it may be a delightful souvenir to send to your mother.

   COMPANY MANAGER and GENERAL MANAGER   These two people are part of the producer's administrative team. Sometimes one person does both jobs, but the duties are split in a large company. The general manager is the business administrator for the production and handles most money and logistical matters. The company manager is his link to the actors. Normally, the company manager will come to rehearsals once a week to bring you your pay and to get you to sign for it. Your pay may come as a check or in cash, depending on the agreement your agent reached with the producer. The company manager will also assist you with job-related problems, such as how to find accommodations if you're away from your place of residence, what banks will honor your checks, what doctors, hospitals, and dentists you should contact in case of emergency, how to file for Worker's Compensation in the event of accident, and a myriad of other problems that arise. He is engaged to assist you. He will be your contact for tickets if friends or agents wish to see the show. (You'll have to pay for these, of course. You are paid your salary because seats are sold. But the company manager'll be able to get you seats, even if the house is nominally sold out.) He'll help you get seats to other events in town if you're traveling. He'll arrange your transportation from one city to the next. He'll arrange your hotel accommodations while you're on tour. He'll attend to many of your needs. The company manager is someone who gets emotional rewards from being of service and will go the extra mile for anyone who is pleasant and courteous to deal with. I don't think I need to point out how important it is for you to be on his good side.

FRONT OF HOUSE   You're not likely to have much traffic with the house manager, box office treasurer, or other front-of-house personnel, but it behooves you to remember that they are the permanent cadre in the theatre and that you are the transient guest. When your show closes, they'll be working on the next show in the theatre. (This is true even in institutional and educational theatres.) You will get along with the front-of-house staff if you extend to them the same respect and courtesy you show elsewhere. Then, if you need the house manager to take special care in showing your aged aunt to her seat, you can count on her showing you appropriate respect and courtesy.

YOURSELF   The theatre is a public arena in which creativity and business co-exist through the cooperative workings of many people. You will prosper in this arena if you understand its workings, the relationships between the people who make up its political structure, and the obligation each of us has to respect our fellows and to pull our own weight. And that means, finally, that we must each respect ourselves. You will gain self-respect through attention to your craft, experience, and love of the art that you create. As Stanislavsky taught us many years ago, "Love the art in yourself, and not yourself in art."

Preparing for Rehearsals

"I couldn't find it," you say as you pant into the first rehearsal eight minutes late. Some beginning! Actors are looking at you through weary eyes, the stage manager is silently rehearsing his reprimand, the director has lost the edge he had for his opening remarks, and the company manager is thinking about the five-day clause. It may take you a week of hard work to earn back the company's confidence—all because you didn't prepare properly for rehearsals.

The first thing to do, in the time between learning you got the job and reporting for your first day's work, is to put all your "civilian" duties in order. Pay the bills, write your correspondence, negotiate your leave of absence from your "job-job," cancel any unnecessary medical or social appointments, get your bank account balanced, your clothes laundered, your apartment cleaned, and your grocery shopping done. You're about to enter into a four-week period in which you simply won't have time for the daily exercises of living. In addition to all the preparations that you may need to do to play the role (research the writer, brush up on the manners of the period, learn the lines, analyze the script, secure a dialect coach, etc.), you must make appropriate preparations to go to work.

Next, make certain your rehearsal kit is in order. If it is the same as your audition kit, there may not be a great deal to do, but check it all the same. You may not need as extensive a supply of medical aides, since the stage manager will supply many of your wants, but check to ensure that you have breath mints and aspirin. Make sure your calendar book is up to date, so you won't schedule conflicts with your photo calls, costume fittings, and special rehearsals. Put in a supply of paper and pencils and the like. Prepare your rehearsal clothes. Are you going to need a rehearsal skirt? A double-breasted suit coat? Three-inch heels? A fedora? And what kind of shoes will you want to rehearse in? What PR materials will you need? Photos, for sure. And résumés. A new bio? Well, whatever you can imagine you'll need, get it ready. A rehearsal period is a bit like a trip. You have to pack carefully if you're going to be comfortable on your way.

Scout the terrain. Discover where the rehearsal hall is and how you can get there. Check the comparative rates of parking lots, if you'll be driving. Investigate the traveling time needed by car, bus, or subway. Decide on your best route before you find yourself eight minutes late. Then check out the neighborhood. Are there parts of it that seem unsafe? If so, are there preferred routes to the rehearsal hall and preferred times of day to travel on particular routes? Is it fine to go to the theatre by subway in the daytime but safer to take the bus home if the rehearsal goes past 6:30 p.m.? Investigate the neighborhood for drugstores, restaurants, and bars. Compare prices, so you don't spend your first week's paychecks on lunches alone. At first, any new neighborhood seems forbidding and alien. But you're going to be working in this one for several weeks, and your work requires you to be relaxed, so you'll help yourself by familiarizing yourself with your new haunts before you set to work.

If you're heading out of town, your task is a bit more elaborate. You'll have to find accommodations, learn the transport system, arrange for your telephone, and set up housekeeping. (This is true for stock and LORT engagements; problems you'll encounter on tour will be discussed later.) As a rule, the company manager will be your guide through this, and the finer the company, the finer will be the assistance you'll receive. She'll pick you up at the airport, help you get settled in your apartment, and take you shopping for groceries. But, to paraphrase George Orwell, some company managers are more equal than others, and each experience will be just that: an experience. A friend once described the LORT circuit jokingly as something akin to Solzhenitsyn's Gulag Archipelago in which each theatre has its particular form of torture for its "guests." One theatre has housing that's a mile away from any shops, the next has a rehearsal room that's always too cold, and yet a third rehearses eccentric hours that disrupt your regular meal times and screw up your body-clock: say, from 10:30 to 3:30 and 5:30 to 8:30. But most LORT and stock companies are very concerned about making your life comfortable, and the more thoughtful provide a basket of fruit and other edibles in your apartment as a welcome gift. Most theatres have duplicated information sheets that provide you with the names of reputable doctors, boarding houses, merchants, and restaurants. These frequently list shops that will give discounts to actors and places you are wise to stay away from. In the early days of the Utah Shakespearean Festival, we used to provide arriving actors with a list of bars to avoid. These were frequented by cowboys who were suspicious of strangers, particularly those with long hair and eastern accents, and who loved to have three belts of the hard stuff and then go out "to beat me up a Shakespeare."

If you're heading for a new town, allow yourself ample time to get settled. Don't try to drive in on the morning of the first rehearsal and hope to go to work and get settled simultaneously. It can be done—indeed it's done all too often—but your work will suffer if you try it. Those first three days of rehearsal are tough and they merit and require your 100% attention.

The Daily Work Pattern

The alarm clock rings. You do your morning ablutions, eat a healthy breakfast, and then get ready for the day's work.

Set the day's work in focus. What is going to be done today? Check the rehearsal schedule and recollect what the director said at the end of yesterday's rehearsal. Know what segment of the play is going to be worked and go over it carefully in your head. Then set yourself a goal for the day. "Today I shall fall in love with Othello." This essential aspect of your role hasn't been achieved yet, and without it many of your actions, lines, and emotions are forced, unbelievable. By setting yourself a task, you bring your work into focus. You will do many other things today as well—some will come from the direction you'll receive and others will evolve spontaneously as you work—but with a specific task in mind, you'll be assured of progress during the day's work.

Now do your warm-ups. These may be physical warm-ups for your voice and body or they may be warm-ups for the techniques of your internal process. Will you use emotional recall to help you fall in love with Othello? Then warm up your concen-

tration. Is your task to find your character's physical characterization? Then get out early and observe some civilians. Use your
tools as a way of warming up for the rehearsal and apply them to
the specific goals you've set for yourself.

Lastly, make certain you have everything you need to take
with you. Now go.

Your arrival at the rehearsal hall should be early, quiet, and
cordial. Get to the hall early enough to complete your warm-ups
so that you're ready to work when the stage manager calls,
"Places, please." Greet your comrades cheerfully, but be alert to
the fact that others may already be at work, so don't burst into
the room. Actors may have gotten there early to work together
on a scene; the lighting designer and stage manager may be
writing cues; the writer may be urging changes on the director.
The world doesn't necessarily begin with your entrance. Of course,
if no one is doing anything special, you can make all the noise
you need to.

Every time you come into the rehearsal hall, you should
check for notices. If there's a callboard, check it for costume
fittings, PR interviews, changes in the rehearsal schedule, and
anything that might be new since you last looked. If there's no
callboard, ask the stage manager if there's anything you need to
know. (If you're working in a film, check the shooting schedule
on your arrival. It tells the sequence of the day's shots; there are
almost always changes from the night before.)

Now you're ready to rehearse. The director determines what
is to be rehearsed and how the rehearsal is to be conducted.
There are many standard kinds of rehearsal, each of which has its
own procedures and goals. These include:

> **MEETINGS** These usually deal with business details
> such as the election of an Equity deputy or discussion
> of transportation to another city or theatre. The goal
> is dissemination of information.

> **READINGS** The script is read out loud and dis-
> cussed. Commonly, actors read their own roles, but
> sometimes the playwright or director will read the
> entire script as a way of communicating his feelings

about it. The goals of readings are to hear the entirety of the play as it will be spoken by the voices assigned to each role and to ensure that everyone has the correct script (and this can be of major importance with a Shakespearean text if the director has cut it; you may have lines you didn't realize were yours).

DISCUSSIONS These are always led by the director, though the playwright, designers, and choreographer may be asked to contribute. Primarily, these are rehearsals in which the director and actors explore the nature of characters, intentions of scenes, motivations for actions, and tonality of sequences. The device of discussion is a rational one, and logic and rhetoric are its obvious tools. The goal is to achieve increased understanding of the play.

GAMES These rehearsals are commonly based on the exercises developed by the great acting teacher Viola Spolin. The actors, under the director's guidance, play various childlike games, some of which may relate to the basic action of the play or to one of its scenes. The goals of games are many: to create a relaxed atmosphere in which to work, to kindle the creative spirit, to establish mutual trust, to encounter the play on non-rational terms.

IMPROVISATIONS Like games, improvisations are para-theatrical. Actors, always under the director's tutelage, act out situations that relate to or extend from the characters they play and the situations their characters are in. For example, you're playing Amanda and you return home to tell your daughter Laura how embarrassed you were when you visited Rubicon's Business School. You might improvise your meeting with the headmistress. Or you're doing *Red Noses* and need to have an experience of dealing with the victims of the plague; the director could create an improvisation in which you are nurses at an AIDS hospice. The goal of improvisation is to flesh out the actor's sense of the character's experience.

STAGING or BLOCKING Rehearsals in which the rough outline of the actors' movements are determined. Sometimes this is achieved improvisationally, with the actors following their instincts and the director merely re-shaping what they do. More commonly, the director instructs you where to go and when. The goals are to achieve a beginning physicalization of the play and concurrently to express your character's actions in spatial terms.

WORKING REHEARSALS Rehearsals in which the director and actor work toward a rich, complete, and polished expression of some segment of the play. These rehearsals are the "meat" of a rehearsal period and commonly employ all the techniques at the director's disposal. Discussions and improvisation fuse. Blocking is improvised and readings recur. The distinguishing trait of working rehearsals is *repetition*, as each word, thought, and move is repeated in an attempt to "get it right." The goal is to move slowly toward a deeply felt and externally controlled performance.

SPECIAL REHEARSALS These are rehearsals in which some particular problem is confronted, and they are frequently supervised by one of the director's assistants. Dance and music rehearsals are obvious examples. But rehearsals of nude scenes, scenes of violence, and private coaching sessions are also included. The techniques employed relate to the kind of special rehearsal, though show-and-tell is commonly used. The goal is to select a special task in the production and to refine it toward performance.

RUN-THROUGHS Rehearsals in which the actors proceed through all or a stipulated portion of the play without interruption. Typically, the director sits out front and takes notes, which he later gives to the actors. The goals of a run-through are to provide everyone with a sense of what has been accomplished to that point in the rehearsal process, to identify areas of the play requiring intensive work, and to give the actors a sense of continuity in their performances.

TECHNICAL REHEARSALS Rehearsals in which the scenery, lighting, properties, and sound elements of production are given primary focus. Commonly, a "cue-to-cue" rehearsal is conducted by the stage manager in which the actors are told to "pick it up with your line 'The Queen, my lord, is dead' . . . and GO." And the actors are stopped whenever the technical cue is completed. This rehearsal commonly requires extensive repetition. The goal is to integrate production elements into the action.

DRESS REHEARSALS Rehearsals in which costumes are worn. Commonly, a dress parade will precede a run-through in costume, the two events comprising the first dress rehearsal. The goal is to introduce this element of production into the action.

PREVIEWS Rehearsals of the entire show under performance circumstances, with an audience in attendance. The goal is to discover the audience's responses so that subsequent working rehearsals (usually the following afternoon) can make adjustments in script or action that will lead to an increasingly favorable response.

BRUSH-UP REHEARSALS Rehearsals called after a production has formally opened and usually conducted by the PSM. The goals of these rehearsals are to refresh the actors' performances after a hiatus or to restore to their original execution sequences that have altered undesirably during a long run. Or, as director George Abbott described it, "To take out the improvements."

UNDERSTUDY REHEARSALS Rehearsals conducted

by the PSM to prepare understudies should they have to perform. Understudies are always required to duplicate the performance they are "covering," in respect to movement, interpretation, tempo, and line delivery—to the very best of their abilities.

REPLACEMENT REHEARSALS Rehearsals for all members of the cast who are on stage with a character, when the actor who has been playing her is being replaced by an in-coming, new actor. Usually supervised by the PSM, these rehearsals can be extensive, but the number of hours a week that you can be called for any post-opening rehearsal are stipulated in your contract. Hooray for Equity.

At the end of the day's rehearsal, gather your things together and check for final notices. Read the callboard or check with the stage manager, but make certain you know everything you need to know about tomorrow's work.

You may want to do some socializing with your fellow actors as a way of unwinding; do so. It is very useful to know your colleagues on a social level. All work and no play makes you a dull actor. Two beers at the neighborhood dive is an important part of your working day.

But you still have work to do, so take it easy. After dinner, plan to spend two or three hours doing your homework. (I'll discuss the kinds of homework you might do in a couple of pages.) Before you undertake it, though, reflect on the goal you had set for yourself today. Did you accomplish it? Did you "fall in love with Othello?" If you accomplished your goal, great. If you didn't, you have nonetheless had a focus to your day's work, and you'll have other days to confront that problem again. Not immediately, because it's a poor notion to wrestle with the same problem two days in succession, as it's easy to get obsessive about it or to develop a block—and both are counter-productive.

Now do your homework.

And now . . . relax. You've earned it. It may be hard for you to let go after an intensive day, but you need to. You need to chat with your friends, watch television, read a book, play a game, or otherwise get your mind and body away from your work. A thirteen-hour day is enough! So for a brief time leave the actor in you behind and return to being the pleasant and social creature you really are. It will make the people who live with you a bit more tolerant, and it will help you return to the next day's work refreshed.

And now to sleep. Allow yourself plenty of time for rest. You'll be no good to yourself or anyone else if you stay up half the night working and arrive bleary-eyed at tomorrow's rehearsal. Get a full night's sleep—that's part of your daily work pattern too.

And be certain to set your alarm.

Dismissal, Replacement, and Understudying

"You're fired!" There are elaborate ways of saying it, but when you get down to the truth of it, those are the words that say it clearest. When it happens, it will be the hardest moment in your life as an actor. The rejection you have courted and feared is given concrete reality. You might be able to rationalize why you weren't cast in a show or why you weren't given the role you preferred, but being fired is being fired. It's a blow to your ego, your craft, and your pocketbook.

You might be dismissed for many reasons. Perhaps you've not learned the lessons of this handbook and your professional attitude is poor. You're tardy, lazy, or, like the young actor described in the opening pages, you're an argumentative nuisance. Or perhaps someone in the production has enough "muscle" to get you dismissed because he doesn't like working with you or because he's got a friend he'd rather have playing the role. That is, you could be the victim of politics. But most often, when an actor is fired, it's because the producer wants somebody better. Ouch! You're fired because you're not good enough!

"It isn't fair," you howl. Well, whoever said the theatre was fair? If your training and experience have been in a university, you may have the false impression that rehearsals are for the purpose of your improvement and that if the director would only work with you, you'd *be* good enough. But rehearsals are for the purpose of teaching actors who *are* good enough the particular tasks of this production. You were fired because you couldn't cut it.

When it happens, brevity is the best policy. Don't protest, don't cause a scene, don't try to discuss the situation, don't plead, and don't haggle. Pick up your possessions, find out how you'll get your final check, and go. Any other behavior will cause you extended embarrassment and grief, and you'll embarrass your fellow actors (rupturing your friendships with them). You won't change your fate, and you'll do damage to the production. You must love the theatre more than you love yourself. That's hard to remember when you've just lost your only paycheck, but the show is going to go on without you, so let it.

A few years ago, I had to fire an actor in particularly awkward circumstances. I was directing the premiere of a new comedy in which this actor had a middle-sized role, though a very showy one. The play was there for him to steal. The actor was a fine man, a respected actor with a long and impressive career in theatre and film, and one who was well known to my theatre's Board of Trustees for the excellent performances he had given them in years gone by. In rehearsals, he would be absolutely marvelous at moments, but he wasn't learning the lines. We had been in rehearsal for three full weeks and we opened in five days. I had done everything I knew to help the actor. I had scheduled him to rehearse only in the afternoon so that he could get a lot of rest—he was in his mid-sixties. I had provided an apprentice to help him run lines each morning. I had focused exclusively on his scenes when he was at rehearsal to use his time efficiently. I had asked him repeatedly if there was anything I could do to assist him. He hadn't indicated that there wasn't anything anyone could do, but he was confident that he would know the lines by opening night. During the second week of rehearsals, I lost confidence in him and so did the young playwright, whose first professional production was in danger of being a disaster. And so did the other actors. The Equity deputy came to my office to plead on their behalf that I do something.

So I asked another actor from our company, but one who wasn't in the production, to walk through the role in the morning rehearsals, so that the play could be rehearsed properly and so that the other actors could prepare their roles. While this second actor always carried the script and tried to keep up the ruse that he was merely helping us to rehearse, privately I asked him to learn the role—against the possibility that I might have to make a change. Come the end of the third week of rehearsals, I knew I had to do just that. I will forever be thankful to my managing director, who accompanied me to the actor's apartment and gave me emotional support for this truly painful scene in which I had to tell a fine man and a talented and experienced actor that he was fired. "Why?" he demanded to know. There was no way to be indirect. "You haven't learned the lines," I heard myself saying, "and the playwright is distraught, the other actors are in a panic about opening night, and I just can't take the chance. We have more than 10,000 subscribers and I have to think of them. I'm sorry. I wish I knew something else to do. I don't." My managing director had brought a check for the two weeks' severance pay that the actor was entitled to with him, and he added that the actor could stay in the company's apartment until he made arrangements to return to his home in California. The actor got hostile for a brief moment, then morose, and finally he grew very gracious and accepted the reality. He understood that the producer can hire and the producer can fire. And we actors have little recourse except what our contract stipulates—severance pay. An actor gets fired because the boss wants to hire somebody else.

This story does not have a sad ending. The actor returned to California and continues to work in television and films, where his difficulty in learning lines doesn't impede him and where his talent is welcome. Age or illness or the lack of practice in learning lines may have made it unlikely he'll work on stage, but he can continue his life as an actor. And I am eternally grateful that he handled our awkward situation so well and that he knew how an actor behaves.

How can you help yourself after you've been fired? First, calmly discern why you were fired. If you can honestly conclude that you were the victim of politics, or if you know you were canned because you couldn't sing well enough and you'd told the director at auditions that you weren't a trained singer, then your ego need not be too bruised. If you were released because you were deficient in some skill, set about improving your skills: take classes, work to broaden your employability. But if you conclude you were canned because you weren't good enough, you have some hard thinking to do. Are you in the right business? Can you cut it as an actor? If you're not a mountain climber, all the desire in the world won't get you to the top of K-2. You must have skills, stamina, courage, and a talent for climbing. As an actor, you must have desire, but desire alone won't get you employment and won't sustain you in a career. Any time you're fired is the time to reflect on your chosen career and to consider other ways of spending your life.

* * * * *

You may be engaged to understudy or to replace. As a beginner, you'll likely be hired to play a small role and also to "cover" one or more larger roles. As an understudy, your individual creativity is not welcome. You're engaged to duplicate what someone else has done, and you're a good employee to the extent that your performance repeats hers. Understudying is a frustrating business.

It is an actor's fantasy that the star will fall sick and you'll go on and become a star. Judy Garland sang the fantasy in *A Star is Born* and the real thing happened when Judy Holliday went into the leading role of *Born Yesterday* in Philadelphia. But it won't happen to you. Instead, you'll be under-rehearsed and ill-prepared. You'll get notice at half-hour that you're going on and you'll panic for thirty minutes, trying to remember the words and trying to fit into a strange costume. You'll bumble through the show, perhaps even playing it for a few performances. At each performance, your name will be announced to the audience and they'll groan, assuming you're an under-rehearsed and ill-prepared second choice. Finally, the principal will recover, start playing her role again, and you'll be back saying, "Dinner is served."

If you are understudying, you must try to be unobtrusive. Many actors are made uneasy by the knowledge that someone is ready to take over for them. Never mind that Equity requires them to be understudied. Never mind that everyone in the show is being understudied. Some actors are so insecure that your very presence at rehearsals rattles them. You can help in two ways. First, don't try to help by discussing the problem. Don't walk up to the actor and attempt to denigrate what you're doing; she'll never believe you and will grow even more nervous. Just leave her to wrestle with her paranoia on her own. (If she's unthreatened and wants to help you, she'll approach you; wait for her to initiate things, then you can open up.) Secondly, give the false impression that you're not taking your work very seriously. Let the actor believe you're slacking and couldn't really do the role, even in an emergency. Then she'll regain her confidence, because she'll realize how much the show depends on her.

Equity stipulates that all understudies must be ready to go on. Understudies rarely are. After a production has opened, there are only two understudy rehearsals a week, not nearly enough to learn a role well. During the rehearsal period, there are never understudy rehearsals. That means you're on your own. When the show opens, you must be ready to step into the role. And you've never been rehearsed in it. Madness? Absolutely. Your only recourse is to watch carefully at rehearsals, use the stage manager's prompt script as often as you can get at it, and work a lot on your own.

If you're hired to replace, you have a bit more flexibility in creating the role than you have as an understudy. If you're replacing during the rehearsal period, you have to pick up the blocking as it's already established and certain general attacks on interpretation, character relationships, and rhythms, but you'll be able to rework everything during the remaining rehearsals, and the performance you give can be largely your own. The only limitation in this circumstance is time. You'll have to work faster than you might like to.

If you replace during the rehearsal period, you walk into a tense situation. Most of the company is anxious for you to do well, as they've been aware of the unsatisfactory work of your predecessor, but others may have been friends with the departed actor. You can help yourself and the company by observing common-sense rules of behavior. Don't talk about the other actor. Work as though you were starting from scratch. Get the basic blocking from the prompt script immediately and learn it. Learn the script as fast as you can. By getting these mechanics out of the way, you'll be able to rehearse the scenes, and you'll assure the rest of the company that they can rely on you. Be extremely flexible in working with the other actors—try to supply them with the line readings and business they request. Once you've caught up with the others and are rehearsing as an equal member of the company, you can assert yourself and work as you would normally. But it is useful to remember that you've been engaged as a medicated bandage. You can't contribute to the show's organic development until you've healed the sore. If you're replacing an actor who's leaving a show, you may get a reasonable amount of rehearsal time. You'll be obliged to repeat the basic interpretation of the departing actor, her blocking, execution of specific business, and anything that seriously affects other performers. But during your rehearsals, and during your early performances, you'll commonly be given a bit of leeway so that you can make the performance your own. In his weekly column in the *Sunday New York Times* on January 12, 1992, critic David Richards wrote about the ways that cast replacements can change a production, for better or worse, and celebrated the energy and variety that new actors bring to a role. He wrote at some length about Jane Kaczmarek and Rosemary Harris, who replaced Tony Award winners Mercedes Ruehl and Irene Worth in Neil Simon's *Lost in Yonkers,* and he invited us to understand that their performances, however much they are externally the same as their predecessors, are inherently different—not better nor worse, just their own. I had the opportunity to watch this phenomenon up close a few years ago when Leonard Frey prepared the title role in Molière's *The Imaginary Invalid* in one week. He was replacing E. G. Marshall because our production had been extended and E. G. had another commitment. Frey worked each morning on his lines. He had a five-hour rehearsal each afternoon with two understudies who played all the other roles and helped him through his various scenes. (The stage manager was conducting rehearsals, of course, and Frey received little that could be called "direction.") He watched each performance from the audience, mouthing along with Marshall. He then had two run-throughs with the full cast, and he was ready. It was a damned dazzling display. His performance was much funnier than Marshall's though his basic business made no changes that would disturb the rest of the cast. Our jobs were to adjust to his performance because he had the title role.

Homework

What can you do between the time you leave rehearsal one day and return to rehearsal the next? What can you do to help yourself? Sadly, many actors can do very little. Oh yes, they can learn their lines and think through some specific business, but most are overly dependent on their directors—and if that's true for you, you're not yet ready to accept employment. A director wants you to come to each rehearsal with something new. "Astonish me in the morning," Tyrone Guthrie used to tell his actors. Can you work on your own? To do so, you need both a method of working and sufficient discipline to make yourself use it. There are two types of work you can do between rehearsals: work on the role and work on yourself. These are your homework.

Your work on your role must begin with an analysis of the script and of your role in particular. Analysis is a rational process, a programmed and sequential investigation that uses established tools and methodology to achieve information and knowledge. You need a method to answer such questions as: what is the play about? what is the story? what does it mean? what does my character want? why'd the writer include this character in the first place? what theatrical style is the text and what influence does that have on how I play this? what are my relationships to the other characters in the play? what are my actions, beats, transitions? And a thousand more. The Stanislavsky Method includes a system of analysis that most young actors read about but can't use. When the Actors Studio fell from fashion in the 1960s, and when games and psychophysical exercises became the core for most courses in actor training, the need for a rational method in creating a role was too often forgotten. As a result, too many actors learned no method. Today, the best training schools have re-integrated analysis and text preparation into their curricula, and yet producers still complain that very few young actors are ready to work. Richard Devin, producing artistic director of the Colorado Shakespeare Festival, recently quipped, "There are only three schools training actors we can use." He may have used hyperbole, but he expressed a common sentiment. Superficiality, inconsistency, and unfocused generalities mark too much of today's acting. This handbook on behavior is not the place to describe a method of analysis. It *is* a place to urge you to learn one. Without a method, all of your work is inferior, and the best of work habits and professional manners will not make you a successful actor.

Let's assume you have analyzed your role. What should you do next? Study! Too many actors are intellectual lightweights. There's a great irony here, since so many of America's younger actors hold advanced academic degrees that suggest they have a body of information and a set of scholarly tools with which to learn more. All those MFAs ought to know their ways around a library. Most don't. Do you? Do you know where to learn about the technique of Expressionist acting before you show up to rehearse *From Morn to Midnight*? Do you know where to learn about the daily customs of late nineteenth-century Russia before you begin rehearsing *Uncle Vanya*? You ought to do three types of research on any play: research on the author and his plays, research on the socio-historical setting of the play's action, and research on the psychological and physiological traits of your character. Let's consider each in turn.

You need to learn a great deal about the author. If he's not alive and well and working with you, you must rely on second-ary sources, and these are mostly in printed form. Back to the library! Begin by reading about his life. Biography is frequently helpful in understanding the playwright's attitudes toward people, human and social values, and even the specific subject matters that appear in his plays. Then read some of the playwright's other plays. You'll play Dr. Astrov better if you know Dr. Chubutykin and Dr. Dorn. You'll learn about the writer's characters, the ideas he expresses, and the tonality of the play you're about to rehearse from his other plays. I was directing Neil Simon's *The Good Doctor* when I discovered that the actor doing the short sketch called "The Audition" had never read Chekhov's *Three Sisters*. Since the character she was playing uses a cutting of the sisters' final speeches, I ended rehearsal early and sent her home to read Chekhov's masterpiece. This actor's research was sorely deficient. Even for such seemingly self-contained work as Neil Simon's farces, research is essential.

You need to learn about the socio-historical setting of the play's action. How did people behave in the era in which the play is set? If you're in a Restoration comedy like *The Country Wife*, it's not enough to know that there was a convention called "breeches parts"; you must learn sufficient details about the costumes of that era so that you can know how Margery deports herself when you dress up like a boy. If you're doing a contemporary play, you may be tempted to assume you don't need to do any research. Nonsense. What if you're the waitress in *Frankie and Johnny*? Have you ever worked as a waitress in a diner? Ever lived in Manhattan? You need to know many things about the world of the play if you are to create your character fully. Some can only be learned in rehearsal, some can only be learned experientially, but some can be learned through research.

Your research can also teach you about the psychological and physiological traits of your character. If the script is written so that you can identify your character with contemporary psychological terminology, you might enrich your performance through a study of the type you're portraying. Is your character a youngest child? a sexually repressed introvert? a dangerous paranoiac? The tools of psychology help us to understand human behavior. Characters in plays are imitations of people. It can be useful to learn about people in order for you to learn about your character. The same applies for physical traits. An actor playing *Plaza Suite* for me researched the symptoms of glaucoma because one of his three characters suffers from the disease. His findings about "tunnel vision" influenced both his physicalization of the role and his interpretation of the character who is suffering from an emotional tunnel vision as well.

Research is an unending process, and you must use your common sense about it and not get so research-happy that you never get around to preparing your role. As long as the research is contributing directly to your work, as long as it is not usurping your time and keeping you from essential or immediate requirements of your work, and as long as you can make specific use of your findings, keep it up. But when these three no longer obtain, it is time to leave the library, close your books, and get about your business.

If you share the widely held belief that acting is imitating human behavior, you can enrich your work by doing some observing. When directing a play about city policemen, I arranged for the actors to visit a police headquarters and to go on patrol one evening in squad cars. I wanted the actors to observe the real police officers' behavior. If your director doesn't arrange it for you, make your own arrangements. Are you in a production of *Marat/Sade*? Do as the original cast did: go to an asylum. In short, imitate life, not someone else's imitation. Don't act the way you've seen an actor portray madness. Go to the primary source.

Perhaps the most important work you can do during the brief hours you have for your homework is to identify the key moments in each scene and prepare them. So be selective. Big emotional moments, entrances, and exits are most worthy of your energies, and in that order. You will commonly use emotional recall to develop your moments of profound emotion. The audience will believe your performance in proportion to their belief in your most exalted moments, so these merit a lot of time-consuming work. If you can achieve credibility in these moments while working at home, and if you bring the fruits of your labors to rehearsals, you'll use your precious rehearsal time productively for your fellow actors as well as for yourself. Rehearsing a new play called *Final Touches*, about the reconciliation of a stern redneck father and a gay son, I was thrilled when Gil Rodgers, playing the father, electrified the rehearsal hall as he sank down on his knees in prayer before his son, seeking a sort of Catholic absolution. He'd done his homework, discovered the word "for-giveness" in the text, and let his talented imagination guide him to this telling moment. More, he had rehearsed it at home and then had just "done it" in rehearsal with no discussion and no forewarning. He's the kind of actor that directors dream about.

But your homework needn't be limited to your "big mo-ments." If you're working on your entrances at home, work on the given circumstances so that you can enter the scene with the fullest sense of its particularities. I was directing a show called *Tug of War* off-Broadway some years back, and one scene called for a husband to arrive at his country home to find his emotion-ally unstable wife in the bedroom and then inquire why she had come, how long she had been there, and what she was doing. One rehearsal, the actor Jack Axelrod entered, looked quietly about the room, walked to his wife's suitcases, lifted them, set them back down, and then went on with the scene. I was fasci-nated, but had no idea what he was doing or why it had seemed so compellingly right. At the end of the scene I asked about the business. "I was weighing them," Jack answered. "I wanted to learn if she had unpacked yet so I'd know if she was telling me the truth when she answered me." These two examples are the work of fine actors. Not stars whose name you will recognize, but excellent actors who have earned long and rewarding careers. It is just such particularized actions, devised outside rehearsals, that mark the fine actor, the actor who knows how to do home-work.

Your private homework also includes such mechanics as learning your lines and working out the timing of business. Prof-itable rehearsals depend on knowing the mechanics of your job as early as you can. Forget all the self-delusions about line-learning as an organic or osmotic process; sit down early and learn the words. Until you have done so, you can't do any acting and your fellow actors are also stalled. Similarly, work out the petty details of where you'll light the cigarette, sip the drink, and turn on the light switch in your speech. Any business that is contained within your own lines and actions and does not affect another's cues should be worked out completely outside re-hearsal hours. Rehearsal time is too valuable to waste on details.

Think about your props. Will it help you to bring particular working props to the rehearsal? Why be dependent on the stage manager? If a particular purse, briefcase, or umbrella is essential to the correct timing of your business, bring one with you. The stage manager will be thrilled, the designer will be delighted to have a specific model of what she needs to find, and you'll make your own work richer. If the working prop is extremely valuable, you'll have to cart it back and forth with you, but if it is not, the stage manager will be happy to add it to the other working props and then return it to you when the real props appear. The objects you handle while acting (and the unique way you handle them) are an important aspect of your performance. You can shape your performance by selecting your props.

Not all the work you do on your role is private. Some will bring you together with others. If, for example, you are in Sam Shepard's *Fool for Love* and you have to speak with a western accent, you might have to engage a dialect coach. Or a juggling coach if you must juggle. Or a gymnastics coach if you must tumble. Or a singing coach if you'll be singing. There is no rule that states that you must receive all of your coaching from either the director or your mother wit. If the role calls for specific skills, you'd be wise to seek the advice, training, and coaching of an expert.

And lastly, you can rehearse! Young actors sometimes have the impression that they are not to rehearse outside formal rehearsals, whereas the truth of most commercial ventures is that you will have adequate rehearsal time only if you and your fellow actors get together on your own, and if you work hard. These rehearsals can happen any place you have enough room to work in, and usually that will mean your apartment. So invite your partner over for dinner, and you can work after dinner. At the least you'll develop a relaxed and friendly relationship that will make formal rehearsals go well; at the best you'll discover rich ways to play your scenes and develop a fine performance. Between those extremes: well, through *repetition* you'll protect yourself from the agony of giving an under-rehearsed performance.

Your work on yourself is equally important. Keep yourself rested, fit, and in top rehearsal condition. Get enough sleep, see a doctor if you feel a bug creeping up on you, get plenty of exercise—jog if you're a jogger or go to an exercise spa if that's your practice—and don't waste your energy in excessive partying. And, as your mother used to say, eat a balanced diet.

Keep your head clear of unqualified "good advice," no matter how well-intended it is and no matter how much it sounds wise. Don't listen to your friends or your dear Aunt Nellie. Every amateur will assume knowledge of what you do professionally, and you'll be told, "That's not how to hold a glass a beer," "You have to trill your Rs more when you talk Scottish," and "You know, of course, that Macduff has been having an affair with King Duncan." Avoid discussing your work with anyone not directly involved with the rehearsals. If you can't avoid it, just smile sweetly, say "thank you" for the advice, and forget it. You must become thick-skinned. Nothing distresses a director more than the insecure actor who alters something from one rehearsal to the next and who, when asked about the change, replies, "They said it didn't look good the other way." There is no "they" qualified to tell you that. Not your coach, not your fellow actors, not even the stage manager or playwright. You may make changes you understand and believe in and for which you have clearly thought-out reasons. But don't think so little of your work that you'll follow the counsel of every self-appointed expert you stumble across. Respect yourself and your director—and that's all.

Finally, continue to live a non-theatre life. If only for one hour a day, forget the play and return to normalcy. Visit with people whose lives, conversations, and interests have nothing to do with the theatre. You need the refreshment such encounters will offer. You need the objectivity such returns to reality will make possible. If only for one hour a day, watch TV, play cards, read a book, or make love. You need the joys of a full life if you are to return to your arduous working day with a sane mind and a healthy body. If only for one hour a day, see something new. Go to a museum you've never visited, meet a stranger, eat an exotic dinner. You need the stimulus that takes you out of yourself and helps you confront the world again.

Remember: acting is like running. The sprint of the performance requires weeks of training. The best actor, like the best runner, is well prepared for the event. The runner must know how to run, and the actor must know how to act. And then both must know how to get ready for the start. The runner for the starter's gun and the actor for the stage manager's "places" call for all "starters." The runner must know how to run and you need to know how an actor behaves.

PERFORMANCES

Near the end of *Franny and Zooey*, J. D. Salinger's extraordinary stories about the Glass family (New York: Bantam Books, Inc., 1969), Zooey tells Franny about the theatre, about acting. Franny is despondent, desperate, and close to a nervous breakdown. She is repeating the mystical Jesus Prayer to herself, and Zooey challenges her to tell him why: "I'd *love* to be convinced—that you're not using it as a substitute for doing whatever the hell your duty is in life." Zooey reminds her of their older brother Seymour's instructions that they should always perform well for the Fat Lady, and then he winds up his argument: "I don't care where an actor acts. It can be in summer stock, it can be over a radio, it can be over *television*, it can be in a goddam Broadway theatre, complete with the most fashionable, most well-fed, most sunburned-looking audience you can imagine. But I'll tell you a terrible secret—Are you listening to me? *There isn't anyone out there who isn't Seymour's Fat Lady.*" For all of us actors, the Fat Lady is out there, at every performance. She is the truest connection we can make. Communion with Seymour's Fat Lady is what performance is all about.

Performances commence whenever an audience first joins your play. You may have ten friends at a run-through, half a house at a dress rehearsal, or three long weeks of sold-out pre-views, but the same rules apply in every case. When there's an audience, there's a performance. Your working habits and your behavior must embrace the presence of that audience from the moment the first stranger walks down the aisle to take a seat, for that first, curious, and expectant viewer is always Seymour's Fat Lady.

The Daily Work Pattern

If you were eight minutes late for the first rehearsal, you should have learned by now the vital importance of being prompt. When do you arrive at the theatre for a performance? Equity stipulates a half-hour call. That means you must be in the theatre and on the job no later than thirty minutes before the curtain rings up. At precisely that minute, the stage manager will check the sign-in sheet and, if you're not signed in, you're not in the theatre. (*Never sign the sheet for another! That's a cardinal rule!*) If you're in the building but haven't signed in, you may think you're there, but you're not. You haven't yet reported for work, and the stage manager has set in motion a sequence of extreme measures that will lead to the show's going on without you. While the ASM phones to learn if you are on your way or if you have been taken to a hospital, the PSM instructs the company of the cast changes being made. Costumes are hastily fitted for the understudy, the conductor makes notations in his score, the prop master makes certain who must get which sword, the house manager prepares a sign for the lobby, and your understudy goes through the agony of the damned. And then you saunter in eight minutes late. "After all," you explain, "I don't even come on stage until thirty minutes into the first act." You're wrong. Oh boy, are you wrong. Your character may come on stage only thirty min-utes after the curtain rings up, but *you* come on the job thirty minutes before it does. Your job and the job of everyone else depends on your being where you are supposed to be when you are supposed to be there. And that means you must be signed in and on the job at the half-hour. On stage, if you are late with a cue in the dialogue, you disrupt the work of the actors on stage with you, the stage manager, and possibly the crews controlling sound and light cues. Back stage, if you're late getting to the theatre, you disrupt everyone's work.

As I write this, I am reminded of the time I was late for my call. It was a summer season, and Sunday performances were at seven instead of the regular eight. I was playing Charles the Wrestler in my own production of *As You Like It*, and since we played five different productions in rotating rep, we had never before had an *As You Like It* on a Sunday—and I had no regularized routine. I ate dinner early and decided to go to the theatre early so that I could do my makeup carefully and relax before show time—instead of rushing in at the half-hour, slapping on my makeup, and dashing to make my first entrance. Instead, I thought I'd saunter into the dressing room more than an hour before curtain—and I found everyone on RED ALERT! The stage manager was trying desperately to teach the wrestling match to a frightened and much too frail understudy, while *his* understudy was trying to learn the songs he would sing shortly when he went on as Amiens. Worse, the entire company was in a tizzy. If the director could be so irresponsible, what other dire events might happen? "The center will not hold" was the mood of the moment. I arrived not sixty-five minutes before curtain, as I assumed, but five brief minutes before the lights dimmed and the audience heard Orlando's opening line, "As I remember, Adam . . ." I apologized, dressed faster than you can believe, and went on. But I felt like an ass for days. And today when I remember what I did twenty-two years ago, I still get the shakes.

Commonly, you'll get to the theatre well in advance of the half-hour. Maybe you have a complicated makeup. Maybe you like to do your warm-ups at the theatre. Maybe you like to check your props carefully, or go over every moment of your performance on the stage before everyone else gets there. Whatever. In these cases, you are your own boss. Your employer only requires you to be there at the half-hour. It's Seymour's Fat Lady who requires you to be there early enough so that you can give her your best performance.

When you arrive at the theatre, be ready to go to work. Don't bring your civilian worries with you. Immediately upon arrival, check the callboard. There may be information posted that will affect your work. A sign may tell you about a party after the show, so you can call your date now and not during that rushed costume change in the middle of Act One. Another sign may tell you the costumes won't be back from the dry cleaners until twenty minutes before curtain, so you don't have to panic when you get to your dressing room and your costumes aren't there. Still another may tell you that a celebrity director will be in the house tonight, so you'd better give your best effort. The callboard is your communications link to the company's administrators and it is your responsibility to be informed of all notices posted on that board. Only the stage manager or company manager will post things. It is not for your private use.

Now it's time to do your warm-ups: your vocalizations and your stretches. Try to find someplace other than your dressing room because many actors don't want to listen to you. When you're warmed up, go over any notes you received from the director (if she's still around) or the stage manager. Don't make the same error two performances running. If a note affects someone you play a scene with, find that actor and go over the note with him so that no one is surprised on stage during the performance. Go over your own notes as well. Many actors keep journals or a simple note pad at their dressing tables, and, between scenes or after a performance, they write notes to themselves about things they'd like to adjust. Remind yourself of what you wish to do better in tonight's performance.

Check your set, your props, and your costumes. Don't get caught up short in the middle of the performance by the too-late discovery that the door is jammed and you can't get off stage, that the apple you have to eat is rotten, or that the mask you wear for the ball scene has fallen behind the prop table. There are crews to check all these things, but you'll set your mind at ease if you double-check everything yourself. Errors happen; try to protect against them. But be careful what you touch or move. The theatrical unions are very protective about who does what. If you find a problem, tell the PSM. You don't want to cause a ruckus—or precipitate a strike.

Next, put on your makeup. If you work in film or television, someone does this for you. It's quite pleasant and ego stroking to lounge in a barber's chair while someone does your face. But if you work on stage, makeup is a part of your job. You must know how to achieve the effects you desire, and that means you must have studied makeup and that you have practiced this particular makeup extensively. Well in advance of the first dress rehearsal, you should begin to practice your makeup as a portion of your homework. Dress rehearsals should be a time for refinements, not experiments. Commonly, your makeup will be simple and no problems will arise, but occasionally you'll have to wear a wig, a scar, a false beard, or a prosthetic nose. When you design your makeup, keep in mind that you'll be putting it on many times. Avoid details that take hours to apply and only "read" in your makeup mirror. Avoid prostheses that damage your skin. (Playing Macbeth, I put a deep scar on my forehead and I had to move it from one side to the other after every couple of performances so that I wouldn't bruise myself and create a "real" scar. It was a dumb thing to do. Well, I was young.) You have an obligation to yourself, to your fellow actors, and contractually to your employers to do the same makeup every performance. If you're in a long-running show, you'll grow weary of a complicated makeup and strive to simplify it. Do yourself a favor and conceive of the simpler one in the first place. Then you'll be able to give the same face to your performance each time, and the Fat Lady will always be pleased.

You must supply your own makeup. Management pays for unusual items like wigs or prosthetic noses, but you supply everything else. You ought to have a well-supplied makeup kit. Metal fishing boxes are widely used by experienced actors because they have many compartments, making orderly storage of the varying brushes, tubes, pots, boxes, bottles, pencils, sharpeners, puffs, and sponges. Others use shoe boxes and even old plastic bags. What is important is the contents, not the container. You ought to have all the supplies and tools you'll require for a show: scissors, tweezers, cotton swabs, hairpins, safety pins, nail files, clippers, hair curlers and dryers, and any other hardware and appliances you might use. In addition to the things that you need to put your makeup on your face, you must have whatever you need to take it off: cold cream, baby lotion, or soap and water. And cleansing tissues. Well, a soft toilet tissue will work as a substitute, but the kind supplied in most theatre lavatories is coarse, so don't count on using it more than once or you may break into a rash.

There are many unwritten rules of the dressing room, and you will keep it a happy place for everyone if you observe them. Begin by respecting people's time, space, property, eardrums, and superstitions.

If an actor needs the makeup mirror longer than you do (he has an old-age makeup, and he opens the show), give him preferential treatment at the full-length mirror, the sink, and the lavatory. If another likes to go over his lines quietly to himself while he puts on his makeup, respect his time and don't interrupt.

An actor's property is equally inviolate. Don't move another's costumes and don't touch his makeup. Respect your colleagues' property and territorial imperatives. And never muck with his good luck pieces, souvenirs, and totems. For some actors, performance is a combat with the unexpected, and they need to approach it from the security of an ordered space. Don't reach for his makeup, tissues, cigarettes, matches, face towel, hanger, or script without asking permission. If the response comes slowly, don't push the issue. An actor who is forever borrowing tissues, pencils, cigarettes, and change for the soft-drink machine is an indescribable nuisance and quickly becomes a pariah.

Unless he's adored. There's the tale of an endearing old character man at England's Bristol Old Vic Theatre Company who regaled everyone with delightful stories from his long career spent trouping across the country in the glory days of the old stock companies. He used an old cigar box for his makeup and he'd begin his tales and slowly move about the large dressing room, carrying his cigar box from place to place, adding a pencil line here and a dab of rouge there, and enchanting his listeners. By the end of his story, he'd have made the rounds of the room, and he'd have completed his makeup. In the middle of the season, he fell ill and was taken to a hospital. The company was deeply concerned for him, and flowers and visitors went to the hospital regularly. The stage manager gathered up the old actor's possessions and discovered to his astonishment and joy that the cigar box had no bottom in it. The wily old story teller had merely plopped it down on top of someone's makeup and, while holding his listener enthralled with the tale he was unfolding, used whatever makeup he needed—and it all appeared to come out of his cigar box. The actor recovered, no one ever let on that they knew how he did his makeup, and he went on telling tales and "borrowing" makeup till the end of the season. And they all lived happily ever after.

Protect your own property. You cannot be reminded often enough of this truth: *Something will be stolen on every show you work!* No matter the place, the time, or the people, something will be stolen. And the criminal will rarely be caught, because the criminal is commonly among you—some member of the company. On occasions, theatre robberies are outside jobs. A townie once cleaned out every wallet, watch, and purse from the dressing rooms of the Utah Shakespearean Festival while the full company was rehearsing the curtain call—but most theatre thefts happen when many people are about and none of the perpetrators are strangers. You are well advised to leave your valuables at home. If you must bring things of value into the theatre, leave them with the stage manager. Typically, the stage manager will make the rounds of dressing rooms at half-hour and collect "valuables"—the watch you used to get to the theatre on time and the money you will require to get you home again. These will be stored under lock and key until the end of the performance, when they will be returned to you. Sometimes it takes longer for stage management to get your valuables back to you than it takes you to get into street clothes, and you may be tempted to skip this safeguard. You do so at your own peril. Some actors who do a lot of national tours travel with a "safe-hangar" (you'll see them advertised in those magazines the airlines have in the seat pockets). It locks to the clothes rack, can be opened only with a key, and the key can be kept on your person throughout the performance. And it's a safe way to keep valuables in your hotel room as well.

Respect your fellow actor's sound tolerance. You like to talk loud and laugh and flirt with the juvenile in the next dressing room? Fine, except that you're driving the gal on your right to distraction. Many actors like a dressing room to be comparatively quiet. Not a library or a morgue, but not a high-school locker room either. Try to get a sense of your roommates' attitudes and respect them.

Lastly, many actors have superstitions and can't abide singing or whistling in the dressing room. I once saw an actor rise in red-faced fury and threaten to punch out a young man who was whistling quietly to himself as he applied his eyeliner. There is no accounting for the tensions many actors feel prior to a performance, so you must be considerate. Complaints are commonly lodged against whistling, singing, raucous laughter, obscenities, and uttering lines from *Macbeth*.

* * * * *

The stage manager gives calls over the loudspeaker, or by coming around to the dressing rooms: "Fifteen minutes," "Ten minutes to places," "Five minutes, everyone," "Three minutes, everybody, three minutes," "Places, please, places. This is your call to places." It's time to work. Time to do your job. And your job requires you to give your best effort at each performance. Indeed, your contract stipulates quite precisely that you are obliged to duplicate your original effort at all subsequent performances. Your lines and line readings, your blocking and gestures, your interpretation and timing, your relationships and rhythm—yes, even your costumes and makeup must all remain as consistent as your craft makes possible. If you change your performance inadvertently, the PSM will give you notes, and if you don't respond, he'll call a rehearsal to "take out the improvements." Neither you nor your fellow actors will want to come to the theatre for that rehearsal, so pay attention to the notes you receive. If you're continuing your creative work on a role and you find something new you want to try, go to the PSM first and discuss it with him. If it doesn't affect another actor's performance, he may tell you to go ahead and try it, and he may let you incorporate it into your performance from then on if he likes it. But it's the PSM's decision.

If your change does affect another actor, he may discuss it with that person or he may call a brief rehearsal for the two of you before he lets you try your new approach in performance. The PSM's job is to keep the production vital, and he'll probably give you the OK if your change will pump energy into it. But the PSM's job is also to keep the production just the way the director left it, and if your change will distort the show, he'll reject it. Once the show opens, the PSM becomes the arbiter of performances and his word is final.

It takes great concentration to keep your performance at peak level, and in a long run where repetition becomes numbing or in a repertory situation where you're exhausted from performing one show at night and rehearsing another by day, you can lose your concentration. When that happens, you might forget a line or go "dry." Whenever that happens to you, and it will, you have only yourself to blame. You may be skilled at ad-libbing your way out of the situation, or you may be skilled at taking a prompt from the wings, but in either case you'll be sweating, your performance will suffer, and you'll have betrayed your commitment to the Fat Lady. I recall going "dry" in a performance of *Dear Liar*, the two-person play based on the letters of George Bernard Shaw and Mrs. Patrick Campbell. There's no dialogue in the play, merely the exchange of written correspondence, spoken out loud. So there's no easy way to ad-lib and no good way the other performer can help you. One night I went dry; my mind raced in search of the correct line; my eye shot across to the actress, imploring her help, but there wasn't anything she could do; then I looked into the wings where the stage manager—my hope for salvation and a prompt—was flat on his back, sleeping. Panic. Finally, the actress started speaking; she simply jumped to her next speech/letter and the performance lurched forward, leaving the attentive audience more than a bit confused by the gap my "dry" had created. Not my finest hour!

Most productions don't have a prompter, and most actors prefer to work their own way out of the occasional problem that arises because prompters sometimes cause more problems than they solve. There's the tale, attributed to John Barrymore, of the moment in mid-performance when a silence fell on stage as an actor forgot his line. A low whisper from the wings. Nothing on stage. A low mumble from the wings. Still silence on the stage. Finally, from the wings, the very clear voice of the prompter gave the line so that most of the audience could hear it and Barrymore turned to the wings and replied, "We know the line, dear, but who says it?"

Just as poor concentration may make you may miss your lines, so it can make you may miss your entrance. You must protect against this, and the easiest way is to build some exercise or preparation that takes its cue from a line of dialogue some sixty seconds before your entrance into your performance rhythm. Say, for example, you're playing the French Ambassador who will bring the tennis balls to the English King Henry in the second scene of Shakespeare's *Henry V.* Henry is asked if you should be admitted to his presence, and he replies that he must first hear the advice of his counselors. If you take that mention of your imminent entrance as a cue to concentrate on your given circumstances—to imagine the waiting room, to rehearse your message to the king—then you'll have to be in the wings to hear the onstage line, you'll ensure you're in place for your entrance, and you'll nearly preclude missing an entrance. Nearly, I say, because it's possible to be in place and still miss. I was in the wings chatting with an actor during that passion play in Hollywood when I looked on stage and realized the man I was talking with had missed his entrance and that the actors on stage had been looking toward the wings and sweating for about a dozen improvised lines. I turned to my companion. "My god, Jack, you're on!" He smiled at me. "How'm I doing?" and calmly turned and walked into the scene. It must be one of the oldest gags in the business, but it was new to me that night and I let out a sputtering, gasping laugh that must have sounded to the audience like someone in the wings was having a seizure.

Pranks are forbidden! Your job is to act well, not to try to make someone else act poorly. You owe the audience your best work and not your scorn. If you pull a prank, the Fat Lady will think as little of you as you apparently think of yourself. You will hear many stories of the "funny" pranks actors have pulled. Enjoy the stories, but don't add to them. There's the apprentice actor who had to run on stage in a production of *Henry V* to summon the French nobles to battle with the line, "The English are embattled, you French peers." Backstage he had joked about substituting a "qu" for the "p" that begins that final word. He repeated his backstage joke so often that one night he blurted out the wrong line on stage, and the French Constable fluffed his next line. The apprentice spent the rest of the evening apologizing to everyone in the cast.

And then there's the well-known tale of the time the phone rang on a Broadway stage at a point in the action when no phone cue was planned. After the third ring, the actors couldn't ignore it. The husband picked up the phone. "Hello? Yes? Oh, I see. My dear," holding out the phone, "it's for you."

And then there's the time I was doing the Inspecting Officer in a summer stock production of *No Time for Sergeants*. The action called for me to enter the latrine and inspect the toilets the hero had lovingly cleaned. From one to the next, in proper military fashion, I was to approach, bend over from the waist and look searchingly into the bottom of the toilet. Toilet number four revealed an 8x10 glossy of myself looking up at me. For some unknown reason I didn't break up. In character, I straightened up, turned to my guide and remarked, "Particularly interesting that one." He turned upstage and broke up. Later we laughed about it. But we were both guilty of breaking the most sacred trust of the theatre—the trust of the actor and the audience. I tell the tale now with some amusement, but more out of guilt. The Fat Lady was not amused.

The final line of the performance is spoken and the lights fade to black. The audience applauds and it is time for your curtain call. You may love curtain calls, but there are some actors who feel uneasy without their characters to hide behind and don't like to present their naked selves before the audience. Others have a sense of false modesty that argues that their work doesn't merit applause. Still others are so arrogant that they feel the audience should be moved to silence, not applause, by their work. Or that a curtain call intrudes on the aesthetic experience of the performance. Regardless of the reason, they don't want to do a curtain call and, therefore, they do it badly. That is all unforgivable, self-indulgent nonsense!

The audience expects a curtain call. Since it's paying for this event, and one part of what it's paying for is the curtain call, you have an obligation to perform it with the same professional seriousness you apply to all other portions of your job. The director directs the call. She dictates your blocking, your tempo, your mood, and your characterization (do you take your bow as "yourself" or as your character?). Is it a joyous call in which you whoop as you stampede on? Or a stately and formal one in which you don't bow but merely walk into place and soberly stand as the lights dim again? Whatever, follow your directions. Play an action: to acknowledge the audience's applause. Curtain calls normally require you to move swiftly and with great precision. Don't talk to your neighbor, wink at a friend in the audience, show your contempt for your performance or the audience, or begin taking off your costume or your makeup. Respect your work and the audience sufficiently to do the call well. It is the final image the audience takes away with it. Do you want people to tell their friends to buy tickets so that you can continue to get your weekly paycheck? Then leave them with an image of your best professional manners. Do the curtain call with precision and energy.

Show's over. Time to leave the theatre? First you must strike your costume. Hang it up neatly and report any problems to the wardrobe department. Now strike your makeup. There are few breaches of professional behavior more obviously amateurish than leaving the theatre with your makeup still on or your hair still grayed from the white shoe polish you've applied to make you look old. Of course you want to leave swiftly, to join your friends or your guests and to get to the bar for a rejuvenating drink. But plan into your daily work pattern the time necessary to strike your makeup. Shampoo your hair, if necessary. If you were a mechanic who worked around and under cars all day, you would scrub off the oil and grease before joining friends for dinner. Well, acting is just another job that gets grease all over you, and it's wise to clean up before you leave the job. If you want people to admire you because you're an actor, act well, and they'll come to see your work. But don't advertise your profession to them in restaurants and bars. Those are not the places for you to seek the strokes your ego needs. Save your acting for the stage.

Time to leave the theatre? Almost. Check the callboard for messages. You may be called for a photo session, an understudy rehearsal, or a costume fitting. Whatever is on the callboard, you're responsible for it. It must be your last stop on the job each day.

Opening Night

The opening is the most important performance you will give, and you must focus all your energies on doing it well. The director will bring the entire production to a peak so it is "right on the night." To your surprise, that may mean he will call a line run-through or even a full dress rehearsal on the afternoon before opening—in order to dissipate the unwanted rush of adrenalin that opening-night excitement can produce. You may want to do something different that afternoon, but the director knows best. The director will attend to the directing; you attend to your acting.

Make certain you have rested well and that you are operating on real—rather than nervous—energy. Attend to all the details of your social life in advance so that you don't spend the final hours flapping about on tangential business and wearing yourself out. If you need a particular dress for the opening night party, get it days in advance. If you have tickets to deliver to your opening-night guests, do so well in advance. If you have presents or cards to buy for people, do so before the final day. Opening-night day ought to be lived as though it were any other performance day, and the daily work pattern you've established ought to remain unbroken so that you can arrive at the moment in peak condition.

In many companies, opening-night gifts are a common ceremony. Some actors give a token gift to everyone working the show—from star to doorman. Others give to their close friends only. Others give nothing. You may do whatever you wish, but be careful not to offend anyone. If you give a split of champagne to an old friend of yours, will that unnerve the actor who shares his dressing room and who has received nothing? Theatre people are cloyingly sentimental about opening nights and opening-night gifts, and the best guideline to your behavior I can offer is this: all or nothing. Either give a card and/or token gift to every-one, or give nothing. If you want to give a gift to a special few friends, do so outside of the theatre. Avoid creating an awkward scene. Actors arriving to their dressing tables on opening night can be very much like eight-year-olds in school on Valentine's Day. The quantity of cards each receives becomes important. The quantity of people who profess to love them is of more moment than the quality of that love.

Quite recently, a new practice has developed. Someone in the company—the Equity deputy or the stage manager—will post a note saying that anyone who wishes to do so is encour-aged to contribute the money that they would have spent on opening-night cards or gifts in the company's name to the Equity Fights Aids fund. This worthy cause is of and for the theatre, and, if you make a contribution, you will have met your opening-night obligations in a manner that helps the profession. The Fat Lady would approve.

Now give the best performance you can.

Now celebrate. Begin by giving and accepting the congratu-lations that the company shares. At the inevitable party, be sup-portive, congratulatory, and cheery. Remember, everyone is as scared of the impending reviews as you are, and you all need to help buoy each other up. Have a good time, but remember you have a show the next day, so don't drink yourself into an oblivion from which you can't return in time for tomorrow's half-hour.

Now wait for the reviews.

Reviews

It is a sad reality of our commodity-oriented society that theatre reviews assert the influence they do. It is irritating to realize that audiences will respect the "consumer report" of a single journalist who may have shockingly little training in or sensitivity for the theatre. It is deplorable that a so-so review from a powerful critic can lead a producer to close a Broadway show after only one performance. It is a shameful reflection upon our public that they will heed the 300-word opinion of an unqualified reviewer and not their own responses. Yet the sad reality remains: reviews influence the size of our audiences.

In a commercial venture, a show can close after one night if it is badly reviewed or run for three years if it is given raves. In an institutional theatre, the reviews will have a less dramatic impact; the show will have its scheduled run, regardless—but the size of the audience and (almost inexplicably) their enthusiasm will fall off it that reviewer doesn't like what he sees.

It is essential for you to judge your judges. Who is writing the review? Some major cities have perceptive, informed, and literate critics. In most cities, most reviewers are imperceptive, uninformed, and illiterate. This charge is made only because I've read reviews in dozens of cities in several countries over thirty years— and also because I've taught dramatic and theatrical criticism for a dozen or so years. I offer more than a sour-grapes opinion here.

Take for example, the instance I came upon recently of a young journalist who wrote in a very large American city about a production of Ibsen's *Ghosts*: "When Ibsen wrote 'Ghosts' as a novel, it was deemed controversial and took a long time before it was allowed on bookshelves, let alone on stage. 'Ibsen wrote his stories in book form,' (the producer) Gandy said, 'and then if theater companies wanted to perform them, they would adapt the books into plays.'" I wasn't involved with this production in any way, but the poor writing and the entirely incorrect information prompted me to write to the newspaper's editor:

> You have my sympathy in that you are obliged to retain on your staff persons who are underqualified to write about the subjects they are occasionally assigned.
>
> I don't know which is more depressing to those of us who wish to educate the public in the realm of theatre, a theatrical producer who doesn't know that the great Norwegian playwright Henrik Ibsen did not write novels or an

under-educated journalist who also doesn't know. I refer to
Lori Buttar's column "Seldom produced Ibsen play comes to
S.L." in yesterday's Sunday *Tribune*.

A very sweet girl, Miss Buttars, but not really knowl-
edgeable enough to write in a public forum.

Both these well-intentioned persons should read a book
sometime. In this case, Michael Meyer's biography *Ibsen*
would be a good place to start.

Yours in curmudgeonly good spirits,

I've left in the names, to finger the guilty, and I hope you'll
agree that no actor should heed that young journalist's review.

Sadly, too many of the reviews that appear in daily newspapers around the world are as foolish as this one from *The Advertiser*, the major daily of Adelaide, Australia.

OLD-STYLE THEATRE

The Murray Park Performance Group last night staged
one of its largest productions—Sophocles' "Oedipus Rex."

As the play opened, the chorus, representing the people
of Thebes infested with the plague, dragged themselves about
the stage and through the audience screaming for Oedipus to
help them.

In true Greek-theatre style, the play was performed on
the steps in the centre of the College Playhouse, surrounded
by the audience.

John Castle interpreted Oedipus on many levels—the ques-
tioning of his birth, the disillusioned discovery of his background, and the final banishment from Theban society because he was found guilty of the murder of his father so he
could marry his mother.

The legend on which the play is based is old, strange and
implausible, but nevertheless the Group did well to adhere to
the dramatically right conclusion, as written by Sophocles,
and not to introduce various neat and unconvincing "morals"
that people have tried to import into his play.

Miri Zlatner

As an actor, you know too painfully well that your job, your
career, and your ego are subject to the remarks of the reviewers.
Attacks on your ego can be handled by judging your judge. Do
you really care what someone like Miri Zlatner thinks of your
work? Or Lori Buttars? Are their opinions any more valid than

your Aunt Bessie's? The best way to deal with reviews is to ignore them. Don't read them. Don't let people read them to you. Don't dignify them with your attention. Unless you believe the critics are qualified professionals whose remarks might give you insight into your work, you are better off disregarding their existence entirely. Indeed, it is now standard practice in America's LORT theatres for the management to prohibit the posting of any reviews, but to provide the actors with packets of all the show's reviews after the run has ended. That way the actors may read them or not, as they desire, and may use the good words when seeking their next job and not let their performances be affected by the bad words. It is pleasing to note how few actors pay much attention to the reviews. I recall the late Michael O'Sullivan remarking acidly that he knew the good and bad parts of his performance and didn't need some refugee from the Obits Department to tell him his job. Attacks on your ego are painful, but you can avoid them or dismiss them.

Attacks on your employment can be combated in a different manner. If a production or a performer has been panned and if the show is not closing as a direct result, the company has an obligation to itself, its investors (or administrators if it's an institutional theatre), and its audience to give the best possible performance day after day. The Fat Lady requires it. If you believe the critics and lose enthusiasm for your work, your performance will indeed become what the reviewers alleged—boring. But if you attack your work with energy and commitment, you may find that the audience does not share the critics' views and that the word-of-mouth on your production may produce more calls to the box office than the journalist's column can discourage. The best way to deal with poorly written reviews is to denigrate them swiftly and then disregard them. Don't engage in lengthy gripe sessions with your friends. Don't dissect the reviews for the inanities of their ideas or the imprecision of their grammar. Don't question the function, literacy, or parentage of the reviewer. Just say firmly and briefly that you disregard the review and the reviewer and that you have better things to do with your time than to dwell on such banalities, and one of the better things is to get on with your job. Then proceed to do so, despite all supplications to join in the general lamentations. Your clear-minded commitment to your job can do more to improve company morale than any reasoned disputation with or about a reviewer.

Attacks on your own work are harder to ignore, but you can do so if you will just ACT WELL! The reviewer may be unqualified to judge your work, but you are equally unqualified to judge his. On rare occasions, an actor or group of actors will foolishly engage a journalist in printed debate over his review of their work. Such an action is foolish for two reasons. First, actors are not qualified critics. You are not necessarily educated in dramatic theory, criticism, and aesthetics. Nor are you experienced in literary or journalistic writing. In short, if you write a letter to the editor, you reduce yourself to the level of the very writer you complain about. Second, you never saw the show he reviewed. You never entered the theatre, sat in your seat amid a paying audience, and experienced the two hours' traffic on the stage. All you know is what you imagine the show to be like, what you hope it is like, and what you intend the audience to experience. But the audience may have been every bit as bored as the critic claimed. Or they may have been in total disagreement with the critic. Or several critics may have been in fundamental disagreement with one another. But one thing is true—you never witnessed the event.

But wait a minute, you say, you just quoted from a letter to the editor that *you* wrote. True, but I was not involved in that production and I was not defending my work. And there's more to that story. The editor must have spoken to the young journalist because she telephoned with a very polite apology, which I accepted with grace. And then I wrote her this letter:

> Permit me to share with you the stance I take as an old curmudgeon. I believe journalists and reviewers have every right to express any opinion whatsoever on the work of those of us who are hubristic enough to place our work before the public. You will never find me objecting to any opinion expressed about the theatre in the press. As I have directed plays and given performances that have been roundly panned, I have tempered the rod of my position in the fire of experience.

But I do hold the press accountable for facts. If I read that George Bush is the Secretary of State, I write to the editor. If I read that Ibsen wrote novels, I write to the editor. There are not a lot of areas in which I feel competent as an expert, but theatre is one. As an educator, I will always blow the whistle when I read misinformation in a public forum.

In this vein, one thing that angers me extremely is the misidentification of an artist's name in print. If a reviewer gets the name of an actor wrong, it is damaging to that actor's livelihood. Actors have a tough enough time making a living as it is, without the added impediment of a careless mistake from a journalist. I have not encountered this in Salt Lake City but I have seen it often enough elsewhere for me to name it in my list of "red flags" that drive me to the typewriter to express my displeasure.

When I wrote about your *Ghosts* column, I was wearing my educator's hat, not my artist's hat. If I can educate you, along with your readers, I am doing my job. So, I thank you for your apology . . . and I will write you a supportive fan letter whenever first I am able.

Cordially,

When your own work is attacked, what can you do? If you've made the mistake of reading the reviews, extract any comments on your own work and consider their validity. Once in a while the reviewer will help you. If he says your accent is unbelievable, go find a dialect coach. And if that professional agrees with the critic, work to correct that flaw in your performance. If the review says you are dull, re-think your performance beat-by-beat to consider if you're making choices that are both true and imaginative. If the review says that you're not funny enough and a re-reading of the play convinces you that the character is not intended as a comic one, disregard that criticism. And if the critic is patently incorrect on other remarks, ignore him again. Critics can be wrong. They can be unqualified.

Critic bashing is a lot of fun for us actors. We are so frequently hurt by what they say about us that it is fun to get a bit of our own back and to show them up for what they truly are. You've probably heard the definition of the critic as the eunuch in the harem who watches the trick done each night, but knows he can never do it himself. Well, here's a true tale about critics that you might enjoy.

Many LORT theatre managements try to find ways to upgrade the quality of reviewing in their communities and to raise the consciousness of the audience about the caliber of the reviewing they should demand from the local critics. While I was in Virginia, I was keen to do that. TheatreVirginia hosted a series of "talk-backs," informal Sunday afternoon discussions that we invited subscribers to attend, and one of these was on the subject of reviewing. We invited the critics from the newspapers, television, and radio to join us, on stage, and explain how they saw their function and responsibility, and what criteria and standards they used when writing about a production, and then to participate in an open-ended question-and-answer session among themselves and the audience. Predictably, some presented themselves well and others poorly; some had a clear vision of their standards and obligations and others had none. Well, one of the chaps who volunteered to participate was the reviewer from an outlying small town's newspaper who had been writing about local productions for some years and who was blind. Really. He came to the productions on his wife's arm and with his seeing-eye dog at his side. He sat on a side aisle seat so that his wife could quietly whisper to him about what she saw. Her whispering was not too great a nuisance, but the dog was because (sweet dog though it may have been) it passed gas frequently. Over the course of each season, we would have requests for a change of location from subscribers whose seats were close to the dog. Most folks didn't know the man was a critic and were probably happy to see a blind man at the theatre. You may think it ludicrous for a blind man to review a visual art like theatre, but there you have it: life imitating metaphor. At the "talk-back," I introduced the critics as they came out on stage, and the last one in line was the blind critic. His dog preceeded him onto the stage, and he needed help to find his chair. Many in the audience thought this was a vulgar and tasteless joke that I was playing— that I was offering my snide opinion of the critics on the stage by likening them to a blind man. If Tom Stoppard had written a blind critic into his funny play *The Real Inspector Hound* to join his characters Moon and Birdboot, the audience would have howled with laughter at the ludicrousness of the conceit. But the truth was too ludicrous for them to accept. They couldn't believe what they saw. As I told one of the theatre's trustees later, if there was a rude joke being perpetrated, it was on the newspaper's readers and not on the audience, and it was by the critical fraternity and not by me. The "talk-back" went smoothly, once everyone was seated, and I believe critics and audience alike learned something from the experience, but the most "theatrical" part of the event was the enduring image of a row of critics, seated in chairs, with the four-footed one on the end punctuating his assessment of the afternoon's discussion by passing gas.

The only assessment of your work that matters is the audience's. If the audience believes you, likes you, applauds you, you're doing your job well. If the audience likes you, you'll be hired again. Your reputation depends much more on the assessments that audiences and producers make of you than the one critics write of you. If you behave professionally and do your job as well as you can, you can dismiss the critics. I was being interviewed for an acting job once and the producer wanted to see my portfolio. "Do you have any reviews?" he asked. "Sure," I replied, "but you won't be surprised to discover that I only keep the nice ones."

The Audience

How do you feel about your audience? Is it your father from whom you seek approval? your mistress from whom you want love? your enemy from whom you fear violence? your judge from whom you expect punishment? or your partner with whom you seek communion? Each actor has a particularized feeling for an audience, and that feeling will lead each of you to particularized behavior. Do you disdain your audience because you fear its judgment, and do you sneer during curtain calls as a result? Do you lust after your audience and, as a result, do you hang around the lobby until half-hour in the hopes of being recognized, and do you hang around the stage door following a performance in the hopes of being congratulated? Are you afraid of your audience and do you bolt from the theatre when the curtain comes down and scurry home to the protection of your apartment? Whatever your relationship to your audience, you must understand its expectations of you, and you must behave accommodatingly.

In performance, the audience expects your best. It doesn't wish to see you fumble your lines, break character over a joke, or "phone in" your matinee performance. The audience has paid money and taken the trouble to come to the theatre to watch you be what it wishes it were. You must fulfill its need for fantasy. That is an unwritten part of the contract that is made when a ticket is purchased. A portion of that finest work requires you to feel emotions yourself—you must cry when your character cries and you must laugh when your character laughs. Through the miracle of *mimesis*, the audience shares with you the emotions that you have as an actor, as you both become the fictionalized character. A communion is expected between you, and the medium for that communion is the character. You must both believe in it for the contract to be honored, the audience gratified, the communion reached. You will gain from the spirit and energy the audience invests in the character as it will gain from the spirit and energy you invest. In this happy instance, the audience's need is your need. Its fulfillment is your fulfillment.

The curtain call is the mutual acknowledgment of that joint need and joint fulfillment. It is the ceremonial affirmation of the communion that was sought. You bow to the audience in thanks for its contribution, and it applauds yours. Like many ceremonies, this theatrical one is frequently empty, a vestigial reminder of what the theatre has been, can be. A bored audience claps out of a memory of previous fulfillments and a politeness supported only by habit. The actor bows out of civility and tradition. But on occasions, the ceremony is alive again and celebrates a communion that both actor and audience have relished. At the end of the Royal Shakespeare Company's *Nicholas Nickleby,* the audience and actors arose spontaneously in mutual applause and the actors moved out into the auditorium and thanked the audience. There were no boundaries between performer and spectator. Both had loved the experience, shared in it deeply, and participated in its creation. Both had found a ceremony through which to thank the other. It happened to me once. And maybe once is enough in each actor's life. I was performing Jerry in Albee's *Zoo Story* under Gordon Heath's masterful direction. One performance was in the chapel of an old monastery in Royaumont, about sixty miles north of Paris. The audience was made up entirely of French students of American literature. At the end of the show, following the one scheduled curtain call, the audience began clapping in unison. A steady, rhythmic, incessant clapping. I didn't know what to make of it. It frightened me. The clapping grew louder, more insistent. I looked across to the actor who played Peter as he stood in the opposite wing. He smiled, knowing the French custom. When a French audience truly likes a performance, it will clap in unison until additional bows are taken. It's like an Italian opera audience demanding an encore following a favorite aria. Slowly, fearfully, I came out on stage and joined Peter. We bowed. The clapping continued. We bowed again. I remember I was crying when we came off stage. What was shared at that moment is what the theatre can be and what an audience has a right to expect from each performance. We all know it happens rarely, but we must all work towards it. The curtain call is the shared moment in which we can jointly say thank you for the event.

Away from the theatre, the audience expects you to be a member of its community. When you leave your job, return to your home, and go to your neighborhood shops, you are just another worker. Your work may make you a public figure, recognizable to many, but you are also a part of the social fabric of your community. And you are needed. You help the image of the theatre, and you add to the worth of your community when you put aside your defenses and those pretenses that separate you from your neighbors: when you become a "citizen-actor."

Paradoxically, your audience expects you to be forever a part of its fantasies, forever the character they saw you portray, forever the "artiste"—that romantic outsider. This is made clear when you consider the phenomena of groupies, autograph hounds, star gazers, celebrity seekers, and wannabes. These folks are the avant-garde, the exponents of a general public interest, those who act publicly on the urges that more timid members of the public repress. Your behavior to this part of your audience is an important aspect of your life as an actor—an important part of how an actor behaves.

I was standing with Richard Chamberlain one evening on the steps of a newly dedicated theatre in the small college town where we had gone to school a decade earlier. It was intermission of a student performance of Marlowe's *Dr. Faustus.* A small crowd of fans clustered about Chamberlain, seeking his autograph. How did he feel about all that, I asked. How did he feel about those intrusions on his privacy that stardom demanded. "It's all a portion of my job," he answered. "I earn my living from these kind people. I need them. I'm flattered they know me." I can't recall hearing a clearer explanation of the actor's obligations to his audience than Chamberlain gave that evening.

The public's admiration is not reserved for stars of Chamberlain's magnitude. Actors in school plays are greeted by strangers as they walk to their classes. Actors at summer festivals are introduced to the druggist's children when they go shopping. At first, you will feel awkward, embarrassed because you are being accorded attention you find disproportionate to your accomplishment, and piqued that your privacy has been infringed. But you must learn to behave correctly in these circumstances. You need these kind people, and they expect you to fulfill their needs as well. Be polite, modest, and warm. Sign an autograph for the child who asks. It is a portion of your job.

For audiences, the theatre is a magical moment in which make-believe becomes truth and the fruits of its imaginations are given physical reality. In the anonymity that a darkened auditorium creates, each individual adult merges into the collective child that is the audience—a child who willingly embraces the lies of the stage. In that magical time, the actor is a wizard, an alchemist, a shaman who makes that mystery happen. When the lights come up at the show's ending and the child diffuses into a crowd of individual adults, the magic has a residual influence. The adult never knew you, though the child knew your character. The adult understands that you exist, knows you are not your character, but as he's never met you, he only sees and recognizes your character, which he knows as an adult does not exist. He carries this ambiguity with him from the theatre, and he is confronted once again with his paradox when he meets you in his adult world. Are you Al Pacino or Michael Corleone? And, equally important, does he want to talk to you or to your character? Soap-opera fans only want to talk to your character. They believe in the fiction of your show so fully that they want to advise you what the villain is going to do to you next week. But more circumspect members of your public feel puzzled when they meet you. You can help them through their puzzlement and get yourself out of a bizarre conversation if you consider in advance how to behave in such a circumstance.

Make the division between self and character clear immediately. Ask, "Have you seen me in anything else?" Or offer remarks like, "I found that role a rewarding one, but let me tell you what I'm working on now." Such opening gambits will make it evident that he's talking to you and not to your character, but that you are pleased he remembered your performance. But if you meet one of those who can't make the separation, you can only smile, be polite, and be brief.

Your Other Job

The show opened, the reviews were raves, and now you're settling in for a long run. For what may be the only time in your career you have a reasonable guarantee of a paycheck each week for months to come. And all for working only about twenty-five hours a week (matinees included)—and most of those hours in the evening. Time to take it easy. To reap the benefits of security and glory that your hard years of preparation have earned you.

Within two weeks you'll be bored to distraction! You'll have wearied all your friends with tales of your triumphs, and you'll have seen every film and museum exhibit in town. Now what do you do? Well, *before* you had this glorious job, you spent most of your time looking for work. Indeed, many actors will tell you that the only career they really have, the only thing they can say that they have done for years and years, is "look for work." "Working" is a disruption of your established routine—and you feel disoriented. Well, the all-consuming rehearsal period is over, your show has opened, you have time on your hands once again, so what do you do? You get another job.

If you're doing stock or if you're working at a resident theatre, you already have another job. An acting job. While you do your eight performances a week, you spend your days rehearsing the next show. In the standard LORT contract, management may work you up to fifty hours a week. That means you'll have your one day a week off—entirely to yourself. But you'll have rehearsals or matinees on each of the week's remaining six.

If you're not with a resident company, if you're on a production contract for a Broadway show or at a LORT theatre for one show only, you've got some twenty-five hours a week to fill, and you'll want to fill them constructively. You can take a job to earn money, you can seek additional acting jobs, or you can invest your time in the job of self-development—improving your skills and advancing your career.

You may need to take a job to earn money. "But I'm earning a handsome weekly check for my acting," you say? Not really. It's probable you're earning minimum or not much above it. At the time of this writing, Equity minimum for a Broadway production contract is $900 a week. After deductions, your take-home will be about $625. At a LORT "B" company (and actors work more weeks under LORT contracts than under Production contracts), your minimum is $505 a week—for a take-home of about $330. By the time you pay your rent, buy your groceries, and pay your miscellaneous medical and clothing bills, you're broke! If you're careful, you can just barely get by on what you earn. But you won't have anything left over to pay back the debts you incurred looking for the job you now have. And you won't have anything left over to save against the day—not too distant—when your show will close and you'll be back pounding the pavements, knocking on doors, and checking your phone messages.

Since you'll be available Monday through Friday (with the exception of Wednesday afternoon for the matinee), you can probably get a decent job. Actors commonly take jobs that permit them a lot of mobility, so they are free to shift if an audition comes up or another acting job develops. Typical jobs include waiting tables, cab driving, sales clerking, substitute teaching, bartending, and word-processing—especially through temporary agencies. Many young actors in New York will tell you the most valuable class they took during their years in acting school was *word-processing*! Depending on your skills, you can earn much more on your "job-job" than you can from your acting job. And if you're practical, you can bank one entire check each week and build some security against the long hot summer when you fail to get an acting job.

If money pressures are not too great or if you're a gambler and like to live on the edge of financial ruin, you may bypass the security of a "job-job" and choose to seek a second acting job. For the most part, that will mean short engagements in front of a camera—the odd day's work on a film, a week's work on a TV soap, a modeling gig, or the much-sought-after commercial. If your performance in the legit show brings you good notices, or if you have a scene that presents you well (no matter how brief it is), you may try to use it as a springboard to additional acting jobs. It is nice to make the rounds of casting directors and leave invitations for them to come see your work. It is nice to mail out a postcard with a snipe announcing your production angled across your picture. The fact that you're employed gives you an edge over all your out-of-work competitors, although it also puts constraints on your availability. Happily, most film and modeling work is somewhat flexible, and frequently schedules can be made compatible. I once performed two different plays in one day and crammed in the filming of a commercial between them. And my experience is not unique.

You may choose to spend your free time advancing your career by improving your skills. You may enroll in classes to develop your singing, dancing, or acting skills. You may use your present job to attract an agent (and that can be a time-consuming pursuit). You may turn your time and energies to other artistic vocations. Have you always wanted to find time to complete enough canvases for an exhibition of your landscapes? prepare the demo you need to secure a recording contract? have the time to write your novel? Now you have it. Marian Seldes's character was killed at the end of Act One of her long Broadway run in *Deathtrap* and she spent her second acts writing a book. You have the time. Do you have the discipline?

The only thing you should not do with your free time is sit around and vegetate. Remember, time is our eternal enemy—in a winged chariot at our backs—and we must run without stop if we are to breast the tape in our race for success.

Touring

The romance of touring is one of the myths of the theatre. On late-night TV you'll see Jack Carson films about the joys of the vaudeville circuit. Old actors' biographies will be filled with colorful tales of Des Moines and Duluth. At school you'll learn of Molière's ten years in the provinces. You may pass a wintry weekend reading Mary Renault's *The Mask of Apollo* and delight in the descriptions of provincial tours in ancient Greece. And over a double Scotch sour some friend will boast of his recent sexual conquests on a bus-and-truck tour of a ninety-minute version of *Oklahoma!* as it wended its way through college towns in the snowbelt of upstate New York. And like all myths, there's a foundation of truth to it. Touring can be a rich and rewarding experience. It can also be a lonely, back-breaking exercise in artistic and economic futility.

If you get work as an actor, if you're one of the few members of Equity who makes a marginal annual income, sometime or other you'll go out on tour. If you're lucky, you'll go with the first national company of a recent Broadway hit. You'll play extended runs in major cities, travel by plane or train, stop in first-class hotels, and live almost entirely on your per diem while you stick your actual paycheck in your bank account. Such good things *do* come an actor's way. But more likely, particularly in the beginning of your career, you'll stick your battered suitcase underneath the chartered bus and climb aboard for a smoke-filled journey from Trenton to Camden—and you'll stay in the Bates Motel. Or worse, you'll sortie out of New York daily, by careening station wagon, to three separate high-school auditoriums. Wherever you're headed, there are some guidelines to behavior that can help make your tour a pleasant one.

The company manager will supervise your tour. He will accompany you from town to town and will be the producer's representative with the traveling show. He will attend to all travel arrangements, all hotel accommodations, and all personnel and financial matters. He'll get you your weekly check, arrange for a bank that will cash it, oversee all public-relations calls, get you a doctor when you have an ache and a dentist when you have a throb, and he'll arbitrate between you and another actor when you give each other a pain. He'll arrange social receptions for you following performances. In short, he's your man on the bus.

You will not normally have any choice about travel arrangements. The company will travel together on common carriers. If a star is aboard, he may have contracted separate arrangements (first-class on the plane or a private room on the train), since some are more equal than others. But you should not expect to make separate arrangements. If there is a day or two off in the middle of a tour and you wish to spend it away from the company (to visit a relative or to go skiing), the company manager will listen to your desires. But his job is to ensure that you are at the theatre each time, ready to perform, so don't get angry if he denies your request for special treatment. He's only doing his job.

Typically, the company manager will give you instructions about the quantity of luggage you may take with you. That is, the amount the management will pay to have shipped. You ought to travel as light as you can, since you don't want to spend your time, muscle, and money shifting unnecessary boxes and bags from bus to hotel to theatre to bus. While you may be on the road for an extended time and may want lots of changes of clothes for the varied occasions you'll experience, be advised against loading yourself down unnecessarily. Remember, in most towns you'll be new to the people you meet, and the same outfit will suffice time after town after time after town. True, your fellow travelers will get to know your wardrobe intimately, but they'll be in the same situation—and you'll know theirs. Besides, if you need a particular item, you can always buy it along the way and mail it home when you no longer need it. The lighter you travel, the happier you'll be. A good idea is to take one large suitcase and one ample shoulder bag. And be certain you can carry *all* of your luggage yourself; otherwise the bellboys and redcaps will earn your salary.

While traveling, you have the responsibility to be where you're instructed to be when you're instructed to be there. True, there'll be a lot of sitting around in bus terminals and hotel lobbies, but those hours are a part of your working week. Don't be the perennial latecomer who angers everyone. As with every other aspect of your working world, promptness is an essential courtesy.

The company manager will arrange your sleeping accommodations, but you may have some choices to make. Do you want to share a room to save money? Do you want a room with a private bath? Do you mind being fifteen minutes from the theatre if you save $10 a day, or does walking home alone in the dark in a strange city frighten you? The company manager may have a variety of accommodations for you to choose from. But all of them will be expensive. Even in cities where you'll play long enough so that a weekly rate can be negotiated, you'll spend an alarming portion of your income on your hotel room. But since you'll spend a lot of time in your room, consider how important it is to you and how much your personal comfort, your frame of mind, and your work on stage will be affected by your choices. Are you, as I am, six foot three, and do you need a king-sized bed? Do cockroaches offend you? Or, are you happy in a YWCA dormitory? Whatever, make your choice wisely. Don't try to save $35 a week and make yourself miserable.

If you are with a tour that will spend many weeks in a particular city, you may be able to make private arrangements once you've arrived. You may want to move out of the hotel (even though a weekly rate makes it affordable and its location makes it convenient) and find accommodations of your own. The company manager may try to help you, but he may know as little about the city as you do, so be prepared to take care of yourself. Here's a good time to use friends. Have you acquaintances in the city? Have you friends in New York who have friends in the city you're playing? Any source of information or advice is welcome. Some cities have social organizations with names like "Friends of the Theatre" whose members will assist you. Or there may be a LORT company in town, and its actors or management may help you. But there are also agencies that help non-theatre people and you can try them: Travelers Aid and The Chamber of Commerce. Also, if the city has a college or university in it, the housing office may be of service. Indeed, many colleges will rent out available dormitory rooms at inexpensive rates on a weekly basis and those are always clean and comfortable—if a bit noisy.

"You are what you eat," goes the old adage. That is never truer than when you're on the road. If you try sampling the epicurean delights of each city you visit, what you'll be is broke. If you try to live on candy bars, sodas, and pizza, what you'll be is fat. If you try to live on "fast food," what you'll be is sick.

If you're on the bus-and-truck tour making one-night stands, you'll discover that finding a place to eat occupies a lot of your waking hours. Hotel food, as a rule, is overpriced. Cafeteria food is bland and depressing. Chinese food is frequently inexpensive and a nice change of pace from the lunch-counter meals that may be your norm. Wherever you eat, try to get some intelligent dietary balance to your meals. Some fresh fruit and an occasional salad may serve to keep your system functioning.

Of course what you really want is a home-cooked meal. If you're adept at meeting people in strange cities, you may be able to wangle your way into their hearts and up to their tables. Good luck. Your alternative is to cook for yourself. Most hotels forbid cooking in their rooms. Most actors cook in their rooms. How to do it? Well, start by being selective of what you cook. Quickly and "smellessly" is the order of the day. An extraordinary ragout with chopped garlic in it may draw the management's attention, but there are less noticeable choices. If the management comes to the door . . . well, you're an actor, aren't you? Let's see that improvisation. Let's see that look of innocence that earned you the acting job in the first place. What will you cook on, you ask? You'll have to carry your equipment in your luggage. An electric frypan is a first-rate substitute for a kitchen range. A picnic basket accommodates all the silver and crockery you might require. You don't want to pack and lug all that unless you're really going to use it, but if you're out on the road for many months, it may prove desirable. I know one actor who constructed a most ingenious electric burner inside what appeared to be a briefcase. He could pack it, carry it, and hide it from the night clerk with remarkable ease.

*   *   *   *   *

The social crucible of a touring company challenges you daily. It is easy to make enemies and have a rotten time. It is easy to become a lonely stranger in a gabbling crowd. It is easy to become a social lion and lose all privacy. No one can provide you with guidelines to the happy life, but there are some questions you can put to yourself at various stops along the route, and the answers you come up with may help you to enjoy your trip.

Are you a part of a social clique? Are there actors on the tour that you like but rarely socialize with? It is likely you'll develop friends on the journey—your roommate, perhaps—but it is limiting if you see only the same, small group all the time. Cliques are divisive, and the morale of the company and the quality of your collective performance may suffer if they become factious. Also, you'll find you're bored if you exchange thoughts and witticisms with only the same, small group day after dreary day. An easy antidote to this is to vary who you sit with. Get on the bus after many have boarded, and pick a seat near someone you haven't spent time with recently. At mealtime, join up with a group you haven't eaten with before. If you establish yourself early on the tour as someone who seeks out a variety of folks to talk with, you can increase your pleasure throughout the weeks you're all together.

Are the sexual or racial lines of the company too sharply drawn? Your social, political, sexual, and racial horizons might be constructively widened on a tour if you will take advantage of the opportunities before you. For once, you may not retreat entirely to the cocoon of your old friends and haunts. You must encounter new places and people; if you will relate to those new folks who share your traveling world, you may enrich your life experience.

Are you enjoying being a tourist? Do you get away from the theatre and the company enough to take advantage of the places you visit? It is easy to grow lazy on a tour and to miss out on the sights that you would otherwise travel miles to see and spend a fortune to visit. If you're in Philadelphia, take in a matinee at the Symphony, visit the Rodin Museum, and see the historical buildings. If you're in Seattle, run up to Vancouver on your day off. If you're in Los Angeles, get out of the bars and off the beach and see the Watts Towers or a bullfight in Tijuana. If you're in Salt Lake City, go on a Thursday evening to hear the Tabernacle Choir rehearse. If you're in Washington, visit Congress in action—it'll be funnier than the comedy you're touring, you can bet on it. In short, take advantage of this once-in-a-lifetime opportunity for a paid tour of faraway places with strange-sounding names. That's the real excitement of touring.

Have you found a daily rhythm that makes you happy? Your schedule probably calls for you to sleep in till mid-morning, eat breakfast at noon, go to the movies in the afternoon, have lunch at dinner time and dinner at midnight. But is your rhythm running you or are you living your life to suit your desires? You *can* get up at 8:00 a.m. if you want to, live the schedule the rest of the world lives, and go to bed shortly after the show comes down. It's up to you to control your world.

Do you enjoy your privacy? Do you have any privacy? If you are with the company too much, you may feel stultified, restless. You must withdraw into yourself regularly. One of the touring actor's greatest challenges is finding the necessary resources within herself to fill the waiting hours that confront her. If you have no such resources, if you are dependent upon others for your fun, if external stimuli like television and card games are your only forms of recreation, you may be uncomfortable on a tour. Tours are filled with hours of waiting—no time for an outing or a formal gathering, just forty-five empty minutes after breakfast and before the bus leaves. Do you know to fill those minutes? The actor who reads is usually the happiest. You'll be startled at the number of books you've always wanted to read that you'll now plunge through.

Are you able to make social contacts outside the company?

On a tour, you will long for a return to a non-theatre life, for conversation about anything other than actors' gossip. If you are comfortable in a cocktail lounge, you'll probably have a place to meet strangers. If you're moderately religious, you may find social contacts through the offices of your church. That Monday evening discussion group may be just what you need to meet someone—and who knows, you might get invited home to dinner. If you're attracted by intellectual environments (or by the attractive men and women who inhabit them), you might find the local college or university a good place to visit. If you drop by the drama department, you'll find you're a celebrity—you're the thing all those students dream of being, a working actor. You'll meet people with common interests who think you're admirable. You'll find out about the good nightspots and cheap restaurants, and you may even engage in a stimulating conversation or two.

But none of these will come to you. You must be the activist, the seeker. You can check into your hotel, eat in its restaurant, walk with your company to the theatre, and retreat to the hotel's television set after the performance. Or you can tour. You can get out and learn about your country, your people, and yourself.

Closing Night

All good things must come to an end. Happily, some bad things come to an end as well. So whether you're closing a turkey before its formal opening or saying farewell to a show that's been your delight and your life for over a year, you know that a life in the theatre is made up of short and intense episodes that all end. Whether happy or sad, these final moments are charged with emotion, and you can reduce your anxieties and discomforts by attending to many details in advance.

You may have business to negotiate with the management in advance of the closing. If you're closing on the road, you must arrange return tickets to your place of origin. The company manager will assist you here. If you're interested in buying some of your costumes, talk to the company manager early so that he has time to explore it with the producer. You might like a dress, a suit, a raincoat, a pair of boots. Well, frequently the producer is happy sell off those items for which he has no further use, and you can get some nice things at bargain rates.

Your final exit from the theatre will be made easier if you cart away all your private belongings before the final show. If you've been in a run that is even two weeks long, you'll find that you have extra street clothes (sweaters, raincoats, umbrellas), books and magazines, souvenirs and totems, and miscellaneous bric-a-brac in your dressing room. Take it home before that final day.

Leave your dressing room in good shape. Hang up your costumes neatly, clean up your makeup, and discard your garbage. Your job may be finished, but there are some members of the company or the theatre staff who still have work to do. Consider them, and show your affection and respect for them through to the final moment.

Tip your dresser! Like others in the service industry—like waiters, cab drivers, and hotel porters—dressers have earned and expect a gratuity. They are paid an insultingly small salary, and your tip helps them pay their rent. How much? A lot depends on how much *you* have been earning. If you get a grand a week, you can afford to be more generous than if you've earned $350. Other considerations include how long your run has been and how much your dresser has done for you. As a rule-of-thumb, actors at LORT companies usually give about $10 a week. A four-week period from first dress rehearsal to closing night would mean a tip of around $40. It's polite to slip your gratuity into an envelop along with a thank-you card and give it to your dresser at the end of the final performance.

Say your farewells. Some of you will be sloppy sentimentalists and cry all over each other's lapels. Others will be lifelong enemies, glad you'll never see one another again. Others will be cool "professionals" and casually walk away from the theatre knowing that another job will lie ahead and that you'll probably run into many of this cast on some future show. However you behave, say your good-bys. Include the stage management and the house crew (or stage-door attendant). And say them briefly. Don't hang around hoping something magical will happen. Don't prolong your gloating over the show's failure or your tears over its final demise. Say "good-by," hope you'll work again, and go.

Well . . . one final stop. Go out onto the darkened stage and silently say good night to the Fat Lady.

BETWEEN ENGAGEMENTS

Acting is your hobby. Your avocation. The thing you do occasionally, when the circumstances permit. Oh, you may believe you're an actor and may tell others you're an actor, but are you? Compare your life as an actor to the life of a doctor, say. Or a fireman. Or any of those who practice what our society calls a profession—a vocation that requires extended training, that deals in social services, that is valued as essential to the well-being of a community, and that is highly remunerated. Ask yourself how much you earn and what proportion of your total earnings comes from your acting. Ask yourself what license you had to secure to become an actor and what standards of competence are required by the acting "profession" (are they comparable to those required of a CPA, for instance?). Ask yourself how much time you spend acting. If you become a pharmacist you'll spend forty hours a week, fifty weeks a year or 2,000 hours a year on the job. If you're lucky as an actor, you may work fifty hours a week fifteen times, or about 750 hours a year. Oh, you may be qualified to be an actor, and you may want to be an actor, but in all probability acting is your hobby. Your avocation. The thing you do occasionally, when the circumstances permit. What do you do with the rest of your life? What do you do "between engagements?"

A portion of your life as an actor is spent preparing to act. The rest is spent in non-theatrical pursuits: earning enough money to live, meeting your obligations as an individual, as a member of a family, or as a citizen of your country. Let's take a look at your life.

Training

Training for acting is a lifelong pursuit. Before you ever embark on an acting career, you must seek some basic training. You're going to need control over your body and voice so you don't bob at the waist and crack into falsetto when you get excited. You must learn to concentrate on what your character is doing so that your eyes don't wander out into the audience when they should be looking at the character stalking you with a knife. You must have a method for recreating physical and emotional states in yourself so that you're not reduced to squeezing onion juice into your eyes when your character is supposed to cry. You must have some method for analyzing a text so you know *why* Hamlet doesn't stab Claudius after you say, "Now might I do it, pat." You must have some ordered methodology for rehearsing so that you don't merely float from one rehearsal to the next, hoping that the director will tell you what to do. You must learn the techniques required on a stage or before a camera so that you can communicate effectively what you think and feel. These are the things you need to learn in basic training.

True, you can announce yourself as an actor without these skills. Thousands do so annually. But they rarely have successful or long careers. The football player turned actor, like Jim Brown, doesn't get hired once his reputation as a football player fades and fans stop buying tickets to see him. Rock stars like Madonna and Sting who venture onto the Broadway stage quickly reveal their inadequacies and are an embarrassment to themselves, to the audience, and even to their fans. Self-announced actors aren't actors. If you are serious about a career in the theatre, if you hope to make acting your profession instead of your hobby, you must have some basic training. There are three common ways to get it: amateur theatre, theatre schools, and private teachers. Let's consider each alternative by imagining three siblings who decide to become actors.

The oldest is Bill, and he falls in love with the theatre while acting in *Our Town* with "The Players Club" at his church. He's getting the most common kind of training for the theatre, but the least good. He's learning by doing, "jumping in the deep end." He'll learn by observing the more experienced folks in the cast, but he'll learn their bad habits along with their good. He'll learn to reach for effects rather than to create truths. He'll learn a set of mannerisms instead of a way to produce behavior. He'll learn some tricks to fool an audience rather than a way to share his experience. Unless he goes beyond what he learns in this sort of experience, Bill's career as an actor will probably peak with "The Players Club."

His sister Barbara sees him in *Our Town* and catches the theatre bug. "I can do better than Bill," she tells her parents. She's just finishing high school and she's trying to decide where to continue her schooling. She talks with the drama teacher at the local college and gets some good advice. She learns that she could go to a conservatory, like the Royal Academy of Dramatic Art in London or the American Conservatory Theatre in San Francisco, or she could major in theatre at any of 200 colleges and universities across the country. She learns that the conservatories probably have the most intensive training but that the universities will provide her with both a broader based education and the option of changing to a different field of study if the theatre bug leaves her after a couple of years. Her advisor gives her some guidelines for choosing between the various conservatories and colleges. One guideline is to consider the duration of the training. A three-year program is better than an eight week crash course, and a department that offers a Bachelor of Fine Arts with a focus on acting is probably better than one that offers only a B.A. in Communications & Speech. Admissions standards are another measuring stick she can use. A program that admits anyone who can pay the tuition is less desirable than one that auditions nationally and admits only two dozen students each year. A third measuring stick is the curriculum, and she can learn about that by reading the brochures and bulletins that the conservatories and theatre departments print. A school that offers a rigorously structured curriculum that guides the students through a progressive sequence of courses is preferable to one that offers the students a wide variety of "electives." "And think about the faculty," she is warned. Are there several teachers and are they specialists in such areas as voice and speech, combat, T'ai Chi, dialects, period dance, mask, and acting—or are there only a couple of teachers? And who *are* those teachers? Are they working professionals who can share the realities of a life in the theatre and who have a firm vision of the quality Barbara will need to demonstrate if she's going to make a career, or did they graduate from the college they're now teaching at and have never ventured out into the competitive world of the professional theatre? "And don't forget to consider *where* the school is," says her advisor as Barbara puts on her coat to leave. "If it's in the Northeast Corridor or in Southern California, there's a greater likelihood you'll meet people who will help you get started when you finish your training than if it's in Oklahoma, South Dakota, or West Virginia." The kindly teacher walks Barbara to her car and gives her a couple of parting bits of advice. "If you want to go into Alternative Theatre or Performance Art, then find a school that focuses on that. And if you really just want to be a movie star, then go to a school that does lots of film projects. But mostly, Barbara, don't go to a *bad* school. There are hundreds of them out there, and frankly they're a waste of your time."

"But what if I don't get admitted to one of the good schools?"

"Then maybe the world is telling you something. Maybe you'll have to discover the hard way that the only one who thinks you should be an actor is you." Barbara gets into Carnegie-Mellon University's BFA program in actor training and she starts a life in the theatre.

Her twin brother, Bart, is in a hurry. He wants to be an actor by the time Barbara gets out of school, so he heads for New York, gets a job waiting tables, and starts taking private classes. He discovers three truths pretty quickly. The teacher he studies with has a speciality, and he's not getting the full range of training that Barbara's letters describe she's getting. Secondly, he's only studying one night a week, and she's slugging away eight hours a day, every day of the week—she even rehearses on Sundays, she writes him. And thirdly, he doesn't like the guy he's studying with and recently heard of another teacher he might be more compatible with. Bart's story is a pretty typical one, and many young actors seek their basic training this way. And some get what they need and begin a life in the theatre—but most find that they don't have the advantages of their friends who got the finest training at the leading conservatory and university training programs: schools like Juilliard, Brandeis, Yale, Southern Methodist, Delaware, Wisconsin-Milwaukee, and a handful of others.

Wherever and however you get your basic training, you must get it. And then it is time for your advanced training. This is the training you continue throughout your professional life. Whether you're in Hollywood or New York, London or Sydney, Toronto or Seattle, you'll want to continue studying with master teachers who can help you meet your particular goals: increase your skills, train your instrument, develop a system of work, or practice your craft.

YOUR SKILLS The more things you can do, the greater your chances for employment. Many actors spend a sizable portion of their time and available funds in expanding the repertoire of their skills. All manner of dance classes, music lessons, singing classes, circus-technique classes, dialect classes, audition-technique classes, acting-for-camera classes, combat classes, and mime classes might be taken. And then there're the para-theatrical courses in yoga, T'ai Chi, and Transcendental Meditation that aspiring actors hope will help them shape an ever more interesting self.

YOUR INSTRUMENT You might take classes to correct deficiencies or to maintain your level of accomplishment. Actors without satisfactory vocal instruments may study to achieve strong breath support, enriched resonances, or unlocalized accents. Others may wish to correct minor speech imperfections such as lateral or sibilant lisps. Others will enroll in a program of physical workouts at a gym or spa—to achieve or maintain a strong and well-toned body.

YOUR SYSTEM OF WORK Too many actors leave their basic training without a clearly defined and readily implemented system for doing their work. They are without the tools they need to analyze a script or prepare a role, so they study with "acting" teachers who offer weekly or twice-weekly classes. Most of these are taught by successful actors who have evolved for themselves a method based on the Stanislavsky system. Fads for teachers come and go, and each season actors will seek the teacher who is recognized as having helped some actor become a success the preceding year. Bill Esper one year, Uta Hagen the next, and Michael Kahn the year after. Teachers who have endured for several years and who have earned the respect of the profession (as have the three listed here) are much in demand and take students by audition only. There are always new teachers, though, and sometimes they are good.

Compatibility is essential to effectiveness with "acting" teachers more than with "skills" teachers. If you get along well with the teacher, great. Many will function as gurus and expect your devotion. If you can't find it in yourself to give it, try a different teacher. It would be nonsense to suggest that one of these teachers is measurably superior to another. It would be safe to assert, however, that *you* will connect better with one than another. Happily, you have the chance to experiment. Unlike the university or conservatory to which you commit yourself for a period of years, most acting teachers will take students for six to twelve weeks at a time. If you find one you like, you can continue those classes for years on end. If you want to shift to another, you can do so easily.

YOUR CRAFT   You like to act. You wish to act. You need to act. Well, if nobody has hired you recently, you're not acting. And your acting skills are like the runner's skills—if you don't use them regularly, they go stale. How do you keep them fresh? How can you demonstrate your sensitivity and versatility in an audition if you haven't acted in several months? The answer is that you must act in classes. You need to maintain or sharpen your acting craft by doing it regularly, and the "scene-study class" is the most common place for actors to do this. There's a cruel irony here. You are a professional because people will pay you to act, and now you're reduced to paying someone for the right to act. In New York, Hollywood, and most large cities where a substantial number of actors live, there are countless scene-study classes, and serious actors attend them regularly. The best known may be the H-B Studios and the Actors Studio, but there are others of comparable excellence. In Hollywood, the standard form is the "workshop" or "showcase" theatre where actors pay up to $100 a month for the opportunity to get together to act— frequently without the supervision of an important mentor. These workshops usually present showcase productions that actors hope will let them parade their talents before casting directors. Whether or not these showcases lead directly to employment, they do give the actors their only chance to act for months at a time.

The problem of finding good instruction is as much a part of the actor's continual nightmare as the problem of finding good audition pieces. You'll rarely be completely satisfied. You'll continue to explore, looking for that teacher who holds the secret you believe you need to become a star. Well, while looking, where do you begin? Some teachers advertise in the trade papers—*Variety, Back Stage, Show Business,* or *The Hollywood Reporter.* You will probably seek the advice of friends, the agent you're hoping will sign you, or someone who has studied with the teacher you're considering. One thing that may help you choose is that many teachers will let you observe on one or two occasions before you must either leave or pay to stay.

* * * * *

However you choose the teacher, you know that you must find a way to keep acting, so make a choice, take the plunge, and move forward. As the dancer must dance and the violinist must play, the actor must act. The road to success is littered with the corpses of those who believed in shortcuts.

Not all of your training happens under a teacher's guidance or in a formal class. Just as you are on your own when the performance begins, you are on your own for a large portion of your training. You will need a clear program for self-instruction and a lot of self-discipline. But if you are to be the actor you wish to be, you will have to spend some portion of each day in concentrated self-instruction. You will have the best chance of success if you regiment yourself and spend the same time on this work each day.

To begin, you must exercise your voice and body each day. If you've had good training, you will know a set of exercises you can employ. If you spend ten to fifteen minutes daily on your voice, it will serve you when you need it. The same is true for your body.

Acting is an imitation of human behavior, and you can broaden your understanding of human behavior by studying the other arts. Take advantage of the museums, galleries, concerts, sculpture exhibitions, dance concerts, operas, and movies that are available to you. Any week that goes by without your visiting a museum or hearing a concert or seeing a classic film is wasted. You will act Shakespeare better if you have heard a concert of madrigals. You will act Sam Shepard better if you've seen an exhibition of Georgia O'Keeffe's paintings. To act Beckett well, you must first have walked among Giacometti's sculptures.

Maybe you can't get out to a museum every week, but you can read every day. Most actors in America today are sadly uninformed about the literature, history, legends, and theory of the art they aspire to serve. They have only their sloth to blame. There is so much to read. Where to begin? By imposing some sort of plan and schedule on your reading. For example, plan to read a play every single week. Plan to read a book about acting every month (a biography of an actor, a study of some theory or style, a history of the craft). Plan to read a book about the history or practice of theatre each month (a discussion of Shakespeare's theatre, a history of the Federal Theatre Project). Do you need help creating a reading list? Write to the theatre department of some reputable university and ask for their Ph.D. reading list; you'll get several hundred titles you can select from. Subscribe to magazines such as *American Theatre, Theater Week,* or *Plays and Players.* In short, set yourself some categories and some goals. A particularly enjoyable way to help yourself is to create a discussion group. Select a handful of your professional colleagues who agree that such a plan is desirable and meet once each month to discuss the book you've all agreed to read. If you screen your members carefully, you'll find the discussions stimulating and you'll also lift your spirits because you'll know that you're doing something constructive about your life as an actor. As Gogo says in *Waiting for Godot*, "We always find something, don't we Didi, to give us the impression we exist."

＊ ＊ ＊ ＊ ＊

Go to the theatre! It is depressing to talk with actors or acting students and discover how rarely they go to the theatre. I may overreact to their seeming disinterest, but I am suspicious of actors who don't see other actors' work. There is much to be learned from watching a brilliant performance, and there is at least something to be learned from watching a poor one—if only that you should never make those same mistakes. See how another actor confronts particular challenges. How would you have dealt with that scene? That monologue? That pratfall? Doctors have operating theatres in which they learn by watching other doctors at work. Football players screen tapes of other teams' games. You should see as much theatre as you possibly can.

See performances more than once. I am puzzled by actors who go to the theatre only for pleasure, as though they were civilians. You should go to learn. To watch, consider, assess, and learn. The best learning is by comparison. Go see Irene Worth in *Lost in Yonkers* more than once. And then go see the show when Rosemary Harris takes over that role. How are they different? Is Roc Dutton different from Delroy Lindo in *Joe Turner's Come and Gone*? How do John Lithgow, Tony Randall, and David Dukes approach the central role in *M. Butterfly*? Don't ask if one is better or worse. But how do they differ? Why are they different? And how will you do it if you land that role in summer stock two seasons from now? And how will you do it in scene-study class next month? Think of the many recordings of a Beethoven symphony you might listen to. That's how many variants there can be on a performance. You can learn from all of them.

"But it's expensive," you moan. True. But can you afford *not* to go? And there are some ways to reduce the expense. In New York, the Equity office distributes free tickets to card-carrying members almost every day. If you know people working on a show and if you select a slow night (Tuesday for example), the stage manager might be inveigled into "walking you in"—bringing you through the stage door and into the auditorium, to occupy an empty seat as the house lights dim. There are also reduced rates for New York shows through the TKTS booth at Duffy Square (47th St.). And, if all else fails, you can "second act it" and back in at the intermission. True, you'll miss the first act, but if your goal is to learn by observation, seeing part of the performance is better than sitting in front of your TV like a couch potato. All you do is inquire at the box office what time the intermission begins, stand outside, and as the audience filters out, you filter in. Once in, wait until the house lights dim for the second half of the show and either grab any empty seat or stand at the back. Once in a while you'll get caught and ejected, and your pride may be bruised, but mostly you'll spend an hour or so studying your profession—for free.

Looking for Work

You're a migrant worker. And just like other migrant workers, you go where the work is, stay there as long as it lasts, and desperately look about for the next place you can work. You go to St. Louis to plant a little Shakespeare, to Phoenix to plow a little Chekhov, to Richmond to fertilize a little Sondheim, and to Salt Lake City to pick a little Simon. Like other migrant workers, you're always on the road, always looking for your next job, always underpaid, always living in temporary digs, always worrying about your health insurance, always planning your next unemployment compensation claim, and always hoping for something more secure. This image came to me when I was running a Shakespeare festival in Maine. Except for the Equity actors whose union contract ensured better for them, the entire company lived in a large old farmhouse on the commercial apple orchard of one of the theatre's trustees. Designers, technicians, and non-union actors had rooms in the same house and shared a common kitchen. What was the house used for the rest of the year, I inquired? To house the migrant workers who picked the apples each September. Which was why the theatre staff had to get out before Labor Day. The theatre season had to end early to accommodate the apple season. One set of migrant workers followed by another.

Like other migrant workers, you're out of a job most of the time. Looking for the next one. During these fallow times, it is very easy to contract an acute case of the "upfers," a disease endemic to the acting profession and one that strikes young actors with its most virulent strain. The symptom is heard in every bar, coffee shop, waiting room, and party where actors gather. "I'm upfer a role in that show." "My agent is sending me upfer a commercial next week." "I was upfer that pilot, but it didn't sound right for me." The cause of this disease is the actors' need to feel a part of the profession that they sense is happening all around them but which they are not yet actively practicing. Actors feel a need for self-delusion, they need to give themselves the impression they exist as actors. If they can persuade themselves that employment is imminent, they can use Stanislavsky's "magic if" and project themselves to the enviable condition of being a "working actor." They have tired of that other self-delusion by which young actors proclaim they are serious actors and not interested in commercials, or television, or repertory, or musicals, or whatever is the form of theatre employment under discussion—which by coincidence they have not yet been asked to do. They have come to accept the grizzled veteran's explanation that there are only two kinds of actors—those who get work and those who don't. There is only one cure for the "upfers." Employment. In the parlance of the medical profession, employment is a miracle cure. One injection and the "upfers" are over. At least for a while. Like malaria, it is a recurring disease.

How do you get that cure? That employment? Well, the first problem is to locate the clinics where it is dispensed. Once there you can follow the established ceremonies of auditions. But you've got to find out where to go, first of all. There are public channels and private channels.

The public channels include all published notifications of interviews and auditions. The New York and Hollywood Equity offices have callboards that list upcoming auditions for stage work. Equity requires an open call for every show under its jurisdiction. These are general calls and frequently they turn out to be cattle calls, but the information posted is accurate and actors will be seen and, despite rumors to the contrary, do occasionally get hired from open calls.

The trade papers (*Variety, Hollywood Reporter, Back Stage, Show Business*) also list casting news, and frequently the concise notes at Equity are fleshed out in the trades with descriptions of the types being sought, names of directors and writers, projected opening dates, etc. The trades also have listings for non-Equity jobs—showcases, non-Equity stock and dinner theatres, commercials, and student TV and film jobs. Information in the trades is not always accurate but you have to follow it up anyway. Sometimes the press release a producer has sent to a trade is printed too late to do you any good. On other occasions the show has been entirely or largely cast and the notice is the producer's way of meeting his contractual obligation to Equity. But sometimes there are "jobs in them thar hills" for actors who will prospect long enough and hard enough.

In the fifteen years since an earlier version of this book was written, there's been a major change in the employment of American actors. Today, actors work more weeks each year on the LORT Contract than they do on what Equity calls its "standard contract," by which Equity means the Production Contract used for Broadway and national tours. The LORT Contract covers the more than eighty resident theatres that have formed into an association called the League of Resident Theaters, which is widely known by the acronym LORT. How do you learn about auditions for LORT theatres? Several ways. To begin, you can get the October issue of *American Theatre*, which lists the annual productions at most theatres: the titles, dates, and directors. If you find theatres that are doing plays in which there are roles you might play, you'll want to audition for them. The theatres' addresses and phone numbers are available in the *TCG Theatre Directory* published annually by Theatre Communications Group, the service organization for America's expanding not-for-profit theatre that publishes *American Theatre* among its other services. You can write (or phone) the theatres to ask who their New York casting director is, and you will discover that there are roughly a dozen active casting agents: from those who service TV and film along with the flagship LORT companies like the Long Wharf and the Guthrie to those that service only a few of the smaller LORT theatres. You can send your photo/résumé to the casting director and ask to be seen at the auditions for the play or plays you think you have a chance for. If you drop by their offices and meet them personally, you increase your chances. A real human is more memorable than just one more impersonal photo/résumé. An even stronger way to get into those auditions is for your agent to send your photo/résumé to the casting director. But your agent may not think to do so, or may not want you to go out of town, or may have other clients she wants to send "upfer" that audition. So if you learn about the audition, you ought to nag your agent until she submits you to the casting director.

Another way into the LORT theatres is through the LORT Lottery, which Equity holds three times during the year. By contract, each LORT theatre is obliged each year to hold three days of open auditions in New York (or any city in which Equity maintains an office). Equity works cooperatively with LORT to facilitate this and to make it efficient and economical for theatres and actors alike. Any member of Equity (and any Equity membership candidate) can send a postcard to Equity requesting a slot in the next LORT auditions. By a lottery-styled drawing, Equity selects the persons who may audition. The theatres send a representative to the auditions, and they see the roughly 100 actors a day who can strut their stuff for a maximum of five minutes. Theatres send anyone from the artistic director down to a casting director who is there representing a half-dozen theatres simultaneously, but the actors *do* get auditioned, and this does occasionally lead to employment. If you are a young actor just arriving into the casting pool, or a mature actor who has been living somewhere else for long enough that everyone in the casting business has forgotten you, the LORT Lottery is an excellent place for you to be seen. Sadly, the overwhelming portion of the auditioning actors are terrible, but that will only make you look good by contrast. The inferior quality of many Equity members speaks to the truth that Equity is only a labor union and not a professional organization that imposes standards for membership.

A lot of funny and painful stories are told about the LORT Lottery. Currently, the New York auditions are held in a large room in the Equity offices (165 W. 46th St.), but there was a time when they were held on the stage of a "dark" Broadway theatre—frequently, as I recall, the Golden Theatre. One day a pudgy young man strode out to do a big speech from *The Rainmaker*—a singularly inappropriate selection, as it turned out. In addition to looking more like Mr. Toad than Starbuck, he had a noticeable "w"/"r" confusion in his speech and sounded remarkably like the cartoon figure Elmer Fudd—the one who is always chasing the "wascally wabbit." The young actor labored through the speech and cranked himself into a frenzy that culminated in his bellowing to the heavens, "I go down to the hollow and I look up and I say: 'Wain! Dammit! —*please!*—bwing Wain!'" Some forty artistic directors slid under their seats in muffled laughter.

Casting notices for store-front and workshop theatres in New York and Los Angeles frequently never reach such formal publications as the trade papers. Scribbled notes on the callboards of bookstores and bars, two printed lines in underground newspapers, and notices posted on the doors to lofts are sometimes your only way of learning about the auditions. As you can't possibly cover all the bases you might like to; you'll have to be selective, and you'll find you rely heavily on word-of-mouth.

That's the private channel. Whether it is a casually overheard remark by the gal in front of you on the subway or a message on your phone machine from your agent, word-of-mouth is the most common source of information about auditions. It stands to reason that the more people you talk with and the more places you circulate, the better your chances of finding the audition that will ultimately lead to your landing a job.

Remember the early chapter when I wrote about your "contacts?" Well, they are your major suppliers of information. The best contacts are those who are a bit more experienced than you, and these are frequently found in your classes. If there were no other reason for taking dance lessons and scene-study classes than to learn about forthcoming auditions, the money you pay would still be well invested. One way of choosing a teacher might be to investigate how many of her students work with any kind of regularity. If they're working, and if you pal about with them, you may work.

Another source of contacts is the "old school tie." If you went to Carnegie-Mellon, Yale, the Circle-in-the-Square School, or any of the many other schools that have been in operation for a long time and whose students have been out in the business for some years, you can seek some assistance from them. You are usually young enough to not be their competition, and there is a sentimentality that guides us to help our schoolmates. Some schools— Southern Methodist University comes quickest to mind—have well-organized groups in New York that provide advice and even showcases for newly arrived alumni.

A major source of information is the informal exchange that happens at theatre restaurants and bars. (This is much truer in New York than in Hollywood, where distances are so great that actors don't gather with the same regularity as they do in Manhattan.) For each level of theatre, there are different hangouts, and the popular spots change from year to year. Currently in New York, Sam's on 45th St. and Joe Allen's on 46th are the most frequented. The downtown theatres of off-Broadway and off-off-Broadway have their haunts as well. It will behoove you to make the rounds of these watering spots with some regularity. I'm not suggesting you become a bar-hopper and spend each evening panting desperately from stool to stool trying to overhear secrets that will make you a star on the morrow. I am suggesting that these are the places where you can meet your friends casually and learn from each other.

Parties are fine places to meet people, develop friendships and learn about jobs. However, you may have a stay-at-home temperament and not be a party person, but you can help yourself by defining going to a party as a part of your working day— as significant as reading the trades and making the rounds. Go when you can—you may do yourself some good. And once in a while you might even enjoy yourself.

One of the least enjoyable and most tiring ways of looking for work has been dignified with a lot of romantic jargon. You'll be told to "go out on the street," "pound the pavement," and "make the rounds." These are all elegant ways of saying that, since no one will come looking to hire you, you've got to do the looking. It means that you must walk into as many offices as you can: agents' offices, casting directors' offices, producers' offices, television networks' casting offices. Anywhere you can find someone to whom you can present yourself. It can be embarrassing to make the rounds for days on end and never get past the receptionist. It can be demoralizing to pound the pavement for days on end and receive nothing but rejection. "Nothing today." "We're not casting anything this month." "Mr. Jones doesn't ever hire your type." "We only see people submitted by agents." The phrases vary but they all boil down to a simple "No! We don't want you!"

Enterprising actors who've pounded the pavement before you are making a small amount of money by making your task easier. They have catalogued the names and addresses of most producers, casting directors, agents, television network casting departments, advertising and modeling agencies, and their published directories are for sale at performing arts bookstores in both New York and Los Angeles. Some are collated alphabetically and some by address—so you can go from building to building and save yourself a great deal of time and shoe leather.

Just as actors suffer from the "upfers," so employers suffer from "short memoryitis." That agent you left your photo with two weeks ago has no idea who you are today. The director who told you he liked you but had nothing for you in the show he was casting last month no longer knows your name. If you hope to work as an actor you must continue to look for work throughout your entire career. I was seated in a filthy hallway in New York, readying myself for an audition for a production of *Volpone* to be presented in Philadelphia (where I lived, but where no auditions were being held). Alongside me was a student of mine, a young actor in his early twenties on one of his first auditions. Across from us sat an older actor, perhaps in his mid-sixties. His turn came and he went into the audition. The young student turned to me. "Is that me in forty years? Will I be waiting in cold hallways, trying to find six weeks' work out of town?"

"If you're good enough to make it," is all I could reply. "And if you've got the stamina."

If I'd have known it at the time, I'd have shared with him the wag's description of *the five stages of an actor's career.* When you're a youngster just starting out, the stage manager says to the director (as was no doubt said once about Barbra Streisand), "How about hiring Barbra Streisand?" and the director replies, "Who's Barbra Streisand?" When you have some success, the director says, "Get me Barbra Streisand." When you become so successful your salary goes through the roof, the director says, "Get me a Barbra Streisand type." As you reach the late middle ages, you overhear the director whisper to the stage manager, "Get me a young Barbra Streisand." And as you're sitting in that dark New York hallway, you hear the stage manager say to the director, "How about hiring Barbra Streisand?" and then the director replies, "Who's Barbra Streisand?"

Fame is fleeting, and the loss of fame is painful. Fritz Weaver told a story on a TV talk show one night. Weaver may not be a household name or an international superstar, but he has had a significant career on stage and in films and he continues to work prominently. In 1991, he played Governor Danforth in Tony Randall's National Actors Theatre production of *The Crucible* and won praise for his fine performance. At the time he told the story, he was enough of a celebrity that he was an appropriate guest for a late-night talk show. As he told it, Weaver was in a taxi in Manhattan, and he could see that the driver was eyeing him in the rear-view mirror, trying to place him. Weaver was eager to be recognized. What actor isn't? But the driver didn't quite know who Weaver was, and said nothing. The taxi reached its destination and Weaver got out to pay. The cabby reached through the window to accept the fare, looked up, and asked, "Didn't you used to be Fritz Weaver?"

One of the many clichés of the theatre is that you're only as good as your last job. "What have you done lately?" is asked more often than you'd believe. So you need to keep your name and your successes in front of the casting community. There are several ways to do this. As suggested earlier, you can create a mailing list of all your contacts and send periodic reminders of your interest and availability. You can send these to every theatre in the *TCG Theatre Directory* if you wish, or at least to those you think might genuinely be open to hiring you. And you can make the rounds from time to time. Particularly if you've just returned home from an out-of-town job. Presenting yourself in person is more influential than sending a mailer.

One final thought about looking for work. The telephone is your best friend and constant companion. You must have a phone and you must have an answering machine that you can call to get your messages from any remote location. You need to be able to call people, and they need to be able to call you. If you have found out about a job and sold yourself in an audition, you don't want to lose the job because you're not at home when the casting director telephones.

Looking for work is a full-time job. You can make the rounds each day, seek out your contacts each night, go to classes, read the trades, stop by Equity, and hit every audition you can get into. And you still may not find work. Common sense will tell you that the harder you look, the greater will be your chances of finding. And that would be true, if all other things were equal—which they aren't. The theatre is an unfair business in which jobs are granted to friends, sex objects, nerds off the street, untalented celebrities, and occasionally to the most qualified candidate. Since the grounds for qualification are largely subjective, it's hard to measure your successes and your rejections. But one truth remains immutable. *You cannot get a job unless you look for one.* There are many cases of so-so actors who work steadily because they are terrific job finders. And there are the opposite—talented and trained actors who don't work very often because they are terrible job finders. Your career is very much yours to control. Follow your own best urgings.

Agents

Only the beginning actor believes that an agent is the key to success. The working actor thinks that the agent is a necessary evil who gets paid for doing nothing. The successful actor's agent may be both a friend and a business advisor. For all actors, the agent is a puzzlement. Objectively, he's a guy trying hard to make a living by rendering services. What do you pay the agent to do?

To find you work. Your agent will apply himself in direct proportion to his possible earnings. If you're a beginner, he knows he can't make much for his services, so he will probably spend very little time on your behalf. Since you're not likely to earn more than minimum at the beginning of your career, he can't expect to earn much. If he spends valuable time working to get you jobs, it's in the hope that one day you'll become a big earner and he'll have invested his time wisely. The truth is, for beginners, you have to find the jobs yourself.

You pay your agent to negotiate contracts for you. This he will do responsibly, and you can trust him to get as large a salary for you as can be hoped. Your contract includes more clauses than the basic weekly pay, of course, and the agent is particularly skilled at negotiating these items: residual fees, raises after a specified number of weeks, vacations, billing, out clauses, fees for recordings, percentages from endorsements, etc.

Your agent gives you professional advice for free: advice about your image, your photography, jobs it is wise or stupid to accept, showcases to perform, audition pieces to prepare, and a thousand other items ranging from advice on your income-tax return to parties you should attend. Your agent only gets remunerated if you earn something. He views his advice as an investment in his potential earnings if you become a major earner, so when you are tempted to complain that he's doing nothing for you, remember the things he *is* doing for you—even though those may not currently include getting you a job.

Sometimes actors find their agents are keeping them from getting work, and this gets them angry. Your agent may want you to stay in town and try to get a high-paying commercial rather than going to Syracuse to earn $505 a week for a seven-week engagement—never mind that you've always dreamed of playing Ruth in *A Raisin in the Sun*—and so he does not submit you to the casting director. And you hear from the director who's an old school chum that she was disappointed you didn't want to audition! You're angry and you're right. What to do? Make certain your agent understands what *you* want to do, and if he can't endorse that, get a different agent. There's the celebrated instance of Edward Albee submitting the script of his new play *Who's Afraid of Virginia Woolf?* to Henry Fonda's agent—who never told Fonda about it. Much later, when Fonda learned about this, he was enraged. He loved the script and would have done it. The agent had "albumin on the visage," Albee was frustrated, and the only person who liked the way things had gone was Arthur Hill, who got to create the part. The moral? Make certain your agent lets *you* make all your career decisions. Hear his advice, don't dismiss it hastily, but do your own thing.

In New York, an agent is less significant to the beginning actor than in Hollywood. If you are headed for New York, you can get a list of all authorized agents from the Equity office. If you desire an agent, select a few names from that list and send them your photo and résumé with a covering letter explaining that you have just arrived in town and will call their offices in a few days to seek an appointment. Follow up that letter with a call. You'll get the receptionist. Perhaps she'll tell you to come for an appointment, but more often she'll say that the agent is "not taking on any more clients just now," or that "he asked me to tell you to let him know any time you're in a show and he'll try to come see it." If you get a warmer reception than that, you are fortunate indeed.

At some point, you will be admitted to an agent's office. Perhaps he has seen your showcase performance, or perhaps he's in a slow season and can take time to look for new clients. Once there, you'll learn that he is not interested in signing you to an "exclusive" contract, but that he'll send you up for things and be happy to represent you on any job you find yourself. That's useful to you, as you can now tell people at an audition that they can call your agent, Joe Doakes, if they'd like to engage you, and they will infer you are worth hiring, because why else would Doakes bother with you? It is common for you to have informal working relations with several agents at once. Typically, one will handle TV and film work, another commercials, and a third will focus on stage work. But those divisions are arbitrary and no general rules apply.

Any time that you get a job that an agent has sent you to, he

will claim his percentage. Any time you use the agent to negotiate a contract for a job you found yourself, he will claim his
percentage. But you are free to negotiate any jobs you find on
your own, and the agent has no claim on you. Sometimes, of
course, it is politic to give an agent a commission on a job you've
gotten without his services. If he believes you are going to commit to him, he may commit to working harder for you, and you
both may increase your earnings substantially.

If you begin to get work regularly and the agent believes that
your income will be large enough to make his percentage
worthwhile, he may want to sign you to an exclusive contract. All
that means is that you may not work through other agents and
that you must give your exclusive agent a commission on all
work you do, whether or not he had anything to do with your
getting it. If you sign, your agent will negotiate all your contracts.
The only reason you should sign such an agreement is if you
believe the agent will work hard to find you work. As his income
is dependent on yours, he probably will. But if he doesn't, your
agreement can be canceled after a specified time (usually six
months), so check that clause of the agreement carefully before
you sign. Know how to get out of a bad situation, and know
equally well the ease with which the agent can drop you.

If Hollywood is your destination, different guidelines apply.
In the TV and film world, all contracts *must* be negotiated by
agents, and a very high percentage of all work is secured through
agents. (True, you may still ferret out jobs on your own, but the
agent will enter into the negotiations early and will work with
you to land the job.) While in New York you might go for years
without even trying to get an agent, in Hollywood you must sign
with one before you can hope to get work.

Hollywood agents are in a position to gamble on newcomers
more often than New York agents because of the huge salaries
that are paid to film and television actors and because acting
skills are less significant to your potential employment than your
personality and bone structure. The legend used to be that you
could get discovered on a drugstore stool at Schwab's in Hollywood. And there are many true stories like the one about the
undergraduate student at the University of Utah who was seen by

a visiting Hollywood casting director who liked the student's "quality" and recommended her over hundreds of more talented and better-trained young actors for the plum role of the older sister in *Life Goes On*, the hugely successful prime-time series. A star was born. That particular star committed career suicide about six months later by asking to be written out of the show. She was lonely and wanted to go home. Had she stayed with it, she would have been rich for life. Instead, she returned to her nest in Utah and disappeared. Well, Hollywood attracts strange creatures. As a result of the reality that stars can be born from the most unlikely wombs, agents are willing to consider newcomers, and it is not too difficult for you to get an appointment with an agent on the West Coast. And anyway, Schwab's has been torn down.

The West Coast agent will want to see something of your work and will either give you the same "let me know when you're in a showcase and I'll try to get over to see it," or he'll ask to see "some tape." That means, quite simply, he wants to see what you look like on camera. He knows his business well enough to know that your acting skills, live personality, and experience are less important than your image on the screen, and he wants to find out what *that* is before he spends time on you. He also knows that he can use a tape to sell you because casting directors can look at it and judge your quality and appropriateness for themselves.

You contact an agent in Hollywood the same way as in New York. Get a list of agents from the Screen Actors Guild office, send some photos and a covering letter, and follow those up with phone calls. If you can say in your letter that you have "some tape," you will very likely be asked to drop it by the office. Where do you get it? Try doing a film for students at a film school. Directors at NYU or UCLA are always seeking actors for their class projects. Some are very talented and highly skilled, and with some persistence you can very likely get some excellent product. Another method is to work up a scene with a friend and hire one of the many studios that will shoot it for you—but it's not cheap! Look in the trades for ads. If you have "some tape" and an agent sees it, you have a reasonable chance of getting representation.

All agents' contracts in Hollywood are "exclusive." Indeed, the standard contract ties up more than your acting talent. It will include all modeling, writing, and composing you do as well. While some agencies focus only on TV and film work, all have a working arrangement to handle commercials, and many large agencies have agents in their offices who deal exclusively in commercials. All these contracts have a time clause to them, and if you find you've signed with an agent who is doing nothing for your career, you can move after a few months. What you *won't* find in Hollywood are agents who deal exclusively in stage work. It doesn't pay enough to make it worth their while. Most agents will send you on auditions for stage work if you bring it to their attention, but don't expect them to show much interest.

Which agent should you sign with? In most cases, the first one that offers. But if you have a choice, you should consider if a small or large agency is in your best interest. The small agency has fewer clients and may, therefore, work for you more often. However, it may not have as many contacts or as great a muscle in negotiations as the large agency. The large agency has so many clients that you might get lost in the shuffle, but it also is able to create "packages" for producers, supplying writers, directors, stars, and (yes) bright new talent for the small but choice role of the reporter who interviews Glenn Close. It is not possible to weigh the pros and cons of the choices in the abstract, but it is safe to say that you will not have a choice at first and that, when you do, you'll be experienced enough in the profession to make a wise choice.

There are many jokes about agents and most are as cruel, as accurate, and as funny as the one told earlier about the actor who did bird imitations. Just think of how Hollywood portrays the breed. Remember Sidney Pollock's performance as Dustin Hoffman's agent in *Tootsie*? The jokes result from the actors' resentment of the fees paid to agents. That's an unfair resentment, if you consider how little the agent earns and what real services he does for you at contract time. Yet agents remain the butt of actors' frustrations. You want to work, you don't get work, and you blame it on your agent who is "earning 10% for doing nothing." That's dumb reasoning, since the agent knows full well that 10% of nothing is nothing. But the out-of-work actor is impatient and the agent is a convenient scapegoat.

You will get along well with your agent if you keep in mind that he is a business person in a world peopled with arrogant, self-nominating artists. He is the voice of sound economics trying to moderate between a director whose producer can't afford to pay your fee and an actor who looks upon all businessmen as insensitive parasites. You might also remember that he will be more inclined to work for you if he likes you than if you behave badly toward him or if you nag him all the time. You might also remember that he knows as well as you that he is a middle man, a wholesaler, a dealer in your talents, and that he may be embarrassed by that truth. While he takes pride in doing his job well—negotiating a good contract, sending the right actor on the right audition, putting together the right package—he gets frustrated when he can't get work for his clients. You will get along well with him, and do yourself a good turn, if you will think of him not as the butt of a new joke but as a necessary proper adjunct to your career.

Your Other Job

Acting is the hobby you do 750 hours a year, right? What is the job you spend your other 1,250 hours a year doing? How do you earn your living while you're making the rounds? What do you do to make enough money so you can support your theatre habit?

An actor's life requires your non-theatre job to be flexible, and you need mobility so that you can take a morning off to attend an audition, take four weeks off to rehearse a play, and arrange a weekly schedule that permits you to attend classes and make the rounds. Not many employers will cooperate with you, and those that will are likely to exploit you by paying poor hourly wages. But there are some jobs you can pursue.

The best of all is to be in the inheritance business. Get born into a family that can afford to support you during your initial years as an actor. If you did not have the foresight to arrange that, get someone to keep you. A husband or wife, a lover, or even a patron who fancies the notion of "owning" a struggling artist. Any source of income that leaves you entirely free to pursue your career is devoutly to be wished. Some young actors spend a couple of years working two jobs and save a nest egg so that they can come to New York or Hollywood with enough of a bankroll to last a year or more. That requires a great degree of self-discipline, but it can be preferable to arrangements that make you dependent on other people's money.

If you have to take a job, and most of us do, consider one on the swing shift. If you go to work at midnight and get off at eight in the morning, you can get a good sleep from nine to three in the afternoon and be up in time to make auditions and rounds in the late afternoon and classes in the early evening. Of course, that throws your meal schedule into a tizzy and you can follow that upside-down schedule only if you live alone. If your roommate or spouse holds a day job and you pass each other in the hallway as you come and go, your relationship won't last a month. The swing-shift solution is only for the solitary stalker with a flexible metabolism. But it pays well. Word-processors who work the swing shift in New York's investment industry can earn twenty bucks an hour. Figure it out: 20 x 5 days a week x 8 hours a day = $800 a week. Remember the old lyric? "Nice work if you can get it, and you can get it if you try."

Other hourly jobs were suggested in the earlier chapter: cab driver, bartender, waiter, telemarketer, etc. These are typical jobs for wannabe actors, and you'll find ads for these positions in the trade papers. There are two problems with these jobs: they don't pay much and they're dreary. If you're paid by the hour and if you work an irregular week, your pay packet will be thin. You probably won't be able to get along without dipping into your savings. After word-processing, probably the best paying jobs are in bars. Making and serving drinks is a big business in New York and Hollywood, and our nation's current economic depression doesn't seem to have hurt it. If you are not disturbed by working in a lounge or pub, you'll bring home more money for less hours than you will from other job-jobs, and you can retain a fair amount of flexibility in your hours. But this sort of work isn't for everyone, and it can be pretty depressing after a while. It takes a strong sense of self to continue at this kind of job for long.

The job you choose must not depress you, must not make you lose your love of the theatre. The theatre will bruise you enough. You'll lose out in auditions. You'll be in flops. You'll be rejected. You need some portion of your life that is cheery. You need to get up in the morning with something pleasant to look forward to—and that ought to be your job-job. You ought to find a position that interests and challenges you and in which you can take some pride.

There is a paradox here, of course. But the theatre never promised you a rose garden.

Unemployment Compensation

Most actors count their unemployment compensation as a portion of their annual income. You receive it as regularly as any paycheck, you pay the rent with it, and you pay income tax on it. So what else is it if it's not a part of your annual income? A sector of the American psyche tells us that unemployment compensation is only for failures, for misfits who can't make a living, for scroungers. If you were brought up to believe that, get over it! If your parents believe that, try to educate them to the realities of their society. Unemployment compensation is a part of your life as a migrant worker.

Unlike the governments of other industrialized nations, our federal, state, and city governments are not very good about subsidizing the arts. Apparently the people we elect to govern us don't believe that the arts are as important to the quality of life as roads, education, and health care. By way of comparison, you might be intrigued to know that several large cities in Germany spend more annually to support the arts than our entire federal government. Small wonder that we American artists feel unwanted, disrespected, and disenfranchised. Equally small wonder that many American artists define unemployment compensation as an indirect governmental subsidy of the artist. It's a very healthy view to hold.

Policies for collecting unemployment compensation vary from state to state and are subject to change on short notice. A visit to the appropriate office will provide you with all the current information you need to file your claim. There are a couple of general guidelines that might be helpful to know, however.

The unemployment office has the right to send you out on job interviews. If their file indicates that you are a word-processor, you'll be obliged to go on any interviews they set up for you and to take any job you can't prove is inappropriate. To avoid this problem, whenever you make your first claim, do everything you need to do so that forever after you are defined in the federal government's computer banks as an ACTOR. There's another perk that will derive from this categorization. You won't want to waste a half-day each week standing in line to sign a form that says you couldn't find a job! Well, happily the news that there is no work out there for actors has reached the clerks who work in the unemployment compensation office, so you will very likely be excused from having to come to the office, in person, each week to verify that you tried but failed to find a job. That's a half-day saved in which you might look for work, or earn money at your job-job.

Most states have reciprocal arrangements so that if you work elsewhere than where you live, you can still file a claim based on the work you did away from your home state. Check your local office for accurate information.

In New York, to qualify for benefits, you must have worked a minimum of twenty weeks during the previous fiscal year. Then you qualify for twenty-six weeks on the dole. The number twenty can loom large in your life, and sometimes you must choose between acting jobs on the basis of how many weeks you will be employed rather than how much you will earn or what roles you will play. Any old salt or grizzled veteran can guide you through the maze of this aspect of your career, so find a friend, learn the ropes, and get with the program.

The unemployment office in Hollywood is one of the more amazing places you'll visit. The California regulations are very different from the New York ones. They don't expect you to have worked twenty weeks because they understand that work in film and TV is irregular and short-term. Accordingly, you can qualify for benefits if your gross income in the same fiscal quarter of the preceding year was above an established figure. That means that actors whose annual earnings are in the six figures can qualify for benefits any week they are not on a job. You'll be amazed who you'll see there, driving up in expensive new cars, dressed in the height of fashion, and collecting their weekly check. (If you have relatives who want to see a real, live movie star, tell them to go to the Hollywood unemployment office and they'll thank you forever afterwards.)

Taxes

You need a tax consultant. Even if your earnings are modest, you'll be astounded what a large refund a good tax consultant can arrange for you. Here is a partial list of items you can legitimately deduct. Theatre tickets. Movie tickets. Business lunches. Postage. Photography. Printing of stationery and other materials related to your profession. Telephone and answering-service charges. A percentage of per diem expenses for all the time you are on a job away from your home or residence. Makeup supplies. Theatrical wardrobe and maintenance, including dry cleaning. Scripts, scores, sheet music. Demo tapes and commercial prints. Trade advertisements. Classes, coaching, lessons. Records. The list is longer than I know or can recount.

Tax preparers charge in proportion to your gross income, and you can find a reasonable one by chatting with other actors. Some are better than others, some more expensive than others, and some more pleasant than others. You'll have to do your own scouting around, but good tax people are well known, well respected, and easy to locate.

Don't knowingly break the law. With the aid and advice of a theatre-wise tax consultant, you should find enough deductions to achieve a sizable annual refund without breaking the law [See R. Brendan Hanlon, *The New Tax Guide for Performers, Directors, Designers and Other Show Biz Folk* (New York: Limelight Editions, 1991)].

Going to the Theatre

When you go to the theatre, you have obligations to the audience and to the players. You can make the theatre a rich and rewarding place to be, you can encourage audiences to return, and you can help the performers do their jobs if you will reflect in advance about your obligations and if you will behave as an actor behaves.

Today's audiences are reared on television, not live theatre. As a result, they are prone to talk during the performance, rattle candy wrappers, and otherwise detract from the collective event. They do not *assist* in the event, as Peter Brook suggests they ought to in his concluding remarks in *The Empty Space*. They come only to watch as distanced observers and to be "entertained." You have the obligation to offer a role model. Practice the golden rule and behave unto audiences as you would have them behave unto you when you are up there acting.

Dress appropriately. People who don't go to the theatre regularly are frequently uneasy about how they should dress. Provide them with a good example so that the next time they attend, they'll be a role model for others. We are a society that respects uniforms. The policeman in plainclothes confuses us and the businesswoman who dresses like a leather freak is unlikely to gain the respect of her peers. Audiences want to know what the theatregoer's uniform is, and you have the chance to show them. So don't dress flamboyantly to draw attention to yourselves as actors. And don't dress sloppily as though you had no respect for the special event that going to the theatre can be. Costume yourselves as the characters you are that night: Mr. and Mrs. Ideal Playgoer.

Be a supportive audience. Don't be absurdly disproportionate. Don't hoot and stamp your disapproval of an inept performance that the audience finds embarrassing and is polite enough to endure quietly, and don't guffaw like a jackass at some mildly amusing quip. And, worse, don't sit huddled insider yourself as though you were pretending to be somewhere else. The audience needs your laugh, your applause, and your presence.

Be polite, mature, and firm to those rude or ignorant people around you who are disturbing everyone. Today's audience is accustomed to talking during a TV program that is beamed into their bedroom, and most have no awareness that the audience and the performers might be bothered by their chatter. They will probably shut up if you let them know they are disruptive. If someone is talking, offer a subdued but tersely authoritative, "Please do not talk."

The performers need your assistance also. Don't disrupt their work or distract their concentration by letting them know you are present. Try to select seats that aren't immediately visible from the stage if you have acquaintances in the show. Don't tell people you're coming to the show if you feel it would make them self-conscious to know you're out front. Don't go backstage before the show; they have enough to do getting ready without having to deal with you.

Tickets are a tricky matter. It's best if you purchase them because you don't want to put your friends in the awkward position of having to pay for your tickets and pretending that they were complimentary. If your friend offers to have the house manager walk you in, fine. Otherwise, buy your tickets. When you're acting, you can't afford to buy tickets for all your acquaintances. Nor can they for you.

You ought to go backstage after a show. I know there are times you really don't want to, when you really hated what you saw, and I know we've all felt that way. Indeed, I prefer to buy tickets rather than to be given comps because I believe I have bought the right to go home at intermission if I'm in pain. But if you can possibly go backstage, do. If you're stuck for something to say, play at being a reporter. "The couple next to me loved it." "I overheard a woman at intermission tell her friends she was puzzled but was absolutely wrapped up in what would happen next." Ultimately, your acquaintance will want to hear what you thought of her. No. She'll want to hear that you liked her work. So tell her so. Lie, if need be. Later, some other month, you can be honest. For now, consider your obligation to the theatre. The audience deserves the best show it can get. The show will be best if the actors believe they're doing it well. So serve the theatre now. And later you can serve the god of integrity.

If you liked a show, go backstage, even if you don't know anyone in the cast. Actors love to hear compliments from other actors, and you can help the performers and the theatre (and yourself in the long run) if you will take a few minutes to say a kindly word or two to the actors who have just tried to do a good job. In this ego-riddled profession, a flattering word from a fellow actor can offset the most damaging review from some flippant journalist. My companion and I didn't know anyone in the cast of the off-Broadway production of *To Gillian On Her 37th Birthday*, but we greatly admired the show and the acting and went backstage at the Circle in the Square to say so. Rarely have I been so welcomed. The cast, led by the wonderfully compelling David Rasche, knew the show was not selling well and might soon close, despite the love they felt for it. And they were buoyed up by our gesture and talked about the show with us for a half an hour. Little did I anticipate that the following summer I'd be offered a job directing the script in stock and that my discussions with the original cast would help me when it came my turn to select a cast. Serendipity derived from good manners.

This Is Your Life

"Life upon the wicked stage ain't nothin' for a sweet, young girl," warns Oscar Hammerstein's lyric. And it ain't much for the guys either. It's a hard, frequently unrewarding, frustrating, and treacherous life, but it's the one you've chosen. You believe the rewards of fame or creative fulfillment will balance the payments you'll make in hard work and emotional self-sacrifice. Well, I hope for your sake that you're right. It is your life to live and if you want to dedicate it to the muse Thalia, go right ahead. Just two final notions.

First. Your talent is singular, but the business of show business is a collective one. You will serve yourself best by serving the theatre best. The rules of the unions and the practices of the profession are there to provide you with guidelines so that you and your fellow actors can thrive together in your common work.

If the rules seem wrong, try to change them. But keep in mind that until such change comes about, you are well advised to respect and bide by those that exist. The theatre can give you much. You, in turn, must give the theatre its due. The theatre is a very small world. Soon you'll know many of its citizens. Make certain you are a responsible citizen of that theatrical world yourself.

Second. You'll serve Thalia best by serving yourself. If you live your life richly, you'll help yourself to act with vitality and creative vibrance. You are the imitator of human actions, and the more you know and experience of human activities, the more you will imitate with accuracy, specificity, economy, and passion. If you live a reclusive life, surrounded only with friends and artifacts of the theatre, you will not know enough of life to represent it. You must live a varied life. You owe it to yourself and your art to realize that you can behave well as an actor only by behaving well in life.

Be a political animal. Know something of the laws, government, and society you imitate in your work. You need not be a political activist, carrying banners for candidates. You don't need to run for office yourself. Don't be so egotistical as to try parlaying your public's knowledge of your image into a quest for offices you're not qualified to perform. But you ought to be informed on issues. You ought to accept your obligations to vote and to serve on juries. You ought to be a citizen-actor. To hide behind a shield of artistic immunity is to do yourself and your world an unforgivable disservice.

Be culturally alert. Know what painters and composers are doing. Read the contemporary novelists. See the important new films. Read the newspapers and magazines that reflect your world. You have much to learn from these artists, and if you will inform your art with their wisdom, they, in turn will have much to learn from you. Together, you may help to create a better world.

Be a social creature. Know friends from many professions and economic classes. Don't limit your circle of friends to those who share your background and interests. Learn about life through the people you move among.

Travel. See new places, customs, cultures. Shed the deforming cloak of provincialism and don the enriching robes of inquiry.

"In the time of your life, live," wrote William Saroyan, "so that in that good time there shall be no ugliness or death for yourself or for any life your life touches. . . . In the time of your life, live— so that in that wondrous time you shall not add to the misery and sorrow of the world, but shall smile to the infinite delight and mystery of it."

Actor, this is your life. Live it so that you may act. Act so that you may be alive. Behave in your acting as you would behave in your life, for (and here comes the book's final maxim) *life is a continual rehearsal for a show that closes out of town.*